Mastering Azure Analytics

*Architecting in the Cloud with Azure Data Lake,
HDInsight, and Spark*

Zoiner Tejada

Beijing · Boston · Farnham · Sebastopol · Tokyo

Mastering Azure Analytics

by Zoiner Tejada

Copyright © 2017 Zoiner Tejada. All rights reserved.

Printed in the United States of America.

Published by O'Reilly Media, Inc., 1005 Gravenstein Highway North, Sebastopol, CA 95472.

O'Reilly books may be purchased for educational, business, or sales promotional use. Online editions are also available for most titles (*http://oreilly.com/safari*). For more information, contact our corporate/institutional sales department: 800-998-9938 or *corporate@oreilly.com*.

Editor: Shannon Cutt	**Indexer:** Ellen Troutman
Production Editor: Kristen Brown	**Interior Designer:** David Futato
Copyeditor: Rachel Monaghan	**Cover Designer:** Karen Montgomery
Proofreader: Charles Roumeliotis	**Illustrator:** Rebecca Demarest

April 2017:   First Edition

Revision History for the First Edition

2017-04-04:   First Release

See *http://oreilly.com/catalog/errata.csp?isbn=9781491956656* for release details.

The O'Reilly logo is a registered trademark of O'Reilly Media, Inc. *Mastering Azure Analytics*, the cover image, and related trade dress are trademarks of O'Reilly Media, Inc.

978-1-491-95665-6

[LSI]

Table of Contents

Foreword

"Every 25 milliseconds, a turbine emits 10 distinct data points..." began almost every customer conversation about big data and advanced analytics that I've been a part of over the last six years. A simple story about the data needs of a wind farm highlighted the evolving size, speed, and shape of data that is representative of customers across industries. Over time, the technology names, the integration scenarios, and the guidance would evolve, but a few things remained consistent despite the ever-increasing pace of change:

- Customers are faced with a rapidly expanding amount of data, in a variety of shapes and sizes, generated and stored throughout their environment.
- Deep understanding of customers, of purchase patterns, of machine performance, of transaction streams, and more, is fast becoming table stakes as competitors are doing the same.
- The pace of innovation from vendors, and more importantly the ecosystem, is operating at what feels like a record high.

The value that customers get from advanced analytics, big data, and machine learning can transform businesses, but there are still a lot of pieces that need to come together. I've been fortunate to have had such an immensely exciting, rewarding, and simply fun time building products customers can use to solve these challenges. These technologies have, in many cases, enabled people to build solutions that simply weren't possible 5 or 10 years ago.

The addition of the Azure cloud in these scenarios has given customers an entirely new level of flexibility. Cloud services such as HDInsight make it faster, easier, and cheaper to experiment with a wide range of software and hardware combinations, make it possible to finely tune the consumption of cloud resources to the specifics of a given project, and to scale up and down as required. Additionally, the economic model of the cloud is fundamentally different than acquiring and operating these tools on premises, which enables scenarios that are simply not possible on premises. We've seen Azure customers scale out to a large number of GPU-enabled machines to conduct training using the latest deep learning libraries, and then take that output and deploy it to their web services (as well as to devices running anywhere), paying only for the few dollars' worth of compute they used when they did so. Now, with this flexibility comes the need to manage and orchestrate across these systems, which can quickly become a key challenge.

This book takes the reader through the same workflow you'll see for implementing an analytics project in the real world—building a data pipeline. By first walking through ingesting and storing data, you'll set the stage in Azure for a rich set of insights to derive from that data. Once you've ingested the data, processing can occur in real time, in offline batch scenarios, and while using tools and languages that you're familiar with. The next stage is in acting on the insights gained, whether through dashboards or further integration into other applications and services. Oftentimes, the analysis that we want to be able to do may also involve machine learning to bring structure or predictions to the data. It is said that most machine learning projects are 80% acquiring and processing the data prior to performing any machine learning, and the tools shown throughout this book can be used for this. Finally, we must deal with a set of very real operational aspects of any production data pipeline, such as security and data governance, which need to be considered throughout any project.

Zoiner's perspective on this space is one crafted through years of hard work, walking hand in hand with customers who are looking to transform their businesses with the power of data. Zoiner and I met nearly 10 years ago while we were both working in the distributed systems space, where we shared a passion for orchestration engines and messaging layers. Since then, I have always appreciated his ability to work with fantastically complicated technologies and distill down the key choices and aspects of a solution into simple guidance that anyone can understand. I'm excited to see him applying that same approach to a topic that's so near to me, and I'm excited to see what all the readers can do with the knowledge they will gain.

— Matt Winkler
Group Program Manager,
Big Data and Machine Learning
Microsoft
Woodinville, WA

Preface

If you are building software solutions today, odds are that you have a data problem. You might even have an advanced analytics problem or one that requires machine learning. The trouble is that the world of software development and those of big data and advanced analytics seem like they are light years apart—they use different software stacks, different terminology, and often different engineering approaches, and there are lots of choices. The aim of this book is to provide you with a map of the galaxy that helps you chart your course to wrangling insights and guidance out of your data—irrespective of whether that data is arriving at warp speed from IoT sensors or at the glacial pace of decades of historical data.

The structure of this book is designed along the path of a data pipeline that aims to ingest, process, store, and deliver data along both real-time (hot data) and batch (cold data) paths. The waypoints in the map to your data pipeline are groups of Azure services, and each is covered in one or more chapters. We describe each service and tool that you should consider for a particular step in your pipeline. Another way to think about it is to look at each phase of the analytics pipeline as a toolbox onto itself: which Azure service would you use for long-term storage? We show you how to use Azure Storage and Azure Data Lake Store. What about storage of streaming data? We give you the options—including Azure Stream Analytics, Azure HDInsight with Storm or Spark, and the Event Processor Host—and show you how to program them.

Of course, without a specific destination in mind, a map is not that interesting. To motivate our journey to build analytic data pipelines in Azure, we provide a fictitious business scenario looking to manage the data for airports, and give you all the sample data and code you will need to cement your understanding of the covered services.

Approach this book as you would a tour guide: you can read it from cover to cover, but you can also pick and choose the areas of most interest to you and dive into those. The map we build provides a narrated tour of the constellations of the various Azure services and tools you can use to build your data pipeline. In some cases, these constellations are complex, deep, and robust. In other cases, they are simple purpose-built solutions to a narrow set of problems. They might contain open source code bases, or they might be proprietary innovations from Microsoft. In all cases, by the end of this book you should have built your guide to the galaxy, will know which services and tools to use for which purpose, and will be well on your way to mastering Azure analytics.

Conventions Used in This Book

The following typographical conventions are used in this book:

Italic
> Indicates new terms, URLs, email addresses, filenames, and file extensions.

`Constant width`
> Used for program listings, as well as within paragraphs to refer to program elements such as variable or function names, databases, data types, environment variables, statements, and keywords.

`Constant width bold`
> Shows commands or other text that should be typed literally by the user.

`Constant width italic`
> Shows text that should be replaced with user-supplied values or by values determined by context.

> This element signifies a tip or suggestion.

> This element signifies a general note.

> This element indicates a warning or caution.

Using Code Examples

Supplemental material (code examples, exercises, etc.) is available for download at *https://github.com/ZoinerTejada/mastering-azure-analytics*.

This book is here to help you get your job done. In general, if example code is offered with this book, you may use it in your programs and documentation. You do not need to contact us for permission unless you're reproducing a significant portion of the code. For example, writing a program that uses several chunks of code from this book does not require permission. Selling or distributing a CD-ROM of examples from O'Reilly books does require permission. Answering a question by citing this book and quoting example code does not require permission. Incorporating a significant amount of example code from this book into your product's documentation does require permission.

We appreciate, but do not require, attribution. An attribution usually includes the title, author, publisher, and ISBN. For example: "*Mastering Azure Analytics* by Zoiner Tejada (O'Reilly). Copyright 2017 Zoiner Tejada, 978-1-491-95665-6."

If you feel your use of code examples falls outside fair use or the permission given above, feel free to contact us at *permissions@oreilly.com*.

O'Reilly Safari

 *Safari* (formerly Safari Books Online) is a membership-based training and reference platform for enterprise, government, educators, and individuals.

Members have access to thousands of books, training videos, Learning Paths, interactive tutorials, and curated playlists from over 250 publishers, including O'Reilly Media, Harvard Business Review, Prentice Hall Professional, Addison-Wesley Professional, Microsoft Press, Sams, Que, Peachpit Press, Adobe, Focal Press, Cisco Press, John Wiley & Sons, Syngress, Morgan Kaufmann, IBM Redbooks, Packt, Adobe Press, FT Press, Apress, Manning, New Riders, McGraw-Hill, Jones & Bartlett, and Course Technology, among others.

For more information, please visit *http://oreilly.com/safari*.

How to Contact Us

Please address comments and questions concerning this book to the publisher:

O'Reilly Media, Inc.
1005 Gravenstein Highway North

Sebastopol, CA 95472
800-998-9938 (in the United States or Canada)
707-829-0515 (international or local)
707-829-0104 (fax)

We have a web page for this book, where we list errata, examples, and any additional information. You can access this page at *http://bit.ly/masterAzureAnalytics*.

To comment or ask technical questions about this book, send email to *bookquestions@oreilly.com*.

For more information about our books, courses, conferences, and news, see our website at *http://www.oreilly.com*.

Find us on Facebook: *http://facebook.com/oreilly*

Follow us on Twitter: *http://twitter.com/oreillymedia*

Watch us on YouTube: *http://www.youtube.com/oreillymedia*

Acknowledgments

A book with a scope this large needs a village to support its creation, and I was honored to be supported by so many great experts along the way. I would like to thank Lynn Langit for her hypercritical eye for anything unclear or ambiguous—her challenges and pressure helped this book emerge from a diamond in the rough. I am honored to have had technical reviewers from Microsoft: thanks to Nishant Thacker, Ted Way, and Rama Ramani for lending their specific areas of expertise to this effort.

I would like to recognize one outstanding citizen of the Azure MVP community: Tom Kerkhove. Thank you for your meticulous attention to detail in testing the code and making modifications so that readers have a smooth implementation experience.

Thanks to Matt Winkler for lighting the way forward from those workflow days into this amazing new world of data, and teaching me both how to drink from the firehose and control it.

I would be remiss not to mention the caring, insightful, and helpful support I received from my editor Shannon Cutt on this journey of more than a year. Similarly, I am most appreciative to Kristen Brown for helping catch the places where my fingers didn't quite transcribe my thoughts at the speed I was thinking them. Thank you both for making my first O'Reilly authoring experience an amazing one.

Finally, thank you to my wife Ashley for tolerating the many late nights and boring weekends we spent "together" writing this book. Your understanding and patience were the ultimate gesture of love.

CHAPTER 1

Enterprise Analytics Fundamentals

In this chapter we'll review the fundamentals of enterprise analytic architectures. We will introduce the analytics data pipeline, a fundamental process that takes data from its source through several steps until it is available to analytics clients. Then we will introduce the concept of a data lake, as well as two different pipeline architectures: lambda architecture and kappa architecture. The particular steps in the typical data processing pipeline (as well as considerations around the handling of "hot" and "cold" data) are detailed and serve as a framework for the rest of the book. We conclude the chapter by introducing our case study scenarios, along with their respective data sets, which provide a more real-world context for performing big data analytics on Azure.

The Analytics Data Pipeline

Data does not end up nicely formatted for analytics on its own; it takes a series of steps that involve collecting the data from the source, massaging the data to get it into the forms appropriate to the analytics desired (sometimes referred to as *data wrangling* or *data munging*), and ultimately pushing the prepared results to the location from which they can be consumed. This series of steps can be thought of as a *pipeline*.

The analytics data pipeline forms a basis for understanding any analytics solution, and thus is very useful to our purposes in this book as we seek to understand how to accomplish analytics using Microsoft Azure. As shown in Figure 1-1, the analytics data pipeline consists of five major components, which are useful in comprehending and designing any analytics solution.

Source
    The location from which new raw data is pulled or which pushes new raw data into the pipeline.

Ingest
> The computation that handles receiving the raw data from the source so that it can be processed.

Processing
> The computation controlling how the data gets prepared and processed for delivery.

Storage
> The various locations where the ingested, intermediate, and final calculations are stored. Storage can be transient (the data lives in memory only for a finite period of time) or persistent (the data is stored for the long term).

Delivery
> How the data is ultimately presented to the consumer, which can run the gamut from dedicated analytics client solutions used by analysts to APIs that enable the results to integrate into a larger solution or be consumed by other processes.

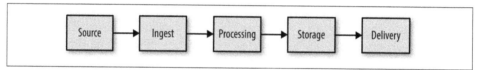

Figure 1-1. The data analytics pipeline is a conceptual framework that is helpful in understanding where various data technologies apply.

Data Lakes

The term *data lake* is becoming the latest buzzword, and is following a path similar to how *big data* grew in popularity, and at the same time its definition has become more unclear as vendors attach the meaning that suits their products best. So let's begin by defining the concept of a data lake.

A data lake consists of two parts: storage and processing. Data lake storage requires an infinitely scalable, fault-tolerant, storage repository designed to handle massive volumes of data with varying shapes, sizes, and ingest velocities. Data lake processing requires a processing engine that can successfully operate on the data at this scale.

The term *data lake* was originally coined by James Dixon, the CTO of Pentaho, wherein he used the term in contrast with the traditional, highly schematized data-mart:

> If you think of a datamart as a store of bottled water—cleansed and packaged and structured for easy consumption—the data lake is a large body of water in a more natural state. The contents of the lake stream in from a source to fill the lake, and various users of the lake can come to examine, dive in, or take samples.

In this definition, a data lake is a repository that intentionally leaves the data in its raw or least-processed form to allow questions to be asked of it that would not be answerable if the data were packaged into a particular structure or otherwise aggregated.

That simple definition of a data lake should serve as the core, but as you will see in reading this book, it belies the true extent of a data lake. In reality, a data lake includes not just a single processing engine, but multiple processing engines, and because it represents the enterprise-wide, centralized repository of source and processed data (after all, it champions a "store all" approach to data management), it has other requirements such as metadata management, discovery, and governance.

One final important note: the data lake concept as it is used today is intended for batch processing, where high latency (time until results ready) is appropriate. That said, support for lower-latency processing is a natural area of evolution for data lakes, so this definition may evolve with the technology landscape.

With this broad definition of data lake, let us look at two different architectures that can be used to act on the data managed by a data lake: lambda architecture and kappa architecture.

Lambda Architecture

Lambda architecture was originally proposed by the creator of Apache Storm, Nathan Marz. In his book, *Big Data: Principles and Best Practices of Scalable Realtime Data Systems* (Manning), he proposed a pipeline architecture that aims to reduce the complexity seen in real-time analytics pipelines by constraining any incremental computation to only a small portion of this architecture.

In lambda architecture, there are two paths for data to flow in the pipeline (see Figure 1-2):

- A "hot" path where latency-sensitive data (e.g., the results need to be ready in seconds or less) flows for rapid consumption by analytics clients
- A "cold" path where all data goes and is processed in batches that can tolerate greater latencies (e.g., the results can take minutes or even hours) until results are ready

When data flows into the "cold" path, this data is immutable. Any changes to the value of particular datum are reflected by a new, timestamped datum being stored in the system alongside any previous values. This approach enables the system to re-compute the then-current value of a particular datum for any point in time across the history of the data collected. Because the "cold" path can tolerate a greater latency until the results are ready, the computation can afford to run across large data sets, and the types of calculation performed can be time-intensive. The objective of the "cold" path can be summarized as: take the time you need, but make the results extremely accurate.

When data flows into the "hot" path, this data is mutable and can be updated in place. In addition, the hot path places a latency constraint on the data (as the results are typically desired in near–real time). The impact of this latency constraint is that the types of calculations that can be performed are limited to those that can happen quickly enough. This might mean switching from an algorithm that provides perfect accuracy to one that provides an approximation. An example of this involves counting the number of distinct items in a data set (e.g., the number of visitors to your website): you can either count each individual datum (which can be very high latency if the volume is high) or you can approximate the count using algorithms like HyperLogLog. The objective of the hot path can be summarized as: trade off some amount of accuracy in the results in order to ensure that the data is ready as quickly as possible.

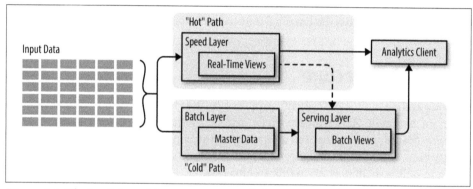

Figure 1-2. The lambda architecture captures all data entering the pipeline into immutable storage, labeled "Master Data" in the diagram. This data is processed by the batch layer and output to a serving layer in the form of batch views. Latency-sensitive calculations are applied on the input data by the speed layer and exposed as real-time views. Analytics clients can consume the data from either the speed layer views or the serving layer views depending on the time frame of the data required. In some implementations, the serving layer can host both the real-time views and the batch views.

The hot and cold paths ultimately converge at the analytics client application. The client must choose the path from which it acquires the result. It can choose to use the less accurate but most up-to-date result from the hot path, or it can use the less timely but more accurate result from the cold path. An important component of this decision relates to the window of time for which only the hot path has a result, as the cold path has not yet computed the result. Looking at this another way, the hot path has results for only a small window of time, and its results will ultimately be updated by the more accurate cold path in time. This has the effect of minimizing the volume of data that components of the hot path have to deal with.

The motivation for the creation of the lambda architecture may be surprising. Yes, enabling a simpler architecture for real-time data processing was important, but the reason it came into existence was to provide human fault tolerance. In effect, it recognizes that we are moving to a time when we actually can keep all the raw data. Simultaneously, it recognizes that bugs happen, even in production. Lambda architectures offer a solution that is not just resilient to system failure, but tolerant of human mistakes because it has all the input data and the capability to recompute (through batch computation) any errant calculation.

Kappa Architecture

Kappa architecture surfaced in response to a desire to simplify the lambda architecture dramatically by making a single change: eliminate the cold path and make all processing happen in a near–real-time streaming mode (Figure 1-3). Recomputation on the data can still occur when needed; it is in effect streamed through the kappa pipeline again. The kappa architecture was proposed by Jay Kreps based on his experiences at LinkedIn, and particularly his frustrations in dealing with the problem of "code sharing" in lambda architectures—that is, keeping in sync the logic that does the computation in the hot path with the logic that is doing the same calculation in the cold path.

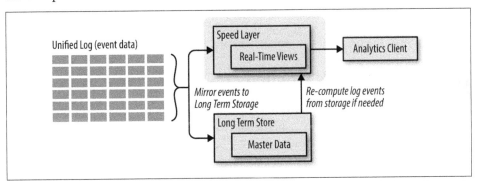

Figure 1-3. In the kappa architecture, analytics clients get their data only from the speed layer, as all computation happens upon streaming data. Input events can be mirrored to long-term storage to enable recomputation on historical data should the need arise.

Kappa architecture centers on a unified log (think of it as a highly scalable queue), which ingests all data (which are considered events in this architecture). There is a single deployment of this log in the architecture, whereby each event datum collected is immutable, the events are ordered, and the current state of an event is changed only by a new event being appended.

The unified log itself is designed to be distributed and fault tolerant, suitable to its place at that heart of the analytics topology. All processing of events is performed on the input streams and persisted as a real-time view (just as in the hot path of the lambda architecture). To support the human-fault-tolerant aspects, the data ingested from the unified log is typically persisted to a scalable, fault-tolerant persistent storage so that it can be recomputed even if the data has "aged out" of the unified log.

Kreps on Kappa

If you're interested in reading more about kappa architecture, take a look at *I Heart Logs* by Jay Kreps (O'Reilly), as Kreps applied it toward event log processing and analytics.

If this architecture sounds vaguely familiar to you, it is probably because it is. The patterns employed by the kappa architecture are the same as those you may have come across if you have used the Event Sourcing pattern or CQRS (command query responsibility segregation).

Choosing Between Lambda and Kappa

Arguing the merits of lambda architecture over kappa architecture and vice versa is akin to arguing over programming languages—it quickly becomes a heated, quasi-religious debate. Instead, for the purposes of this book we aim to use both architectures as motivations to illustrate how you can design and implement such pipelines in Microsoft Azure. We leave it to you, the reader, to decide which architecture most closely matches the needs of your analytics data pipeline.

The Azure Analytics Pipeline

In this book we will expand on the analytics data pipeline to understand the ways we can build the one required by a particular scenario. We attempt to do this in two directions: first, by broadly showing the lay of the land for all the Azure services in the context of where they apply to the pipeline; and second, by taking on specific scenarios that enable us to apply a subset of the services in implementing a solution for that scenario. We will explore the concepts of data lakes, lambda architectures, and kappa architectures in our solutions, and show how we can achieve them using the latest services from Microsoft Azure.

Throughout this book, we will tease out the analytics data pipeline into more and more granular components, so that we can categorically identify the Azure services that act in support of a particular component. We will expand our analytics data pipeline (source, ingest, storage, processing, delivery) with the following subcomponents, as illustrated by Figure 1-4.

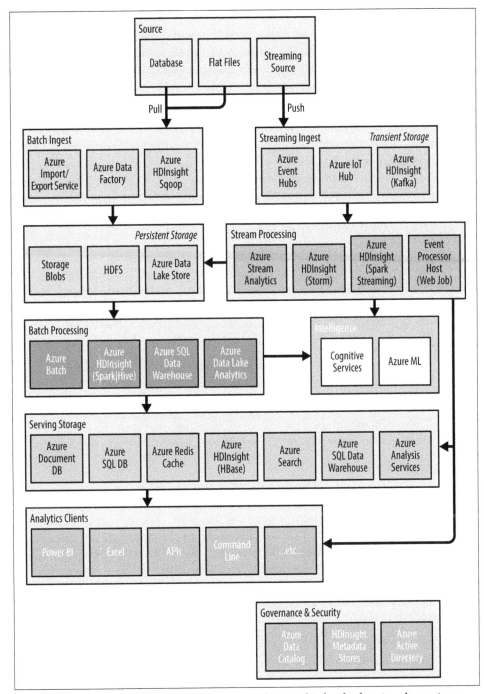

Figure 1-4. The Azure analytics pipeline we explore in this book, showing the various Azure services in the context of the component they support.

Source

For the purposes of this book, we will look at three different source types: an on-premises database like SQL Server, on-premises files (like CSVs in a file share), and streaming sources that periodically transmit data (such as logging systems or devices emitting telemetry).

Ingest

In Chapter 2, we cover the components that act in support of getting data to the solution, either through batch ingest (bulk data loading) or via streaming ingest. We will examine loading from sources that use push-based approaches to ingest, such as receiving streaming messages into Azure Event Hubs or IoT Hub. We will also examine pull-based approaches, such as using the Azure Import/Export Service to send a disk full of files to Azure Storage or using Azure Data Factory agents to query data from an on-premises source.

Storage

In Chapter 3 we explore the components that are used to store the ingested, intermediate, and final data, such as queue-based and file-based approaches. We place the storage options in three different contexts: transient storage, persistent storage, and serving storage.

Transient storage

This can take the form of multiconsumer queues with a duration-based expiry to their content, as in Event Hubs and IoT Hub.

Persistent storage

These components are capable of storing their content indefinitely and at scale, as seen in Azure Blob Storage, HDFS, and Azure Data Lake Store.

Serving storage

In Chapters 7 and 8 we will also cover storage that is optimized for serving results to the ultimate client of the analytics processing pipeline, generally to support flexible, low-latency querying scenarios. In some cases, this might be the direct landing point for data processed in real time; in other cases, these serving storage services are the repository for the results of time-consuming computation coming from batch processing. Among these components, we cover Azure Document DB, Azure SQL Database, Azure SQL Data Warehouse, Azure Redis Cache, Azure Search, and HDInsight running HBase.

Processing

In Chapters 4–8, we cover the components that process and transform the ingested data and generate results from queries. We explore the gamut of latencies, from the high-latency computations of batch processing, to the shorter latencies expected with interactive querying, to the shortest latencies of real-time processing. With batch processing we will look at Azure HDInsight running Spark or using Hive to resolve queries, and we will take a similar approach to applying SQL Data Warehouse (and its PolyBase technology) to query batch storage. Then, we will look at the unified capabilities that Azure Data Lake Analytics brings to batch processing and querying. Finally, we will cover the MPP option Azure offers for batch computation, in the form of Azure Batch, as well as how to apply Azure Machine Learning in batches against data from batch storage.

Delivery

The analytics tools covered in Chapter 12 actually perform the analytics functions, and some of them can acquire their data directly from the real-time pipeline, such as Power BI. Other analytics tools rely on serving storage components, such as Excel, custom web service APIs, Azure Machine Learning web services, or the command line.

Governance components allow us to manage the metadata for items in our solution as well as control access and secure the data. These include the metadata functionality provided by Azure Data Catalog and HDInsight. They are covered in Chapter 10.

Introducing the Analytics Scenarios

To motivate the solution design, selection, and application of Azure services throughout the book, we will walk through a case-study scenario for a fictitious business, Blue Yonder Airports. Following the process of creating a solution from the case study will provide you with some of the "real-world" challenges you are likely to face in your implementations.

Let's imagine that Blue Yonder Airports (BYA) provides systems for airports that improve passengers' experience while they are in the airport. BYA services many of the larger airports, primarily in the United States, and provides them with logistics software that helps them "orchestrate the chaos" of moving passengers through the airport.

The Federal Aviation Administration (FAA) classifies airports that provide scheduled passenger service and serve at least 10,000 passengers per year as *commercial primary airports*. Commercial primary airports are further classified by the volume of passenger boarding they have per year:

- Nonhub airports account for at least 10,000 and less than 0.05% of total US passengers boarding.
- Small hubs account for between 0.05% and 0.25% of all US passenger boarding.
- Medium hubs account for between 0.25% and 1% of total US passenger boarding.

- Large hubs account for at least 1% of all US passenger boarding.[1]

As of 2014 there were 30 large hub and 31 medium hub airports in the United States.[2] BYA's business focuses on optimizing the experience for passengers traveling through many of these medium and large hubs.

To put the volumes in perspective, on any given day in their largest large hub airport, BYA sees upward of 250,000 people through the airport in response to over 1,500 flights per day, and manages the passenger experience at over 400 domestic and international gates.

Of late, BYA has realized they have a significant opportunity to deliver the "intelligent airport" by capitalizing on their existing data assets coupled with newer systems that provide airport telemetry in real time. They want to apply intelligent analytics to the challenges surrounding the gate experience.

They want to maintain passenger comfort while there are passengers waiting at a gate for their departure, or deplaning from an arriving flight, by maintaining an ambient temperature of between 68 and 71 degrees Fahrenheit. At the same time, they want to aggressively avoid running the heating or cooling when there are no passengers at the gate, and they certainly want to avoid the odd situation where the heating and air-conditioning cycle back to back, effectively working against each other.

Today, many of BYA's airports have their heating and cooling on a fixed schedule, but BYA believes that by having a better understanding of flight delays, being able to reasonably predict departure and arrival delays, and having a strong sensor network, they will be able to deliver the optimal passenger experience while saving the airport money in heating and cooling costs.

Blue Yonder Airports has reviewed their data catalog and identified the following data assets as potentially useful in their solution:

Flight delays
> BYA has collected over 15 years of historical, on-time performance data across all airlines. This data includes elements such as the airline, the flight number, the origin and destination airports, departure and arrival times, flight duration and distance, and the specific causes of delay (weather, airline issues, security, etc.).

Weather
> BYA relies on weather data for its operational needs. Their flight delay data provides some useful information regarding historical weather conditions for arriving and departing flights, but they also have partnered with a third party to

---

1 *https://en.wikipedia.org/wiki/List_of_airports_in_the_United_States*

2 *https://en.wikipedia.org/wiki/List_of_the_busiest_airports_in_the_United_States*

provide them not only current weather conditions, but weather forecasts as well. This data include elements like temperature, wind speed and direction, precipitation, pressure, and visibility.

Smart building telemetry

BYA installs smart meters and gateways that provide real-time telemetry of systems running the airport. Initially, their smart meter telemetry focuses on heating/cooling and motion sensors as they look to optimize costs while maintaining passenger comfort. These provide time series data that includes the temperature from each device at a given point in time, as well as activation/deactivation events for heating/cooling and when motion is triggered.

Example Code and Example Data Sets

In each chapter that follows, we will provide links to any example code and example data sets necessary to follow along with the BYA content in the chapter. You will want to ensure your environment is set up per the instructions in the next section, however.

What You Will Need

To follow along with the examples in this book you will need the following items.

Broadband Internet Connectivity

Many of the examples are performed directly on Azure, so you'll need at least a stable broadband connection to perform them. Of course, faster connections will certainly be better, especially when you are transferring data sets between your computer and the cloud.

Azure Subscription

A pay-as-you-go subscription or MSDN subscription is highly recommended. A free trial subscription might get you through some of the examples, but you are very likely to exceed the $200 free quota. To see all your options to get started with Azure, visit the Microsoft Azure purchase page (*https://azure.microsoft.com/en-us/pricing/purchase-options/*).

Visual Studio 2015 with Update 1

Visual Studio 2015 with Update 1 is used with the book's examples. Any one of the Community, Professional, or Enterprise editions will work.

If you already have Visual Studio 2015 installed, but not Update 1, you can download Update 1 online (*https://www.visualstudio.com/news/vs2015-update1-vs*). Once the download completes, launch the installer and step through the wizard to update your Visual Studio to Update 1.

If you do not have a development machine already set up with Visual Studio and want to get started quickly, you can create a virtual machine (VM) from the Azure Marketplace that has Visual Studio 2015 preinstalled and then remote-desktop into that. Beyond reducing the setup time, most data transfers will benefit (e.g., they will be faster) from running within the Azure data center. Just remember to shut down your VM when you are not actively using it to keep your costs down!

To set up a VM with Visual Studio preinstalled, follow these steps:

1. Navigate to the Azure Portal (*https://portal.azure.com*) and log in with the credentials you associated with your subscription.

2. Click New.

3. In the blade that appears, under the New heading there is a search text box with the hint text "Search the marketplace." Type in **Visual Studio 2015** and press return (see Figure 1-5).

Figure 1-5. Searching for Visual Studio 2005 virtual machine images within the Azure Marketplace.

4. The Everything blade will appear with a list of VM images that include Visual Studio 2015. Choose "Visual Studio Community 2015 Update 1 with Azure SDK 2.8 on Windows Server 2012 R2" (see Figure 1-6). If this specific version is not available, choose one with the more recent version of Visual Studio and the Azure SDK.

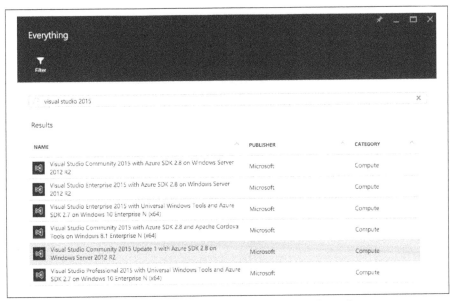

Figure 1-6. Selecting the correct Visual Studio 2015 image from the Azure Marketplace.

5. On the blade that appears, leave "Select a deployment model" set to Resource Manager and click Create.

6. On the Basics blade that appears, provide a name for the VM, the username and password you will use to log in, a resource group name (e.g., "analytics-book") and the Location that is nearest you (see Figure 1-7).

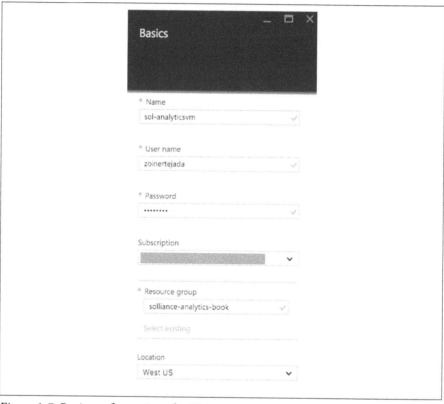

Figure 1-7. Basic configuration of a VM.

7. Click OK.

8. On the "Choose a size" blade, select the instance size for the VM. We recommend an A3 Basic, but any option with at least four cores and 7 GB or RAM will provide a comfortable experience. If you are not seeing the A3 option, click the View All link near the top right of the blade.

9. Click Select.

10. On the Settings blade, leave all the settings at their defaults and click OK.

11. On the Summary blade, click OK to begin provisioning your VM.

12. It may take 7–15 minutes to provision.

13. After the VM is created, the blade for it will appear. Click the Connect button in the toolbar to download the RDP file (see Figure 1-8). Open the file (if it doesn't automatically open) to connect to your VM.

14. Log in with the username and password credentials you specified during the configuration steps.

Figure 1-8. Connect via RDP.

Azure SDK 2.8 or Later

Besides installing Visual Studio, make sure that you have the Azure SDK version 2.8 or later. The following section walks you through the installation.

If you are using Visual Studio on your own machine:

1. Launch Visual Studio.
2. From the Tools menu, select Extensions and Updates.
3. In the tree on the left, select Updates and then Product Updates. You should see Microsoft Azure SDK 2.8.2 (or later) listed there. Click on the item in the listing and then click the Update button (see Figure 1-9).

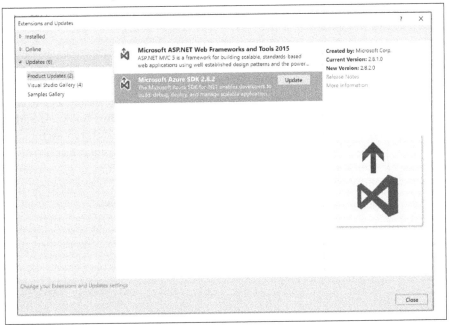

Figure 1-9. Install Azure SDK 2.8.2.

4. Follow the prompts to download the update. Then run the downloaded file, stepping through the wizard until the installation is complete.

If you are using the VM with Visual Studio preinstalled, Azure SDK 2.8.2 or later should already be installed. If you find yourself in a situation where that is not the case, follow these steps:

1. Connect to the VM via Remote Desktop; the Server Manager application should launch automatically.

2. Click on the Local Server tab on the lefthand navigation bar.

3. In the Properties pane, click the On link next to IE Enhanced Security Configuration. If the link already reads Off you can skip the next step, which disables enhanced security for Internet Explorer.

4. Change Administrators to the Off setting and click OK.

5. Launch a browser and navigate to *https://azure.microsoft.com/en-us/downloads*.

6. Click the VS 2015 link under .NET, and when prompted click Run to install Azure SDK 2.8.2. Complete the installation wizard.

You should now be ready to attempt any of the examples used throughout this book.

Summary

This chapter provided a tour of the fundamentals of enterprise analytic architectures. We introduced the analytics data pipeline at a high level. We introduced the concepts behind a data lake, and then illustrated two canonical architectures that implement the data pipeline: lambda architecture and kappa architecture. We got a taste of all the Azure services we will cover (at varying levels of detail) in this book, expanding on our data analytics pipeline with the Azure services that are helpful to each phase. We then introduced Blue Yonder Airlines (BYA), a fictitious company from which we draw a case study that motivates our efforts and examples for the remainder of the book. We concluded the chapter with the prerequisites and setup instructions you will need to follow before attempting any of the book's examples.

In the next chapter, we turn our attention to the first phase of the analytics data pipeline: ingest. There we will explore how we get our data into Azure in the first place.

CHAPTER 2

Getting Data into Azure

In this chapter, we focus on the approaches for transferring data from the data source to Azure. We separate out the discussion into approaches that transfer typically large quantities of data in a single effort (bulk data loading) versus approaches that transfer individual data (stream loading), and investigate the protocols and tools relevant to each.

Using our Azure analytics pipeline as a guide, this chapter focuses on the items highlighted by the red, dashed borders in Figure 2-1.

Ingest Loading Layer

In order to perform analytics in Azure, you need to start by getting data into Azure in the first place. This is the point of the ingest phase. Ultimately, the goal is to get data from a source location (e.g., on premises or another cloud) into either file- or queue-based storage within Azure. In this context, we will look at the client tooling, processes, and protocols used to get the data to the destination in Azure.

To help put this layer in context, let's refer back to the Blue Yonder Airlines scenario. They have historical flight delay data, historical weather data, and smart building telemetry upon which they wish to perform analytics. The first two data sets are candidates for bulk loading, which we will discuss next. The last data set, the smart building telemetry, is a candidate for streaming ingest, which we will examine later in the chapter.

The next chapter will dive into details of how data is stored once it lands in Azure, while this chapter focuses on how to get the data there.

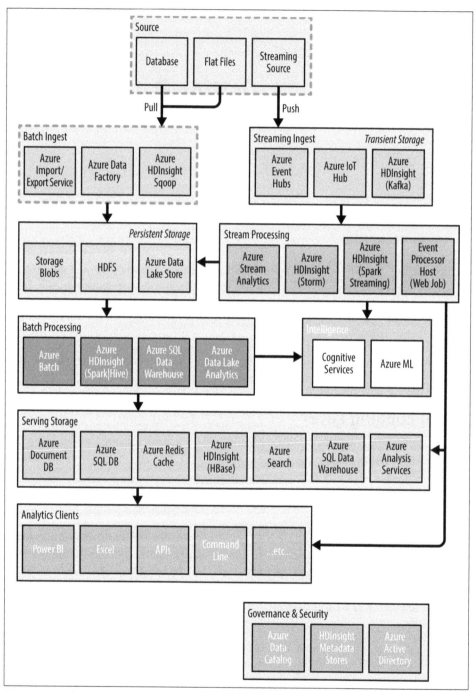

Figure 2-1. The Azure analytics pipeline focus for this chapter.

Bulk Data Loading

Bulk data loading or bulk ingest is the process of loading larger sets of data in batches. The bulk load may be a one-time event (such as loading all historical data into Azure) or it may be ongoing (such as periodically shipping in bulk all telemetry collected on premises over a period of time).

Disk Shipping

Disk shipping is an approach to bulk data loading that is about as direct as it sounds —you take a disk, fill it with the data you want to store in Azure, and physically mail the disk to a processing center, which then copies the data off of your disk and into Azure. Let's return to the Blue Yonder Airlines scenario for a moment to understand why they would consider a disk shipping approach.

BYA has many terabytes' worth of historical flight delay data that they have amassed over the years. This is something they want to transfer in bulk up to Azure, so they have the historical data available before they begin dealing with the current and real-time data. Because the batch of data is sizeable (in the few terabytes range) and because it's likely a one-time event (once the historical data is loaded, updates will be made in Azure directly), it makes sense to ship high-capacity disks loaded with the historical flight delay data.

By shipping disks loaded with data, you do not have to deal with the network setup or the effort involved in trying to secure a reliable connection. You also avoid having to wait for the upload time required: 1 terabyte over blazing-fast 100 Mbps broadband can take a full day to upload, so if you had 5 terabytes' worth of data you would be waiting five days in the best case (assuming the file transfer was not interrupted and that your throughput was consistent). Finally, you avoid the costs associated with setting up and maintaining a performant network connection, especially one that is used only in support of this one-time data transfer.

While the quote may be somewhat dated by the technologies he mentions, I like to think of this option as I heard it from one of my Stanford professors quoting the *New Hacker's Dictionary*:[1]

> Never underestimate the bandwidth of a 747 filled with CD-ROMs.

To perform disk shipping with Microsoft Azure, you can use the Import/Export Service.

---

[1] Eric S. Raymond, ed., *The New Hacker's Dictionary*, 3rd ed. (Cambridge, MA: MIT Press, 1996).

Azure Import/Export Service

The Import/Export Service enables you to ship up to a 6 TB disk loaded with your data to a local processing center, which will securely copy the data from your disk into the Azure Storage blob container that you specify using a high-speed internal network, and ship your disk back to you when finished. You can ship multiple disks if you need to send more than 6 TB of data. In terms of costs, Azure will charge you a flat fee of $80 per drive and you are responsible for the nominal round-trip shipping costs of the drives you send.

Regional Availability

As of this writing, the Import/Export Service is available in most Azure regions except Australia, Brazil, and Japan.

From a high level, the process of loading data using the Import/Export Service works as shown in Figure 2-2 and described in the steps that follow it.

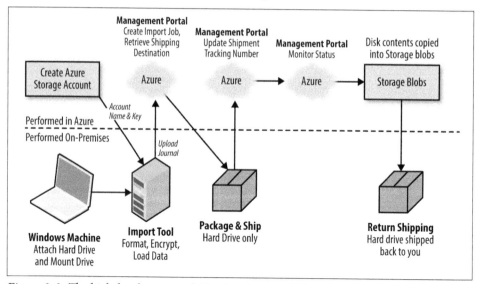

Figure 2-2. The high-level process of shipping data on disk to Azure using the Import/ Export Service.

1. Create your target Azure Storage account and take note of the account name and key.

2. Attach the hard drive you want to ship to a Windows machine. Use the WAImportExport tool (whose filename is *WAImportExport.exe*) to enable BitLocker

encryption on your disk, copy the files over to the disk, and prepare metadata files about the job.

3. Use the Azure Management Portal (*https://manage.windowsazure.com*) to create an import job, where you upload the metadata files, select the datacenter region, and configure shipping information.

4. Package up your disk (just send the disk, without any cables or adapters) and ship it to the processing center whose address you retrieved from the Management Portal.

5. Once you have shipped the disk, update the import job in the Portal with the tracking number used for shipping. You can track the status of the shipping, receiving, transferring, and completion of the import job via the Management Portal.

6. When the import job is complete, your data will be in the configured location in Blob Storage and your disk is shipped back to you.

Requirements for import job.   Before you attempt a transfer, you should be aware of the requirements for the disk you will ship. The hard drive you use must be a 3.5-inch SATA II/III internal hard drive—that is, a drive that is external or USB only will not work. If you, like me, work from a laptop, this means you will need to pick up a SATA II/III-to-USB adapter. To give you an example, I use the Sabrent EC-HDD2 adapter. To use it, you set your hard drive into the adapter like an old video game cartridge and connect the adapter via USB to your computer, after which your computer should recognize the attached drive (Figure 2-3).

Another important requirement is that your hard drive must not be more than 6 TB in size—it can be smaller, just not larger. If you need to send more than 6 TB of data, you can send up to 10 drives per job, and your Storage account will allow you to have up to 20 active jobs at a time (so theoretically you could be copying from as many as 200 drives at a time).

On the computer you use to prepare the drive, you will need a version of Windows that includes BitLocker drive encryption. Specifically, the supported editions include Windows 7 Enterprise, Windows 7 Ultimate, Windows 8 Pro, Windows 8 Enterprise, Windows 10, Windows Server 2008 R2, Windows Server 2012, and Windows Server 2012 R2.

Finally, as of the writing of this book the Azure Import/Export Service supports only Storage accounts created in the Classic mode. That is to say, if you create a Storage account in v2 or Resource Model mode, you will not be able to use it as a target.

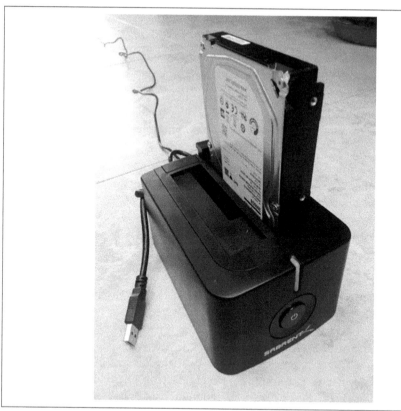

Figure 2-3. An example of a SATA-to-USB adapter, showing the cartridge-like approach to connecting an internal drive to a computer via external USB.

Preparing a disk.   Assuming you have your storage account and compatible disk in hand, let's walk through the steps required to prepare a disk for use with an import job.

1. Download the WAImportExport tool from *http://bit.ly/2mtenkm*.

2. Extract the files to somewhere easily accessible from the command prompt (e.g., *C:\WAImport*). Within that folder you should see the files shown in Figure 2-4.

Name	Type
Azure Import_Export Tool_05-07-2014	Text Document
hddid.dll	Application extension
Microsoft.Data.Services.Client.dll	Application extension
Microsoft.WindowsAzure.Storage.dll	Application extension
WAImportExport	Application
WAImportExport.exe	XML Configuration File
WAImportExportCore.dll	Application extension
WAImportExportRepair.dll	Application extension

Figure 2-4. The files included with the WAImportExport tool.

3. Attach your SATA-to-USB adapter to your computer and connect the hard drive to the adapter.

4. Within Windows, mount the drive (if it's a new drive, you will need to mount and format it). To do this, open an instance of File Explorer and right-click on "My Computer" or "This PC" and select Manage (see Figure 2-5).

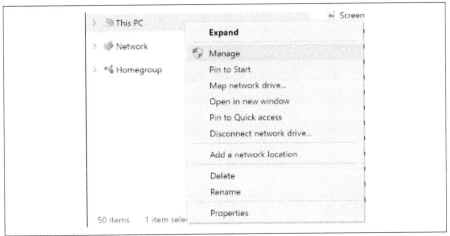

Figure 2-5. Accessing the Manage menu for the local computer.

5. In the Computer Management application, click Disk Management (see Figure 2-6).

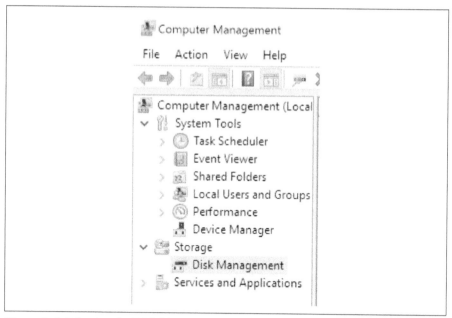

Figure 2-6. Selecting the Disk Management node within Computer Management.

6. In the list of disks, you should see your disk listed (and likely hashed out if it is new). Right-click on your disk and select New Simple Volume (see Figure 2-7).

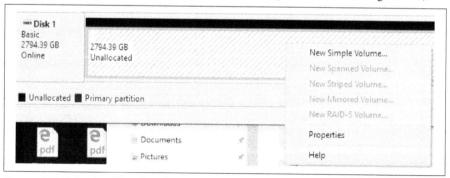

Figure 2-7. Selecting New Simple Volume on an unallocated disk.

7. In the New Simple Volume Wizard, click Next past the first screen.

8. Leave the default size for the volume set to the full size of the drive and click Next (Figure 2-8).

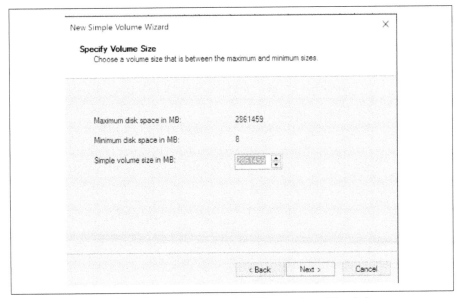

Figure 2-8. Setting the volume size to use the full capacity of the disk.

9. Choose a drive letter at which to mount the drive and click Next (Figure 2-9).

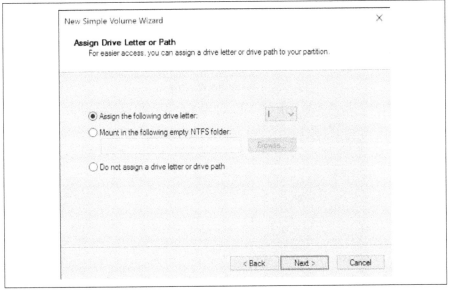

Figure 2-9. Selecting a drive letter to assign to the volume.

10. Leave "Do not format this volume" selected and click Next (Figure 2-10).

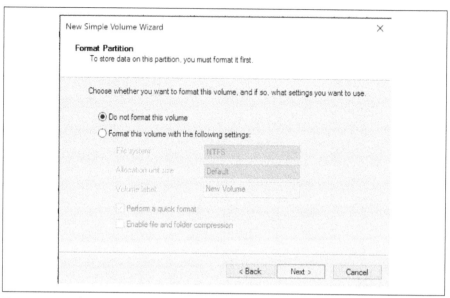

Figure 2-10. Choosing not to format the volume.

11. Click Finish to complete the wizard. Take note of the drive letter you selected, as you will need this in the command-line use of the WAImportExport tool (Figure 2-11).

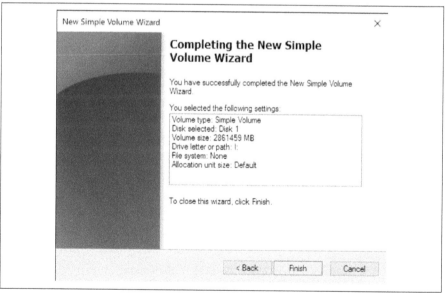

Figure 2-11. Summary screen of the New Simple Volume Wizard.

Run the WAImportExport tool.   Now that you have your disk mounted to a drive letter, you are ready to begin preparing the disk (and copying data to it) using the *WAImportExport.exe* file.

Open an instance of the command line as an administrator (this is important; otherwise, the output will just flash by in a new window and then close) and navigate to where you extracted the WAImportExport tool.

From this point, you can prepare your disk with BitLocker encryption enabled and copy over the files from a single source folder using a single command. The simplest form of this command looks as follows:

```
WAImportExport PrepImport
/sk:<StorageAccountKey>
/t:<TargetDriveLetter>
/format
/encrypt
/j:<JournalFile>
/id:<SessionId>
/srcdir:<SourceDirectory>
/dstdir:<DestinationBlobVirtualDirectory>
```

This command will format and encrypt the drive, and then copy the files from source over to the drive, preserving the folder structure. In the preceding command, the parameters that you need to specify are enclosed in angle brackets (< >). They are:

StorageAccountKey
> The key for the Azure Storage account to which your files will ultimately be copied.

TargetDriveLetter
> The drive letter at which you mounted your external drive that will be used for shipping.

JournalFile
> The name of the metadata file that will be created relative to *WAImportExport.exe*. This file contains the BitLocker key, so it does not ship with the disk (you will upload an XML file derived from it through the portal later). You name it whatever you like—for example, *transfer1.jrn*.

SessionID
> Each run of the command line can create a new session on the external drive, which allows you to copy from multiple different source folders onto the same drive or to vary the virtual path under your target blob container for a set of files. The SessionID is just a user-provided label for the session and needs to be unique.

SourceDirectory

The local path to the source files you want to copy from.

DestinationBlobVirtualDirectory

The path beneath the container in the Azure Blob Storage under which the files will be copied. It must end with a trailing slash (/).

Parameters Used by WAImportExport.exe

For more details on all the parameters supported by *WAImportExport.exe*, see the Microsoft Azure documentation (*http://bit.ly/2mUS9nx*).

By way of example, here is a complete command (with my Storage account key shortened for privacy):

```
WAImportExport PrepImport
/sk:c42fXQ==
/t:i
/format
/encrypt
/j:threetb01.jrn
/id:session#01
/srcdir: "Q:\sources\sampledata"
/dstdir:imported/sampledata/
```

The time required for the process to complete depends largely on the volume of data you have to copy, and the speed of I/O on the machine you are using to perform the operation. For example, in my setup using a 3TB SATA III drive across my adapter to USB, I typically saw around 85 MB/second transfer rates.

When the process completes, you will see on your external drive a folder for the session, along with a manifest file (Figure 2-12).

Figure 2-12. The contents of the external disk after running the WAImportExport tool once.

Within your session folder, you will see the files you selected for copying over with their folder structure preserved (Figure 2-13).

Name	Date modified	Type	Size
zipped	1/25/2016 7:37 PM	File folder	
.DS_Store	1/25/2016 7:37 PM	DS_STORE File	9 KB
cars	1/25/2016 7:37 PM	Microsoft Excel Com...	1 KB
on_time data readme	1/25/2016 7:37 PM	HTML File	12 KB
On_Time_On_Time_Performance_2014_1	1/25/2016 7:37 PM	Microsoft Excel Com...	206,819 KB
On_Time_On_Time_Performance_2014_2	1/25/2016 7:37 PM	Microsoft Excel Com...	188,761 KB
On_Time_On_Time_Performance_2014_3	1/25/2016 7:37 PM	Microsoft Excel Com...	221,592 KB
On_Time_On_Time_Performance_2014_4	1/25/2016 7:37 PM	Microsoft Excel Com...	212,826 KB
On_Time_On_Time_Performance_2014_5	1/25/2016 7:37 PM	Microsoft Excel Com...	219,724 KB
On_Time_On_Time_Performance_2014_6	1/25/2016 7:37 PM	Microsoft Excel Com...	221,705 KB
On_Time_On_Time_Performance_2014_7	1/25/2016 7:37 PM	Microsoft Excel Com...	229,524 KB
On_Time_On_Time_Performance_2014_8	1/25/2016 7:37 PM	Microsoft Excel Com...	223,575 KB
On_Time_On_Time_Performance_2014_9	1/25/2016 7:37 PM	Microsoft Excel Com...	206,383 KB
On_Time_On_Time_Performance_2014_10	1/25/2016 7:37 PM	Microsoft Excel Com...	216,571 KB
On_Time_On_Time_Performance_2014_11	1/25/2016 7:38 PM	Microsoft Excel Com...	203,831 KB
On_Time_On_Time_Performance_2014_12	1/25/2016 7:38 PM	Microsoft Excel Com...	210,865 KB
On_Time_On_Time_Performance_2015_1	1/25/2016 7:38 PM	Microsoft Excel Com...	206,674 KB
On_Time_On_Time_Performance_2015_2	1/25/2016 7:38 PM	Microsoft Excel Com...	188,274 KB
On_Time_On_Time_Performance_2015_3	1/25/2016 7:38 PM	Microsoft Excel Com...	221,697 KB
On_Time_On_Time_Performance_2015_4	1/25/2016 7:38 PM	Microsoft Excel Com...	213,477 KB
On_Time_On_Time_Performance_2015_5	1/25/2016 7:38 PM	Microsoft Excel Com...	213,754 KB
On_Time_On_Time_Performance_2015_6	1/25/2016 7:38 PM	Microsoft Excel Com...	222,089 KB
On_Time_On_Time_Performance_2015_7	1/25/2016 7:38 PM	Microsoft Excel Com...	229,530 KB
On_Time_On_Time_Performance_2015_8	1/25/2016 7:38 PM	Microsoft Excel Com...	224,789 KB
On_Time_On_Time_Performance_2015_9	1/25/2016 7:38 PM	Microsoft Excel Com...	204,326 KB

Figure 2-13. The contents of a session.

Also, in the directory containing *WAImportExport.exe*, you will see your journal file, an XML file (that you will upload to Azure), and a folder that contains the logs (Figure 2-14).

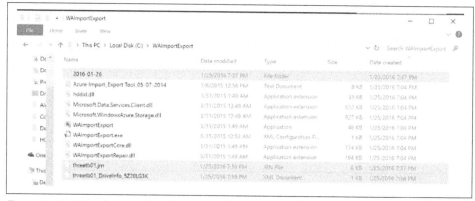

Figure 2-14. Metadata and logfiles created by running the WAImportExport tool.

You are now ready to create an import job in Azure.

Creating the import job. With your disk ready, navigate to the Management Portal (*https://manage.windowsazure.com/*) and locate the Storage account you are using as the target for the copy.

1. Click the Dashboard link for your Storage account (Figure 2-15).

Figure 2-15. The Dashboard for a Storage account, showing the quick glance area.

2. Underneath the quick glance section, click "Create an import job."

3. On the first screen of the wizard, select the checkbox "I've prepared my hard drives, and have access to the necessary drive journal files" and click the right arrow (Figure 2-16).

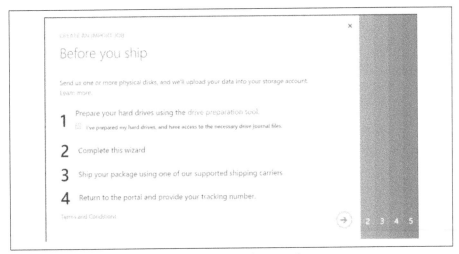

Figure 2-16. Step 1 of the Create an Import Job Wizard.

4. Fill in your contact and return address information. If you desire detailed logs, check the box for "Save the verbose log in my 'waimportexport' blob container." Click the right arrow (Figure 2-17).

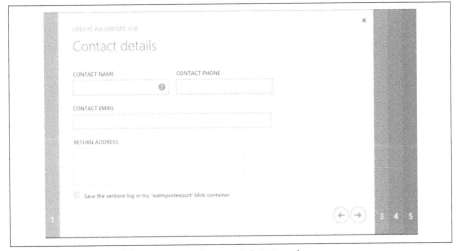

Figure 2-17. Step 2 of the Create an Import Job Wizard.

5. On the Drive Journal Files window, click the Folder icon to the left of "Browse for file," select the journal file outputted by the WAImportExport tool (if you followed our naming convention, it should end in *.jrn*), and click the Add button.

6. Once the file has uploaded, as indicated by a green checkmark, click the right arrow (Figure 2-18).

Figure 2-18. Step 3 of the Create an Import Job Wizard.

7. Provide a name for the job and take note of the address to which you will need to mail your drive (Figure 2-19). The Select Datacenter Region drop-down is automatically set and limited to the region used by the Storage account from which you launched the wizard. Click the right arrow.

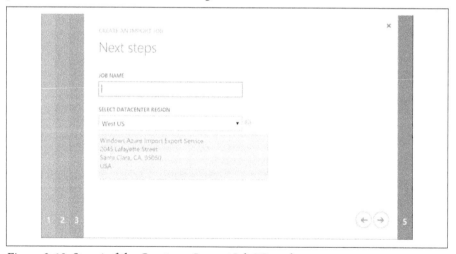

Figure 2-19. Step 4 of the Create an Import Job Wizard.

8. Fill in your shipping details (Figure 2-20). For the United States, the service only uses FedEx, so you will need to be able to input your FedEx account number in the Account Number field. Next, if you wish to provide the tracking number at a later date, you can select the checkbox labeled "I will provide my tracking num-

ber for this import job after shipping the drives." Click the checkmark to complete the wizard.

Figure 2-20. Step 5 of the Create an Import Job Wizard.

9. You should see your new job listed in the portal, with a status of Creating. At this point, disconnect your disk, pack it, and ship it. When you have your tracking number in hand, come back to the screen in Figure 2-21.

Figure 2-21. Viewing your new import job in the Management Portal.

10. Select your job in the list and click Shipping Info (Figure 2-22).

Figure 2-22. The Shipping Info button in the portal.

11. In the wizard, complete your contact information and click the right arrow (Figure 2-23).

Figure 2-23. Completing your shipping information.

12. On the "Shipping details" page, complete the Delivery Carrier and Tracking Number fields and click the checkmark (Figure 2-24).

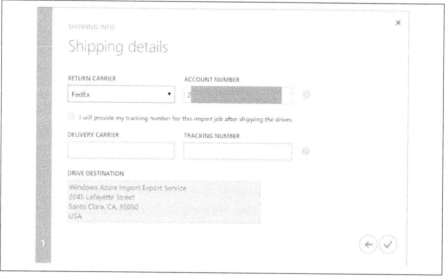

Figure 2-24. Completing shipping information by providing a Delivery Carrier and Tracking Number.

13. Now you wait. A typical transfer can take 3–5 days, consisting of the time it takes for your disk to ship plus the time needed for the transfer to complete. You can monitor the status using the portal (the status will change from Creating to Shipping to Transferring and finally to Completed if all goes well). Once the transfer completes, your data will be waiting for you in your Azure Blob Storage.

End User Tools

In some situations, particularly those dealing with large data volumes, the aforementioned approach of disk shipping is appropriate. There are, of course, multiple options when it comes to tools you can use to bulk-load data into Azure directly from your local machine. In this section, we examine tools that provide a user-friendly interface as well as tools oriented toward programmatic use (such as the command line and PowerShell).

Graphical clients

In this section we discuss the graphical clients you can use to bulk-load data into Azure. Typically, your bulk data loads target either Azure Blob Storage or the Azure Data Lake Store.

Using Visual Studio Cloud Explorer and Server Explorer to bulk-load to Blob Storage.   Visual Studio 2015 comes with two different tools that provide nearly identical support for listing storage targets in Azure (such as Azure Storage and the Azure Data Lake Store). These are the newer Cloud Explorer and the tried-and-true Server Explorer.

Both Cloud Explorer and Server Explorer provide access to the containers in Azure Storage and support uploading in the same fashion. When you get to the point of viewing the contents of a container, the user interface supports selecting and uploading multiple files to a container or a folder path underneath a container in Azure Storage. It can handle four simultaneous uploads at a time. If more than four files are selected, those will be queued as pending until one of the current uploads completes, at which time the pending upload will begin uploading.

To upload a batch of files to Blob Storage using Server Explorer, follow these steps:

1. Launch Server Explorer in Visual Studio, and from the View menu select Server Explorer.
2. Near the top of the Server Explorer pane, expand the Azure node (see Figure 2-25). If prompted, log in with the credentials that have access to your Azure subscription.

Figure 2-25. Server Explorer displaying Azure resources.

3. In a few moments, the tool will list various Azure resources grouped by service. To view your available Azure Storage accounts, expand the Storage node.

4. Underneath the Storage node you will find your Storage accounts, and beneath any one of these you will see nodes for Blobs, Tables, and Queues.

5. Expand the Blobs node to see the blob containers in that account (Figure 2-26).

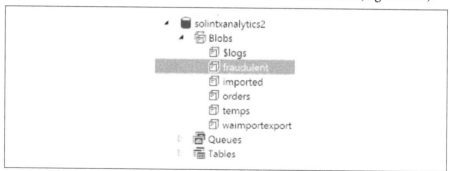

Figure 2-26. Viewing the Storage containers available underneath a Storage account using Server Explorer.

6. Double-click on a container node to view the contents of the container (Figure 2-27).

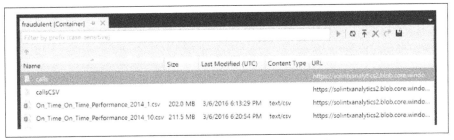

Figure 2-27. Listing of blobs in the container that was opened.

7. Within the blob container document that appears, click the Upload Blob button (Figure 2-28).

Figure 2-28. The Upload Blob button.

8. In the Upload New File dialog that appears, click Browse... (Figure 2-29).

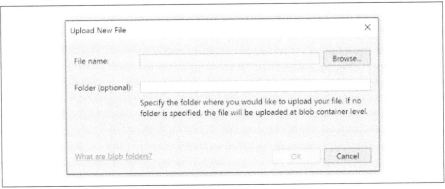

Figure 2-29. The Upload New File dialog.

9. In the Upload Blob dialog, you can select multiple files using either Ctrl to select multiple files individually or Shift to select a range of files. Click Open when you have completed your selection (Figure 2-30).

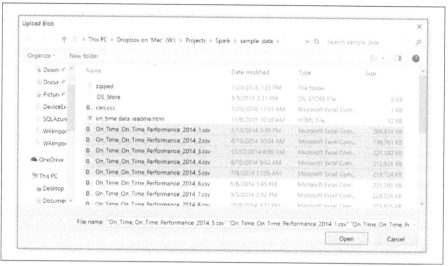

Figure 2-30. Selecting multiple files to upload to Blob Storage.

10. Back in the Upload New File dialog, you can optionally provide a folder subpath that will be used to place the uploaded files below the root of the currently selected container. Click OK to begin the upload process.

11. You can track the status of your uploads in the Microsoft Azure Activity Log that will appear (Figure 2-31).

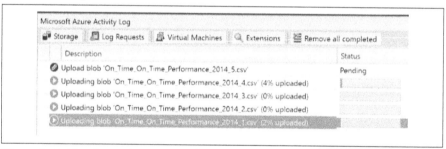

Figure 2-31. The Azure Activity Log showing in-progress uploads.

12. Once finished, if necessary, you can click the Refresh button (next to the Upload Blob button) to update the listing and view the uploaded files (Figure 2-32).

Figure 2-32. The Refresh button.

To upload a batch of files to Blob Storage using Cloud Explorer, follow these steps:

1. Launch Cloud Explorer in Visual Studio, and from the View menu select Cloud Explorer.

2. If prompted, log in with the credentials that have access to your Azure subscription.

3. In a few moments, the tool will list various Azure resources grouped by service. To view your available Azure Storage accounts, expand the Storage Accounts node (Figure 2-33).

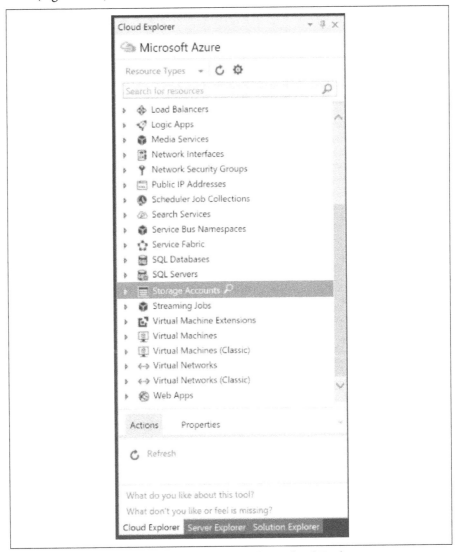

Figure 2-33. Selecting the Storage Accounts node in Cloud Explorer.

4. Expand the Blob Containers node to see the containers in that account (Figure 2-34).

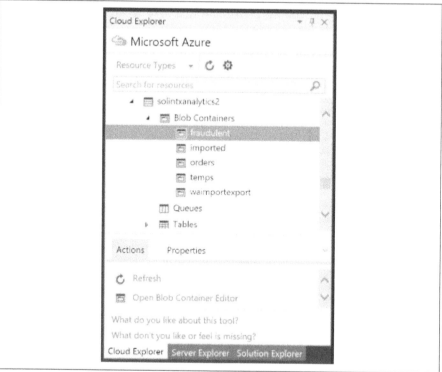

Figure 2-34. Viewing the blob containers underneath a Storage account.

5. Double-click on a container node to view the contents of the container (Figure 2-35).

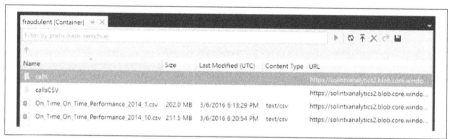

Figure 2-35. Viewing a list of blobs in the selected container.

6. Within the blob container document that appears, click the Upload Blob button (Figure 2-36).

Figure 2-36. *The Upload Blob button.*

7. In the dialog that appears, click Browse… (Figure 2-37).

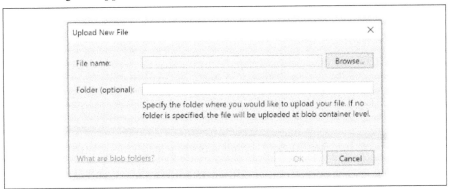

Figure 2-37. *The Upload New File Dialog*

8. In the Upload Blob dialog, you can select multiple files using either Ctrl to select multiple files individually or Shift to select a range of files. Click Open when you have completed your selection (Figure 2-38).

Figure 2-38. *Selecting multiple files to upload.*

9. Back in the Upload New File dialog, you can optionally provide a folder subpath that will be used to place the uploaded files below the root of the currently selected container. Click OK to begin the upload process.

10. You can track the status of your uploads in the Microsoft Azure Activity Log that will appear (Figure 2-39).

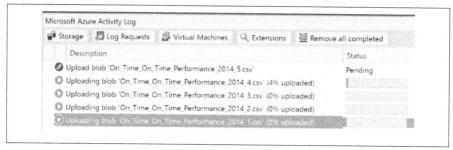

Figure 2-39. Tracking the status of uploads using the Azure Activity Log.

11. Once finished, if necessary, you can click the Refresh button (next to the Upload Blob button) to update the listing and view the uploaded files (Figure 2-40).

Figure 2-40. The Refresh button.

Using Visual Studio Cloud Explorer to bulk-load into your Data Lake Store. Using Cloud Explorer in an approach similar to uploading to Blob Storage, you select a path within your Azure Data Lake Store and upload multiple files at a time. The tool will upload up to six files concurrently and queue the rest. It also gives you the ability to reprioritize queued files.

To upload a batch of files to Azure Data Lake Store using Cloud Explorer, follow these steps:

1. You will need to install the latest Azure Data Lake tools and then restart Visual Studio. To accomplish this, in Cloud Explorer expand Data Lake Store and then select your Data Lake Store.

2. In the Actions pane you will see a link labeled Open File Explorer. Click this, and a link should appear near the top of Cloud Explorer that reads "Azure Data Lake Tools is not installed. Download the latest version." Click the download link.

3. Once the file is downloaded, run the setup executable until completion (there are no options, so it is very straightforward).

4. Restart Visual Studio and return to Cloud Explorer, select your Azure Data Lake Store, and once more click open File Explorer.

5. This time a new document should appear listing the contents of your Data Lake Store (Figure 2-41).

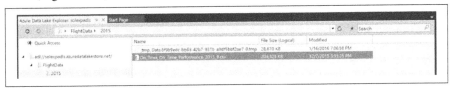

Figure 2-41. Viewing the contents of the Data Lake Store.

6. If you click on a folder in the tree view and then right-click in the whitespace where files are listed, you will be presented with a menu that allows you to upload files (Figure 2-42). Choose "As Row-Structured File" for CSV and delimited text data, or "As Binary" for file types that do not have their line endings preserved.

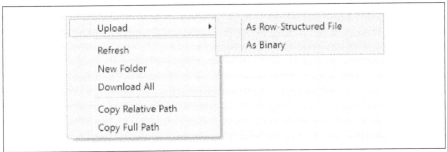

Figure 2-42. Menu showing the options for uploading to the Azure Data Lake Store.

7. In the Upload File dialog, you can select multiple files using either Ctrl to select multiple files individually or Shift to select a range of files. Click Open when you have completed your selection to begin the upload process (Figure 2-43).

Figure 2-43. Selecting multiple files to upload to Azure Data Lake Store.

8. You can track the status of your uploads in the Azure Data Lake Explorer Task List that will appear (Figure 2-44).

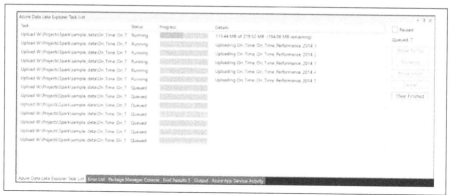

Figure 2-44. Viewing the progress of upload using the Data Lake Explorer Task List.

9. The document listing the files in Azure Data Lake Store will automatically update as your uploads complete.

Microsoft Azure Storage Explorer. This utility, available for free from Microsoft (*http://storageexplorer.com/*), enables you to manage files in Blob Storage without having Visual Studio. In fact, it runs on Windows, macOS, and Linux. With this tool you can upload multiple files in parallel to Azure Blob Storage (Figure 2-45).

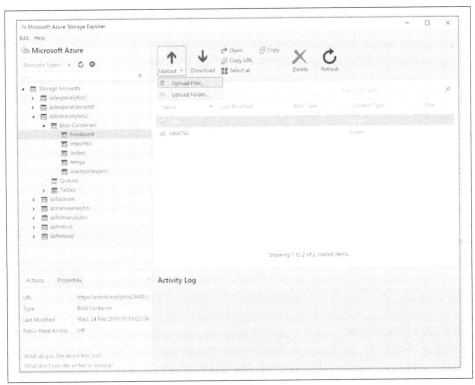

Figure 2-45. The Microsoft Azure Storage Explorer.

Azure Portal. Certain Azure services within the Azure Portal allow you to upload files via the web browser (e.g., Azure Data Lake Store and Azure Files). Unfortunately, the experience tends to be tailored to "single file at a time" approaches, which is of limited use when you are trying to bulk-load data into Azure.

Third-party clients. There are also excellent, free third-party tools that do a great job with bulk data loading. The one I recommend the most is the Azure Explorer from Cerebrata (*http://www.cerebrata.com/products/azure-explorer/introduction*). This tool runs on Windows only, and gives you a Windows Explorer–like shell for dragging and dropping files from your local environment into Azure Blob Storage (Figure 2-46).

Figure 2-46. Cerebrata Azure Explorer.

SSIS Feature Pack for Azure.   If you are already running SQL Server 2012 or later on premises, then you can use SQL Server Integration Services (SSIS) along with the Azure Feature Pack (*https://msdn.microsoft.com/en-us/library/mt146770(v=sql.120).aspx*) to extract data from your local directory on premises and write it out to files on Blob Storage. In short, the Azure Feature Pack comes with an SSIS task called Azure Blob Upload that enables this bulk loading for blobs from SQL Server.

Programmatic clients: Command-line and PowerShell clients

Sometimes the easiest way to bulk-transfer data from your local machine to Azure does not require user interface so much as it does scriptability and reliability. To this end there are a few command-line options that should be part of your toolbox.

AZCopy.   AZCopy is a command-line executable provided by Microsoft that specializes in copying data to and from Azure Blob Storage. While it can also target the Azure Tables and Azure Files services, for our purposes of ingesting data from on premises we are most interested in using it to copy data from a local directory on our filesystem into Azure Blob Storage. It is in this scenario in which it excels, because it offers support for up to 512 concurrent uploads per machine (i.e., it can use as much bandwidth as you can give it) and has an automatic journaling mechanism that enables it to restart failed transfers with minimal waste.

AZCopy is a Windows-only command-line executable. If you need an executable for bulk transfer that can run on macOS or Linux, see "Azure Command-Line Interface" on page 48. You can download AZCopy online (*http://bit.ly/2o50Pb6*). The website is also the primary point of documentation for this feature-rich tool.

Using AZCopy to bulk-load files into Blob Storage. Once you have downloaded AZCopy and installed it, you need to open an instance of the command prompt as an administrator and browse to the directory to which AZCopy was installed (by default this is *C:\Program Files (x86)\Microsoft SDKs\Azure\AZCopy* on 64-bit Windows and *C:\Program Files\Microsoft SDKs\Azure\AZCopy* on 32-bit Windows).

Once you have a command prompt in the AZCopy context, the most basic syntax for copying files from a local directory to Blob Storage is as follows:

```
AzCopy /Source:<pathToLocalFiles>
/Dest:<uriToBlobStorage> /Key:<storageAccountKey>
/S /NC:<numParallelOperations>
```

The parameters used are as follows:

`<pathToLocalFiles>`
> The path to the local file or folder you wish to use as the source.

`<uriToBlobStorage>`
> Has the form *https://<storageAccountName>.blob.core.windows.net/<containerName>/<optionalVirtualPath>*, where the `<storageAccountName>` is the name of your Azure Storage account, `<containerName>` is the name of the target blob container in that Storage account, and `<optionalVirtualPath>` is an optional subfolder path under which your source files will be uploaded.

`<storageAccountKey>`
> The key to your Azure Storage account.

`/S`
> This switch is optional. If it is present, not only are all files in the source directory copied, but so are all subfolders and their contents recursively. If omitted, then only the files in the root of the source directory are copied; subfolders are not copied.

`<numParallelOperations>`
> This is optional, but it enables you to control just how many parallel operations, in this case file uploads, are occurring at once. For most situations there is a point of diminishing returns where having too many upload operations going at once means that collectively all files take a long time to complete. Depending on your file sizes (which for our purposes are quite likely large) and available bandwidth, you may be best served by starting with this set to a low number like 2, 3, or 5. The max you can set it to is 512. By default, AZCopy sets this to a value that is

eight times the number of processor cores on the machine on which it is running (so if you have 4 cores, that means it will try 32 parallel uploads).

For example, here is the command line used to upload all of the files within the *sampl_data* folder on my local machine (without recursing into subdirectories) to my Azure Storage account named solintanalytics2, into the container named *imported* (the key has been shortened for privacy):

```
azcopy /Source:Q:\Projects\Spark\sample_data\
/Dest:https://solintxanalytics2.blob.core.windows.net/imported
/DestKey:gPl/Qf0==
```

Azure Storage Data Movement Library

If you have more programmatic needs, and want to leverage AZCopy in your code, you can use the Azure Storage Data Movement Library, which exposes the functionality as .NET assemblies. See the Azure blog (*http://bit.ly/2ndQ74x*) for instructions.

Azure Command-Line Interface.   If you want a command line that you can use to universally bulk transfer data from macOS, Linux, and Windows machines, you should consider the Azure Command-Line Interface (also known as the Azure CLI) provided by Microsoft and shown in Figure 2-47. The Azure CLI gives you very broad control over everything Azure exposes via its REST API, including Azure Storage.

You can download and install the Azure CLI onto the platform of your choice by following the instructions at *http://bit.ly/2n7QM5T*.

![Screenshot of the Azure Command-Line Interface showing a Windows command prompt with ASCII-art "AZURE" logo and help output]
```
C:\WINDOWS\system32\cmd.exe                                          —  □  ×
Microsoft Windows [Version 10.0.10586]
(c) 2015 Microsoft Corporation. All rights reserved.

C:\Users\ZoinerTejada>azure
info:
info:
info:         _   _____   _ ___ ___
info:        /_\ |_  / | | | _ \ __|
info:   _ ___/ _ \__/ /| |_| |   / _|___ _ _
info:  (___  /_/ \_\/___|\___/|_|_\___| _____)
info:         (_____)           (_____)
info:
info:     Microsoft Azure: Microsoft's Cloud Platform
info:
info:     Tool version 0.9.16
help:
help:     Display help for a given command
help:       help [options] [command]
help:
help:     Log in to an Azure subscription using Active Directory or a Microsoft account identity.
help:       login [options]
help:
help:     Log out from Azure subscription using Active Directory. Currently, the user can log out only via Microsoft orga
nizational account
help:       logout [options] [username]
help:
help:     Open the portal in a browser
help:       portal [options]
help:
help:     Commands:
help:       account        Commands to manage your account information and publish settings
```

Figure 2-47. The Azure Command-Line Interface.

The basic syntax for uploading a file using the Azure CLI is as follows:

```
azure storage blob upload -a <storageAccountName>
-k <storageAccountKey> <localFilePath> <containerName>
```

The parameters are as follows:

`<storageAccountName>`
The name of your Azure Storage account.

`<storageAccountKey>`
The key to your Azure Storage account.

`<localFilePath>`
The path to the local file on your system that will be uploaded.

`<containerName>`
The name of the blob container in your Azure Storage account under which the file will be uploaded.

Note that with the preceding example, we don't need to specify the name of the file (it will automatically infer the appropriate filename to use with Blob Storage).

As a concrete example of using this to transfer a file, here I transfer one CSV file to the fraudulent container (as usual my storage key has been shortened for privacy):

```
azure storage blob upload -a solintxanalytics2
-k gPl ==
Q:\On_Time_On_Time_Performance_2015_9.csv
fraudulent
```

No doubt you have noticed that this syntax allows for uploading only one file at a time. Unfortunately, the current version does not support specifying a directory for upload. The workaround is to incorporate calls to the Azure CLI within your platform's preferred shell scripting approach to create a loop around all the files or folders you wish to transfer.

AdlCopy. In order to move files from on premises into your Azure Data Lake Store, you can use AdlCopy. At present this is not a direct copy proposition (see "Power-Shell cmdlets" on page 50 for other, more direct options); you first need to stage your files in Blob Storage (for example, by using AZCopy or the Azure CLI) and then you can run AdlCopy to transfer the files from Blob Storage to your Azure Data Lake Store.

AdlCopy is provided by Microsoft and can be downloaded from *http://aka.ms/down-loadadlcopy*. It is available only for Windows 10.

The simplest syntax for copying files from a container in Blob Storage into a folder in Azure Data Lake Store is as follows:

```
adlcopy /Source <uriToBlobContainer>
/Dest <uriToADLSfolder> /SourceKey <storageAccountKey>
```

The parameters are as follows:

`<uriToBlobContainer>`
> The URI to your Azure Storage account blob container.

`<uritToADLSfolder>`
> The URI to your Azure Data Lake Store folder.

`<storageAccountKey>`
> The key to your Azure Storage account.

You may be wondering where you provide the credentials for the Azure Data Lake Store. When you run the `adlcopy` command, you will be prompted for them in a pop-up window.

By way of example, here is a complete command line showing how to copy from my imported container within my solintxanalytics2 Azure Storage account, copying only the files under the path *sampledata/zipped* to my Azure Data Lake Store named Solliance to a folder under the root named *imported2*:

```
adlcopy
/Source https://solintxanalytics2.blob.core.windows.net/
imported/sampledata/zipped/
/Dest adl://solliance.azuredatalakestore.net/imported2/
/SourceKey gPlftsdgs==
```

In the preceding example, when specifying the *uriToADLSfolder*, you can use either the `adl:` protocol (as was just shown) or the `swebhdfs:` protocol (which is often shown in the documentation). The `adl` protocol is the preferred option moving forward, but the `swebhdfs` protocol is available for backward compatibility.

PowerShell cmdlets. Azure PowerShell cmdlets can be used to automate the transfer of files from on premises to either Azure Blob Storage or Azure Data Lake Store.

Bulk loading into Azure Storage account blobs. Azure PowerShell enables you to upload a file at a time using the Set-AzureStorageBlobContent cmdlet. You can wrap this with a call to the `Get-ChildItem` cmdlet to upload all the local files in the current directory to a container in Blob Storage:

```
Get-ChildItem -File -Recurse |
Set-AzureStorageBlobContent -Container "<containerName>"
```

In order for this command to properly function, the context needs to be set up with the Azure subscription and Azure Storage account selected. The following shows a complete example of this sequence:

```
Add-AzureAccount

Select-AzureSubscription -SubscriptionName "my subscription"

Set-AzureSubscription -CurrentStorageAccountName "solintxanalytics2"
-SubscriptionName "my subscription"

Get-ChildItem -File -Recurse |
Set-AzureStorageBlobContent -Container "imported"
```

The command executes with the output shown in Figure 2-48.

Figure 2-48. Example output from upload to Azure Storage using Azure PowerShell.

Bulk loading into Azure Data Lake Store.   Azure PowerShell 1.0 and later provides a cmdlet to directly upload files and folder from your local machine to a folder path on Azure Data Lake Store.

At a high level, the syntax appears as follows:

```
Import-AzureRmDataLakeStoreItem -AccountName "<ADLSAccountName>"
-Path "<localFilePath>" -Destination <filePathInADLS>
```

The parameters are as follows:

<ADLSAccountName>
> The name (not URI) of your Azure Data Lake Store account.

<localFilePath>
> The local path to a file or to a folder. The value should end in a forward slash (\)
> to represent a folder.

<filePathInADLS>
> The file or folder name. The value should end in a backslash (/) to represent a
> folder as it should appear in Azure Data Lake Store.

The sequence used to invoke this cmdlet begins with launching PowerShell. After that you will need to use the `Login-RmAccount` cmdlet to gain access. Then, depending on how many subscriptions you have, you may have to use `Select-RmSubscription` to change the active subcriptions used by the context to a different subscription. After this, you can invoke the `Import-AzureRmDataLakeStoreItem` cmdlet. The following shows an example of this sequence:

```
Login-RmAccount

Select-AzureRmSubscription
-SubscriptionName "Solliance Subscription"

Import-AzureRmDataLakeStoreItem -AccountName "solliance"
-Path "W:\Projects\Spark\sample_data\" -Destination /imported3
```

This command will execute with output similar to Figure 2-49.

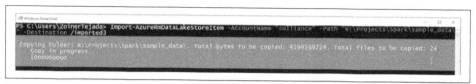

Figure 2-49. Example output of uploading to Azure Data Lake Store using PowerShell.

Network-Oriented Approaches

There are other approaches to performing bulk data transfers that have heavier networking requirements than a simple graphical or command-line client, and so we classify these as network-oriented approaches. In some cases, these approaches center on a particular protocol such as FTP, UDP, or SMB. In other cases, they center on establishing a network tunnel that enables persistent hybrid connectivity—such as establishing a virtual private network between your on-premises location and Azure.

FTP

For many legacy systems, the File Transfer Protocol (FTP) was, and may still be, the key protocol used for batch transferring of data files. There no Azure services that directly support the ingest of files via FTP; however, you can deploy a protocol gateway that enables FTP ingest on the perimeter, which is then backed by Azure Blob Storage.

There are three approaches to this:

- Build a cloud service worker role that exposes FTP endpoints.
- Run a virtual machine, with FTP services installed, that has a Windows service running that transfers the files from the FTP server's folders to Azure Storage.

- Leverage the FTP endpoints already available via the Azure Web Apps service to receive FTP transfers to a monitored location on the filesystem that then transfers the files to Azure Storage.

The cloud service worker role option exists in the community, but the code is very much in need of a refresh. If this approach is preferable to you, I suggest you examine the source available at *http://ftp2azure.codeplex.com/*.

The details of the setup for the VM approach are beyond the scope of this book, but are fairly well documented in the blog post "FTP Server Proxy for Azure Blob Storage" (*http://www.redbaronofazure.com/?p=5781*).

The last option, and the one I prefer, is to use an Azure web app with a Web Job. The web app provides the FTP endpoints and receives files to storage it also provides. A Web Job is used to host code (such as the FileSystemWatcher component from .NET) that looks for new files in the filesystem and then triggers the execution of logic that copies the file to Azure Storage. For the steps to set this up, take a look at *http://bit.ly/2mVH2u2*.

UDP transfers

With the increasing adoption of cloud storage, a clear need has surfaced for optimizing transfers from on premises to cloud storage. Most cloud storage services, such as Azure Storage, are accessed through Transmission Control Protocol (TCP), which relies on bidirectional communication. When you are performing an upload, the communication needs to be largely one way, from the source to the destination, and removing the chattiness incurred by maintaining a bidirectional channel can result in a significant speedup in network transfer rates. To do so, change the protocol used for the transfer: instead of using TCP, leverage the one-way User Datagram Protocol (UDP).

There are no services in Azure that natively offer UDP endpoints, but to fill this void two vendors provide excellent solutions that deploy into Azure to let you upload from on-premises clients to Azure Storage via UDP. While these two solutions are not free, they can be pivotal components of your ingest strategy by enabling reliable, fast, and persistent ingest of large files to Azure Storage:

- Aspera Server On Demand (*http://bit.ly/2nCI5U2*)
- Signiant Flight (*http://bit.ly/2ndDJBD*)

SMB network shares

Another option you might be considering for ingest is to use network shares. On premises these work well to copy files between servers, so what about using the same approach to copy from on premises to Azure? The most common protocol for network shares is Server Message Block (SMB), and there is one service in Azure that supports it natively: Azure Files. Azure Files is a component of Azure Storage that lets you store up to 5 terabytes' worth of files in a network share that is accessible from any authorized device or client application.

With Azure Files you can mount shares from on-premises client services that support SMB 3.0 (basically Windows 8 onward and Windows Server 2012 onward). However, there is a hidden gotcha: many internet service providers block outbound TCP port 445 for security reasons, and this port is required by SMB. In other words, while Azure Files may enable you to make a connection between your on-premises machines and an Azure Files share via SMB, your ISP may prevent you from making that connection. This latter issue typically rules out SMB as an option for on premises to Azure Files.

Hybrid connections and Azure Data Factory

The term *hybrid cloud* refers to the ability to have services that span from an on-premises datacenter to services in the cloud, supporting communication in both directions as desired. One approach to establishing such connectivity is to use site-to-site networking, which we will discuss in the next section. Another approach is to use hybrid connections, as we will discuss here.

Hybrid connections revolve around the notion that you have a service running in Azure that needs to access a service or resources that are available only on premises, and they do this with minimal impact on your network configuration by requiring only outbound TCP or HTTP connectivity. To accomplish this, they deploy a software agent that lives within the on-premises network and acts as proxy for the Azure-hosted services to be able to reach the services desired on the network. The agent is responsible for maintaining a secure connection with Azure, and for proxying traffic from Azure to the target service and from the target service back to Azure. Typical examples of this include enabling an Azure web app to query data stored in SQL Server on premises, or to access a file share that exists only on premises (see Figure 2-50).

The setup typically proceeds as follows:

1. Provision a service that supports hybrid connectivity in Azure.

2. Using the portal, download an installer onto a machine in the on-premises network that contains the service you want Azure to access.

3. After installation, return to the portal to configure the destination the agent should be talking to (e.g., the hostname and port of your SQL Server or the IP address of your file server).

4. Once configured, the Azure services that use this agent can communicate with the machine as if it were local to them.

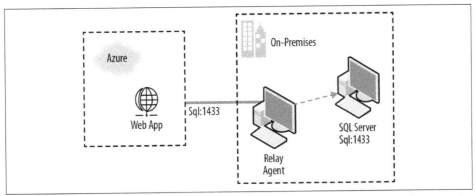

Figure 2-50. Example of a hybrid connection between a web app running in Azure and SQL Server running on premises.

Hybrid connections are available to Azure App Services, which means your websites and Web Jobs running, for example, on a web app can use the hybrid connection to talk to your on-premises SQL Server. This scenario may be interesting to you if you have code that you want to trigger that is hosted within an app service. The setup for an app service hybrid connection is simple, but is outside the scope of this book. For details, see the Microsoft Azure documentation (*http://bit.ly/2mV9GMq*).

The hybrid connections we focus on in this book are those that are tailor-made for bulk data movement from your on-premises resources. The Azure service that provides this capability is the Azure Data Factory (ADF). ADF provides the services and tooling to compose and integrate data, build data pipelines, and monitor their status in real time. It has a broad set of functionality to which we will return a few times in this book, but for our focus on data ingest ADF supports data movement from on-premises sources including a file share, SQL Server, Teradata, Oracle Database, MySQL Database, DB2, Sybase Database, PostgresSQL, ODBC, and HDFS. The data movement can ingest the data to Azure services including Azure Blob Storage and Table Storage, Azure SQL Database, Azure SQL Data Warehouse, and Azure Data Lake Store.

To accomplish the connectivity to the on-premises source, ADF uses the Data Management Gateway, which is a hybrid connection agent as we discussed previously. Once you have the Data Management Gateway agent installed, you configure data sets that represent the source and destination, and construct a pipeline that consists of a single activity, the Copy activity, which moves data between these data sets.

Ingesting from a file share to Blob Storage

Let's look in detail at the steps to create an Azure Data Factory pipeline that copies files from a folder on a network share to blobs in Azure Storage. We begin by creating an Azure Data Factory instance.

1. Log in to the Azure Portal (*https://portal.azure.com*).
2. Click New.
3. Choose Data + Analytics, and then click Azure Data Factory.
4. Provide a name for your new Data Factory, and select an Azure subscription, a resource group, and a region.
5. Click OK to create your Azure Data Factory.

Once your Data Factory has been created, it takes about 20 minutes to provision; the blade for it should automatically open in the Azure Portal. You are now ready to install and configure the Data Management Gateway.

1. Log in to the machine on which you will install the agent for the Data Management Gateway.
2. Navigate to the Azure Portal. If possible, use Internet Explorer for the following steps, because the gateway install is easier with ClickOnce.
3. From the ADF blade, click "Author and deploy" (Figure 2-51).

Figure 2-51. The "Author and deploy" tile on the Data Factory blade.

4. In the blade that appears, click "More commands" (Figure 2-52).

Figure 2-52. The "More commands" button

5. Click "New data gateway" (Figure 2-53).

Figure 2-53. The "New data gateway" button

6. Provide a name for your data gateway and click OK.

7. On the Configure blade, click the link below Express Setup ("Install directly on this computer"). Alternately, click the "Download and install data gateway" link if you are not using IE (when you do this, be sure to copy the NEW KEY value on the blade so you can enter it during the installation). See Figure 2-54.

Figure 2-54. The Configure blade enables you to download the data gateway installer.

8. Follow the onscreen instructions of the agent installer.

9. After a few moments you should see your gateway is connected in the Microsoft Data Management Configuration Manager (Figure 2-55).

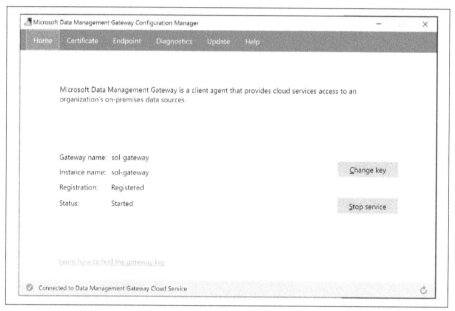

Figure 2-55. The Data Management Gateway Configuration Manager.

10. Back on the Configure blade, click OK and OK again to complete the "New data gateway" setup.

11. You should now be back on the "Author and deploy" blade. Click "New data store" (Figure 2-56) and select Filesystem from the drop-down.

Figure 2-56. The "New data store" button.

12. In the dialog that appears, provide values for the following properties located within the `typeProperties` object (Example 2-1):

host
> Enter the UNC path to the file share you will be uploading from. You need to escape the slashes by doubling them up—for example, *mycomputer\sample-data* would need to be entered as *mycomputer**sampledata*\\.

gatewayName
> Enter the name of the gateway you just provisioned.

Example 2-1. Sample configuration of a linked service

```
{
    "name": "OnPremisesFileServerLinkedService",
    "properties": {
        "type": "OnPremisesFileServer",
        "description": "",
        "typeProperties": {
            "host": "\\\\DESKTOP-ORFJ0P6\\SampleData\\",
            "gatewayName": "sol-gateway",
            "userId": "<Domain user name e.g. domain\\\\user>",
            "password": "<Domain password>"
        }
    }
}
```

13. When you finish entering the `gatewayName`, a button labeled "encrypt creden-tials" should appear (if not, try deleting the quote before `gatewayName` and then re-adding the quote). Click the "encrypt credentials" button. This will download a ClickOnce application called Credential Manager into which you will enter the username and password of a Windows account authorized to access the share. Since this relies on ClickOnce to install the app, you will need to use IE.

14. In the Credential Manager enter the following (see Figure 2-57):

Username
Provide the username in the on-premises environment that can access the share. Be sure to enter it in *domain\username* format.

Password
Enter the password for the user.

Figure 2-57. The Data Factory Credential Manager.

15. Click OK.

16. Return to the linked service you were just editing and click Deploy (Figure 2-58).

Figure 2-58. The Deploy button

Now that you have established connectivity to your file share via the linked service, you are ready to begin constructing the data sets and the pipeline. First, begin by creating a data set that represents the file share.

1. Within the "Author and deploy" blade, click "New dataset."

2. Choose "On-premises file" from the drop-down (Figure 2-59).

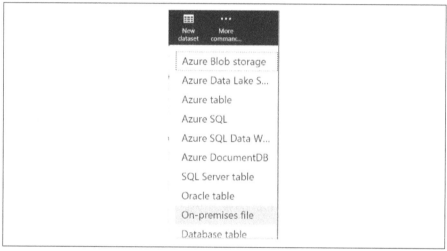

Figure 2-59. Options for a new dataset

3. Specify the following attributes (Example 2-2):

name
: Enter the name of this data set.

linkedServiceName
: Provide the name of the linked service you just created.

folderPath
: Provide the relative path to the folder containing the files you wish to process (relative to the root of the share). Enter the path with double slashes (e.g., *foo \\bar*).

availability.frequency
> Specify the unit for the interval. Valid values are Minute, Hour, Day, Week, and Month.

availability.interval
> Specify the interval as an integer (no quotes around the value because it is an integer and not a string).

external
> This attribute is not present in the template, but you must add it (beneath availability) because the data represented by this data set is produced by a process outside of the pipeline (i.e., it's an input to the pipeline and not a target or sink). Set the value to true.

Example 2-2. Example of an on-premises file data set

```
{
    "name": "OnPremisesFile",
    "properties": {
        "type": "FileShare",
        "linkedServiceName": "OnPremisesFileServerLinkedService",
        "typeProperties": {
            "folderPath": "raw\\"
        },
        "availability": {
            "frequency": "Minute",
            "interval": 15
        },
        "external": true
    }
}
```

4. Click Deploy.

Next, you need to create a linked service that represents the connection information to Azure Storage.

1. Within the "Author and deploy" blade, click "New data store."

2. Choose Azure Storage from the drop-down.

3. Specify the following attributes (Example 2-3):

connectionString
> Provide the AccountName and the AccountKey for the Storage account that contains the blob container you will target.

Example 2-3. Example of linked service to Azure Storage

```
{
    "name": "AzureStorageLinkedService",
    "properties": {
        "type": "AzureStorage",
        "description": "",
        "typeProperties": {
            "connectionString":
                "DefaultEndpointsProtocol=https;AccountName=
                <accountname>;AccountKey=<accountkey>"
        }
    }
}
```

4. Click Deploy.

Now that you have a linked service for Azure Storage, you need to create a data set that represents the data as it will be stored.

1. Within the "Author and deploy" blade, click "New dataset."

2. Choose Azure Blob Storage from the drop-down.

3. Specify the appropriate attributes. Let's assume you are uploading CSV files, so you would delete the structure object and then specify the following (Example 2-4):

linkedServiceName
> Provide the name of the linked service for Azure Blob Storage that you just created.

folderPath
> Enter the container and path to which your files will be written, including the partitions if you specify any in the partitionedBy property (e.g., con tainername/{Year}/{Month}/{Day}).

format
> Enter TextFormat.

columnDelimiter, rowDelimiter, EscapeChar, NullValue
> These can be deleted unless your CSV has something unusual.

availability.frequency
> Specify the unit for interval (Minute, Hour, Day, Week, or Month).

availability.interval
> Specify the interval as an integer (no quotes around the value):

Example 2-4. An Azure Blob Dataset configuration

```json
{
    "name": "AzureBlobDataset",
    "properties": {
        "published": false,
        "type": "AzureBlob",
        "linkedServiceName": "AzureStorageLinkedService",
        "typeProperties": {
            "folderPath": "adfupload/{Year}/{Month}/{Day}",
            "format":{
                "type": "TextFormat"
            },
            "partitionedBy": [
                {
                    "name": "Year",
                    "value": {
                        "type": "DateTime",
                        "date": "SliceStart",
                        "format": "yyyy"
                    }
                },
                {
                    "name": "Month",
                    "value": {
                        "type": "DateTime",
                        "date": "SliceStart",
                        "format": "MM"
                    }
                },
                {
                    "name": "Day",
                    "value": {
                        "type": "DateTime",
                        "date": "SliceStart",
                        "format": "dd"
                    }
                }
            ]
        },
        "availability": {
            "frequency": "Minute",
            "interval": 15
        }
    }
}
```

4. Click Deploy.

At this point you have data sets for both the source (the files on the file share) and the destination (the blobs in Azure Storage). You are now ready to create a pipeline that describes the data movement by way of activities (in this case, a single Copy activity between both data sets).

1. Within the "Author and deploy" blade, click "More commands" and then "New pipeline" (Figure 2-60).

Figure 2-60. The "New pipeline" button.

2. Click "Add activity" (Figure 2-61).

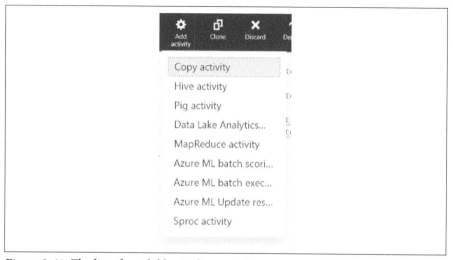

Figure 2-61. The list of available pipeline activities.

3. Choose "Copy activity" from the drop-down.

4. At minimum, specify the following attributes (Example 2-5):

Description
    Provide a user-friendly description for the pipeline.

inputs[0].name
    Provide the name of your file share data set.

outputs[0].name
    Provide the name of your blob container data set.

typeProperties.source.type
Enter `FileSystemSource`.

typeProperties.source.sqlReaderQuery
Delete this property.

typeProperties.sink.type
Enter `BlobSink`.

scheduler.frequency
Specify the unit.

scheduler.interval
Specify the interval as an integer (no quotes around the value).

start
Enter the date when the pipeline should start running, in YYYY-MM-DD format. Set this to today's date.

end
Enter the date when the pipeline should stop running, in YYYY-MM-DD format. Set this to a future date.

5. Be sure to delete the `typeProperties.source.sqlReaderQuery` attribute that was provided by the template as a sample.

Example 2-5. Example of a pipeline

```
{
    "name": "PipelineTemplate",
    "properties": {
        "description": "copies files from a share to blob storage",
        "activities": [
            {
                "name": "CopyActivityTemplate",
                "type": "Copy",
                "inputs": [
                    {
                        "name": "OnPremisesFile"
                    }
                ],
                "outputs": [
                    {
                        "name": "AzureBlobDataset"
                    }
                ],
                "typeProperties": {
                    "source": {
```

```
                "type": "FileSystemSource"
            },
            "sink": {
                "type": "BlobSink"
            }
        },
        "policy": {
            "concurrency": 1,
            "executionPriorityOrder": "OldestFirst",
            "retry": 3,
            "timeout": "1.00:00:00"
        },
        "scheduler": {
            "frequency": "Minute",
            "interval": 15
        }
    }
    ],
    "start": "2015-03-07T00:00:00Z",
    "end": "2015-03-15T00:00:00Z"
  }
}
```

6. Click Deploy.

 Parameter Documentation

For the details on all the parameters available to the Azure Blob
Storage linked service and data set, see the Microsoft Azure documentation (*http://bit.ly/2n80dCr*).

Congratulations! You've just created your first data pipeline that copies data from an
on-premises file share to a blob in Azure Storage. Your data sets should soon begin
processing slices, and you should see your files start to appear in Azure Blob Storage
shortly.

To check on the status of your pipeline, from the home blade for your Azure Data
Factory, click Monitoring App, as shown in Figure 2-62.

Figure 2-62. The Monitoring App tile available on the Data Factory blade.

This will pop open a new browser window that loads the Monitoring App, which lets you inspect the status of your pipeline by activity and time slice (Figure 2-63).

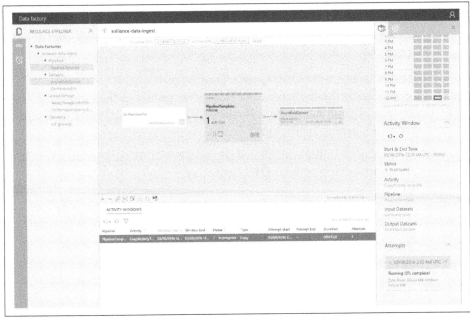

Figure 2-63. The Data Factory Monitoring App showing pipeline activity.

Ingesting from a file share to Azure Data Lake Store

Building upon the on-premises file linked service and data set from the previous section, in this section we show you can also target the Azure Data Lake Store.

Before you proceed with this section, you should have created an Azure Data Lake Store. The details of this process will be covered in Chapter 3, but for our purposes here you can create one using the Azure Portal.

1. Click New.

2. Select Data + Storage.

3. Select Azure Data Lake Store.

4. Provide a name, and choose a subscription, a resource group, and location.

5. Click Create.

Now you are ready to provision the linked service pointing to your Azure Data Lake Store.

1. Within the "Author and deploy" blade, click "New data store."

2. Choose Azure Data Lake Store from the drop-down.

3. In the editor, provide the following properties (Example 2-6):

   dataLakeStoreUri
   > Provide the URI to your Data Lake Store. It will be of the form *https://[data-lakestorename].azuredatalakestore.net/webhdfs/v1*.

   accountName, subscriptionId, resourceGroupName
   > You can delete these if your Data Lake Store resides in the same Azure subscription as your Azure Data Factory. If that is not the case, then you will need to fill these properties in.

4. Click the Authorize button, which will pop up a new browser window that will be used to authorize access to your Data Lake Store.

Example 2-6. Example of a completed Data Lake Store linked service

```
{
    "name": "AzureDataLakeStoreLinkedService",
    "properties": {
        "type": "AzureDataLakeStore",
        "description": "",
        "typeProperties": {
            "authorization":
                "https://portal.azure.com/tokenauthorize?code=AAABAAAAiL9kn...",
            "dataLakeStoreUri":
                "https://<storename>.azuredatalakestore.net/webhdfs/v1",
            "sessionId": "eyJJZCI6bn..."
        }
    }
}
```

5. Click Deploy.

Now that you have a linked service for Azure Data Lake Store, you need to create a data set that represents the data as it will be stored.

1. Within the "Author and deploy" blade, click "New dataset."

2. Choose Azure Data Lake Store from the drop-down.

3. Specify the appropriate attributes. Let's assume you are uploading CSV files, so you would delete the structure object and do the following (see Example 2-7):

   linkedServiceName
   > Provide the name of the linked service for Azure Data Lake Store that you just created.

folderPath
: Enter the folder path to where your files will be written, including the partitions if you specify any in the `partitionedBy` property (e.g., *foldername/ {Year}/{Month}/{Day}*).

filePath
: Delete this when uploading a folder.

format
: Enter `TextFormat`.

columnDelimiter, rowDelimiter, EscapeChar, NullValue
: These can be deleted unless your CSV has something unusual.

compression
: Delete this to leave the CSV files uncompressed.

availability.frequency
: Specify the unit for interval (`Minute`, `Hour`, `Day`, `Week`, or `Month`).

availability.interval
: Specify the interval as an integer (no quotes around the value).

Example 2-7. Example of a completed Data Lake Store data set

```
{
    "name": "AzureDataLakeStoreDataset",
    "properties": {
        "published": false,
        "type": "AzureDataLakeStore",
        "linkedServiceName": "AzureDataLakeStoreLinkedService",
        "typeProperties": {
            "folderPath": "adfupload/{Year}/{Month}/{Day}/{Hour}",
            "format":{
                "type": "TextFormat"
            },
            "partitionedBy": [
                {
                    "name": "Year",
                    "value": {
                        "type": "DateTime",
                        "date": "SliceStart",
                        "format": "yyyy"
                    }
                },
                {
                    "name": "Month",
                    "value": {
```

```
                "type": "DateTime",
                "date": "SliceStart",
                "format": "MM"
            }
        },
        {
            "name": "Day",
            "value": {
                "type": "DateTime",
                "date": "SliceStart",
                "format": "dd"
            }
        },
        {
            "name": "Hour",
            "value": {
                "type": "DateTime",
                "date": "SliceStart",
                "format": "HH"
            }
        }
    ]
},
"availability": {
    "frequency": "Minute",
    "interval": 15
}
    }
}
```

4. Click Deploy.

 Azure Data Lake Store Parameters

For the details on all the parameters available to the Azure Data Lake Store linked service and data set, see the Microsoft Azure documentation (*http://bit.ly/2nnOaDk*).

At this point you have data sets for both the source (the files on the file share) and the destination (the files in Azure Data Lake Store). You are now ready to create a pipeline that describes the data movement by way of activities (in this case, a single Copy activity).

1. Within the "Author and deploy" blade, click "More commands" and then "New pipeline."

2. Click "Add activity."

3. Choose "Copy activity" from the drop-down.

4. At minimum, specify the following attributes (Example 2-8):

Description
: Provide a user-friendly description for the pipeline.

inputs[0].name
: Provide the name of your file share dataset.

outputs[0].name
: Provide the name of your blob container data set.

typeProperties.source.type
: Enter FileSystemSource.

typeProperties.source.sqlReaderQuery
: Delete this property.

typeProperties.sink.type
: Enter AzureDataLakeStoreSink.

scheduler.frequency
: Specify the unit.

scheduler.interval
: Specify the interval as an integer (no quotes around the value).

start
: Enter the date when the pipeline should start running, in YYYY-MM-DD format. Set this to today's date.

end
: Enter the date when the pipeline should stop running, in YYYY-MM-DD format. Set this to a future date.

5. Be sure to delete the typeProperties.source.sqlReaderQuery attribute that was provided by the template as a sample.

Example 2-8. Example of a completed on-premises file share to Azure Data Lake Store pipeline

```
{
    "name": "PipelineOnPremToLake",
    "properties": {
        "description":
          "Copies data from on-premises share to Data Lake Store",
        "activities": [
            {
```

```
        "name": "CopyActivityTemplate",
        "type": "Copy",
        "inputs": [
            {
                "name": "OnPremisesFile"
            }
        ],
        "outputs": [
            {
                "name": "AzureDataLakeStoreDataSet"
            }
        ],
        "typeProperties": {
            "source": {
                "type": "FileSystemSource"
            },
            "sink": {
                "type": "AzureDataLakeStoreSink"
            }
        },
        "policy": {
            "concurrency": 1,
            "executionPriorityOrder": "OldestFirst",
            "retry": 3,
            "timeout": "01:00:00"
        },
        "scheduler": {
            "frequency": "Minute",
            "interval": 15
        }
    }
    ],
    "start": "2016-03-06T00:00:00Z",
    "end": "2016-03-15T00:00:00Z"
    }
}
```

6. Click Deploy.

At this point your pipeline copying files from the on-premises share to the Azure Data Lake Store should be running, and you should see your files start to appear within a few minutes. If you use the Monitoring App from the Data Factory blade, you should see both of your pipelines running, as shown in Figure 2-64.

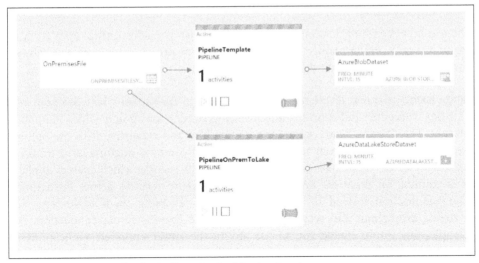

Figure 2-64. Viewing both pipelines in the Monitoring App.

If you get any errors, the best place to see their details is within the Monitoring App. Select a row indicating an error in the Activity Windows panel (the panel at the bottom center) and then in the Activity Window detail panel (the rightmost panel) under Attempts, you will see any errors for the selected time slice. If you expand the error you will be presented with the error details, similar to Figure 2-65.

Figure 2-65. Viewing exceptions in the Monitoring App.

Site-to-site networking

When it comes to bulk loading data, you might also consider setting up a form of site-to-site networking connectivity between your on-premises network and Azure. There are two approaches to this.

Express Route. Express Route lets you create private connections between your on-premises datacenter and Azure, without having connections going across the public internet. The Express Route setup is more involved and expensive than the options presented thus far, but it may make sense for you if you have ongoing large transfers to Azure. Express Route allows you to use Microsoft *peering*, which enables applications running on premises to transmit data to Azure services across the Express Route connection instead of across the internet, enabling them to leverage the increased throughput and security available to the Express Route connection. For example, this would enable you to use any of the aforementioned applications or commands to bulk-transfer data to Azure Blob Storage over your dedicated Express Route connection.

More Info on Express Route

For more information on Express Route, see the Microsoft Azure documentation (*http://bit.ly/2n7UXyC*).

Virtual private networks. Azure Virtual Networks enable you to set up a site-to-site virtual private network (VPN). Unlike Express Route, site-to-site VPN does not have a Microsoft peering option that makes Azure services such as Azure Storage available across a VPN. Moreover, the VPN connectivity to Azure happens over the public internet, so adding a VPN layer on top of it means your bulk data transfers are likely to be slower than without the VPN.

Stream Loading

With stream loading, we take a different approach to ingesting data into Azure, typically for a very different purpose. Whereas in the bulk load scenario, Blue Yonder Airlines was interested in transferring their historical flight delay data, in the stream loading scenario they are interested in collecting telemetry emitted by thermostats (such as the point-in-time temperature and whether the heating or cooling is running) and motion sensors (such as the point-in-time reading indicating if motion was detected in the past 10 seconds).

Stream loading targets queues that can buffer up events or messages until downstream systems can process them.

For our purposes we will examine Azure Event Hubs and Azure IoT Hub as targets, and consider both of them simply as queueing endpoints. We will delve into their function much more deeply in the next chapter.

Stream Loading with Event Hubs

Event Hubs provide a managed service for the large-scale ingest of events. At what scale? Think billions of events per day. Event Hubs receive *events* (also referred to as *messages*) from a public endpoint and store them in a horizontally scalable queue, ready for consumption by consumers that appear later in the data pipeline.

Event Hubs provide endpoints that support both the AMQP 1.0 and HTTPS (over TLS, or Transport Layer Security) protocols. AMQP is designed for message senders (aka event publishers) that desire a long-standing, bidirectional connection such as the connected thermostats in the Blue Yonder scenario. HTTPS is traditionally deployed for senders that cannot maintain a persistent connection. For an example of an HTTPS client, think of devices connected by cellular that periodically check in: cost and/or battery capacity constraints may preclude them from maintaining an open cellular data connection, so they connect to the cell network, transmit their messages, and disconnect.

Events sent to Event Hubs can be sent one at a time, or as a batch, so long as the resulting event is not larger than 256 KB. With AMQP, the event is sent as a binary payload (see Figure 2-66). With HTTPS, the event is sent with a JSON serialized payload.

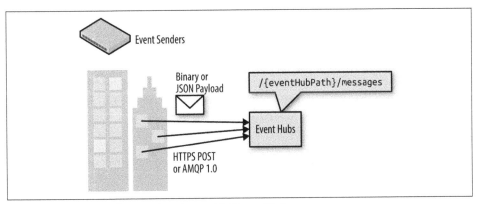

Figure 2-66. Ingest of streaming data with Event Hubs.

Stream loading with IoT Hub

IoT Hub is another Azure service that is designed to ingest messages or events at massive scale. For our purposes in this chapter (focusing on message ingest), the IoT Hub endpoint functions in a similar fashion to Event Hubs (in fact it provides an

Event Hubs endpoint). The key difference is that in choosing to use IoT Hub, you gain support for an additional protocol—MQTT, which is a fairly common protocol utilized by IoT solutions. Therefore, ingesting from device to cloud with IoT Hub looks as shown in Figure 2-67.

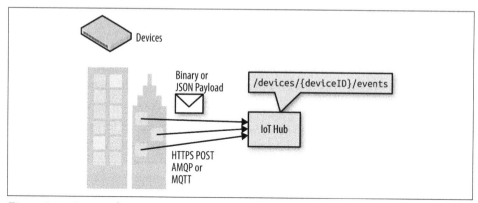

Figure 2-67. Ingest of streaming data with IoT Hub

In the next chapter, we will examine Event Hubs and IoT Hubs in more detail, along with introducing a simulator for Blue Yonder Airlines that simulates devices transmitting telemetry.

Summary

In this chapter we focused on the ingest loading layer, exploring two different approaches. First, we looked at various options for bulk loading data into Azure from on premises. We covered the options broadly, including the Import/Export Service, Visual Studio, Microsoft Azure Storage Explorer, AzCopy, AdlCopy, Azure CLI and Azure PowerShell cmdlets, FTP upload, UDP upload, SMB transfers, hybrid connections, Azure Data Factory, and site-to-site networking options. Second, we looked at streaming ingest of telemetry into Azure and the services that support it, namely Event Hubs and IoT Hub.

In the next chapter we turn our focus to the *target* of the data ingest, or rather where the data transmitted is initially stored.

CHAPTER 3

Storing Ingested Data in Azure

In this chapter, we explore where to land the transferred data and how to choose among the storage options. These options fall into two broad categories: file-oriented storage and queue-oriented storage. The particular category selected impacts the type (and latency) of processing performed at later stages in the pipeline. We intentionally omit other data stores (such as NoSQL or document stores) as the initial landing place for ingested data, as the file and queue options are the simplest and least likely to impose changes on the ingested data before processing can begin.

In terms of our analytics pipeline we are going to examine the storage items outlined in Figure 3-1.

File-Oriented Storage

The more things change, the more they stay the same. This is also true of the innovations in approaches for storing big data used in analytics scenarios—the notion of a filesystem that contains a tree of directories, which in turn can contain files of different formats and encodings, has persisted in storing data at cloud scale. In this section, we examine three such "filesystems" prevalent in Azure: Blob Storage, Azure Data Lake Store, and the Hadoop File System (HDFS).

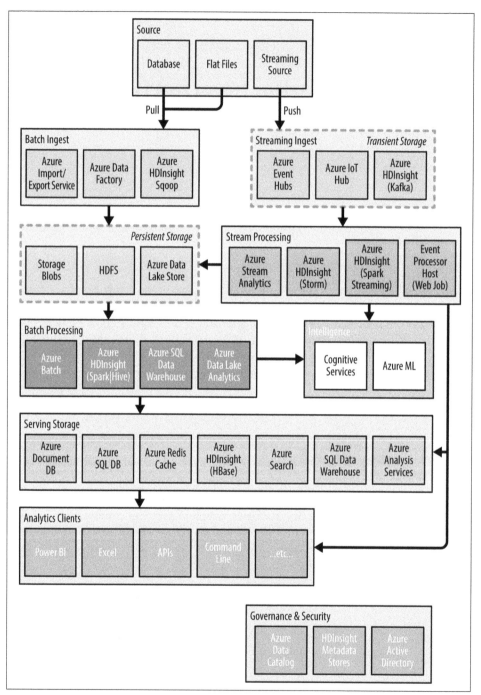

Figure 3-1. Transient and persistent storage services are the focus of this chapter.

Blob Storage

Azure Blob Storage provides highly available, high-scale object storage and allows you to store file data such as text files and binary files. Blob Storage is a component of Azure Storage. In other words, to provision Blob Storage in your Azure subscription you create an Azure Storage account, and within that Azure Storage account are three storage services: Table Storage (a NoSQL key/value store), Queue Storage (a simple queueing service), and Blob Storage—the latter of which is the focus of this section. Blob Storage is used extensively throughout Azure to store things from logs to virtual machine disks.

Blob Storage capabilities

Blob Storage enables you to store files predominantly in three different formats according to your read/write workload.

Block blobs

> Block blobs are optimized for storing text or binary files, allowing for efficient parallel upload/download of a block or list of blocks and modification of a blob at the block granularity. Modifications to an individual blob take a two-phase approach. First, one uploads the changes as a set of blocks. Second, one commits the changes by identifying the list of uploaded blocks. Block blobs are most commonly used for files such as text files, CSVs, and binary files where the typical workload is to read or write the entire file.

Append blobs

> An append blob is a variant of a block blob that is optimized for append-only write workloads, such as logging. It does not allow deleting or updating of existing blocks.

Page blobs

> Page blobs are optimized for predominantly random read/write workloads (such as virtual machine disks) against portions of the blob, where data is stored in pages.

The file structure for a blob in Blob Storage is as follows. At the root of the Storage account, you have a container. A container is a logical grouping of blobs, similar to how folders group files on your local machine. It can be used to set access permissions on the blobs it contains. Within each container you can have an unlimited quantity of blobs.

Each blob (or more precisely, each container and blob pair) identifies a partition. In other words, each file you have in Blob Storage is its own partition.

When you create your Storage account you can define the degree of replication of the data that you desire for high availability and disaster recovery purposes. At minimum data stored within a Storage account is replicated on three separate nodes within a single facility (i.e., building). The replication options are as follows:

Locally redundant storage (LRS)
> LRS stores three copies of the data within a facility (which is naturally within a specific geographic region).

Zone-redundant storage (ZRS)
> ZRS augments LRS by enabling a replica within another facility within the same region. ZRS supports only block blobs.

Geo-redundant storage (GRS)
> GRS automatically replicates your blob storage to another geographic region that is hundreds of miles away from the primary. For example, if your primary Storage account is within the West US region, you can have a secondary replica of it in the East US region. This secondary replica is not readable unless the primary becomes unavailable (and when this happens the failover is transparent to your application, but Azure will send you an email notification). When new data arrives, that data is first replicated to the three local replicas and then asynchronously replicated to the secondary geographic replica (where it is also replicated three times).

RA-GRS
> Read-only geo-redundant storage is a variant of GRS providing a secondary endpoint that enables you to read from the secondary Storage account.

Blob Storage capacity

The capacity of Azure Blob Storage is largely dictated by two items: the universal size limits of the Storage account and the limits specific to block or page blobs (see Tables 3-1 and 3-2). Each blob can also store up to 8 kilobytes' worth of user-defined key/value metadata, which is useful in scenarios where you want to query for the metadata without transferring the entire blob.

Table 3-1. Blob Storage capacity limits

Item	Limits
Storage account size	500 TB
Individual block blob size	4.77 TB
Individual append blob size	~195 GB
Individual page blob size	1 TB
Maximum size of metadata	8 KB

Table 3-2. Blob Storage throughput limits

Item	Limits
Target throughput for a single blob	60 MB/s (~480 Mbps), up to 500 requests per second
Max ingress throughput	In the US: 10 Gbps (with GRS/ZRS) or 20 Gbps (with LRS)
Max egress throughput	In the US: 20 Gbps (with GRS/ZRS) or 30 Gbps (with LRS)

How do we use it in the scenario?

In the previous chapter we introduced many mechanisms for transferring data from on premises to Blob Storage. Now that we have a more complete understanding of Blob Storage, let's look at how it would apply to Blue Yonder Airports. In the introduction, we established that BYA had historical flight delay data. This kind of data is typically a great candidate for bulk storage in Blob Storage. For our purposes, we will use data that's available from the United States Department of Transportation's (DoT) Bureau of Transportation Statistics. They maintain a table of flight delay data (*http://www.transtats.bts.gov/Tables.asp?DB_ID=120*), called *On-Time Performance*, whose contents can be downloaded into CSVs. In this table, you can query for data as far back as January 1987 and as recent as two months back.

Getting the sample data

To save time clicking through the DoT user interface, we have already collected one-year's worth of data (for calendar years 2014 and 2015) and made it available for download from *http://bit.ly/sampleflightdata*.

Download this file and unzip it to view the contents. You should see 24 CSV files, totaling about 4.88 GB (Figure 3-2).

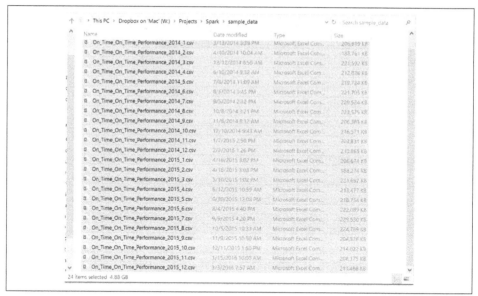

Figure 3-2. Sample CSV files containing flight delay data used in the Blue Yonder Airports scenario.

The schema of the CSV files is described fairly well on the DoT website (*http://1.usa.gov/1qwC9cR*), so we won't repeat that here.

Next, go to Azure Portal and create a new Storage account. You can do so by following these steps (shown in Figure 3-3):

1. Log in to the Azure Portal (*https://portal.azure.com*).

2. Click the New button.

3. Choose Data + Storage, then select Storage Account.

4. In the "Create storage account" blade, provide a unique name for your Storage account (you will be using it throughout this book).

5. Leave "Deployment model" at "Resource manager" and Performance at Standard.

6. Leave Replication at LRS.

7. Verify the Azure subscription selected is the proper one for the Storage account (if you have multiple Azure subscriptions).

8. Set "Resource group" to one whose name you will use throughout the book to logically group the Azure services you create (making them easier to manage or clean up later).

9. Choose a Location that is nearest you.

10. Check "Pin to dashboard" so the account is readily available on your Azure Portal dashboard.

11. Click Create.

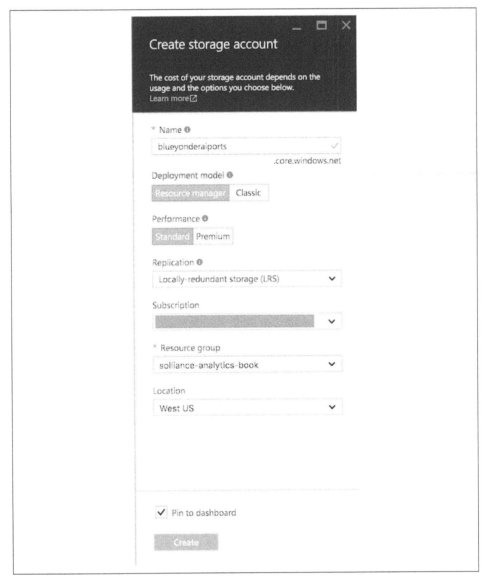

Figure 3-3. Creating a Storage account for the bulk ingest of flight delay data.

Now that you have a new Storage account provisioned, let's briefly discuss the rationale for some of the key settings used. We chose the resource model as the deployment model because that is the new standard for which most new services should be deployed into Azure and should be used wherever possible. We chose the Standard performance tier because we will be working with block blobs; the Premium tier supports only page blobs. Finally, we left the replication set to LRS for the purposes of this book because we do not need the availability guarantees. In production you should strongly consider ZRS (for greater in-region availability) or GRS (for greater multiregion availability).

Transfer the files

Using the approach of your choice from Chapter 2, upload the files individually uncompressed. If you are uncertain of what steps to take, we suggest using either Visual Studio or Azure Explorer (both shown step by step in Chapter 2) to connect to your Storage account and copy over your files. This will go significantly faster if you perform the upload from the virtual machine we recommend you have set up and assumes that the VM and your Storage account are in the same region (e.g., both are in the West US region).

You should upload these blobs as block blobs (which will be the default for most tools) since you will not be performing any random writes against them. This initial upload represents the beginning of your data lake, as you will preserve these as your master data set that is always unmodified and always available no matter what downstream processing you apply.

Once you have the flight delay files in Blob Storage, you are good to go! We will return to them throughout the book.

Azure Data Lake Store

Azure Data Lake Store is a hyperscale data repository optimized for analytics workloads. It enables you to scale your storage capacity without having to reengineer your storage at any point, or even worry about scaling the capacity at all. Its performance is optimized for analytics workloads, providing strong support for parallel reads. It provides a Hadoop filesystem with the familiar notions of folders and files that's accessible via the WebHDFS API, which makes it accessible to many of the Hadoop ecosystem components.

Azure Data Lake Store is built for the enterprise with availability (all data is replicated three times within the datacenter) and security in mind, providing support for authentication (via Azure Active Directory), authorization (via POSIX-style access control lists and firewall rules), and auditing. It also supports encryption at rest (i.e., the data on disk is automatically encrypted on write, and decrypted on read).

Azure Data Lake Store exposes a WebHDFS endpoint that makes it available as a storage substrate for analytics workloads that can leverage the RESTful endpoint provided by WebHDFS. In Azure this means first-class support for analytics workloads running on HDInsight (and of course Azure Data Lake Analytics), but also support for Hortonworks Data Platform (HDP) and Cloudera Distribution including Apache Hadoop (CDH) as well as other clients that are capable of making REST requests against the WebHDFS API (see Figure 3-4).

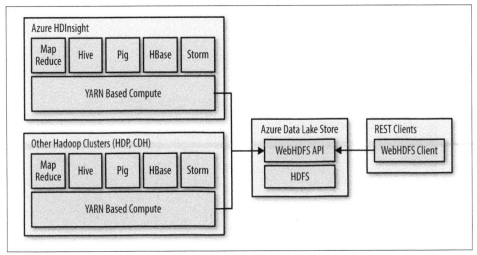

Figure 3-4. Azure Data Lake Store supports a wide variety of analytics workloads and clients.

What's the capacity?

Azure Data Lake Store is intended to allow for storage without limits and "massive" throughput. In practice, this means that the Azure Data Lake Store does not have any limits on the size of an individual file or on the total size of all files it manages. Contrast this with Azure Blob Storage, and you should understand the motivation: Blob Storage has a per-file size limit (4.77 TB for block blobs and 1 TB for page blobs), and has an account limit of 500 TB total for all files stored. Azure Data Lake Store has none of those limits.

Regarding the throughput, as of this writing the throughput targets have not been published by Microsoft.

How do we use it in the BYA scenario?

Earlier, we uploaded the data from on premises to Blob Storage. On its own this is a pretty capable storage area, but as we want to keep flight delay data in perpetuity, we need to be aware that at some point we could exhaust the storage capacity of our Storage account and would then need to reengineer our solution to support using multiple Storage accounts in order to gain the required storage capacity. Alternately, we can use Blob Storage as a staging ground and then copy the files over from Blob Storage to Azure Data Lake Store for permanent storage. This is what we will walk through next.

Provisioning Data Lake Store

Before you can get to the business of using Azure Data Lake Store, you will need to provision one in your Azure subscription. You can accomplish this quickly by following these steps:

1. Log in to the Azure Portal (*https://portal.azure.com*).

2. Click New.

3. Select Data + Storage, and then Data Lake Store (Figure 3-5).

Figure 3-5. Creating an Azure Data Lake Store using the Azure Portal.

4. In the New Data Lake Store blade, provide a name for your new data lake; select an Azure subscription, resource group, and deployment location; and click Create. Your new Data Lake Store should be ready within a minute (Figure 3-6).

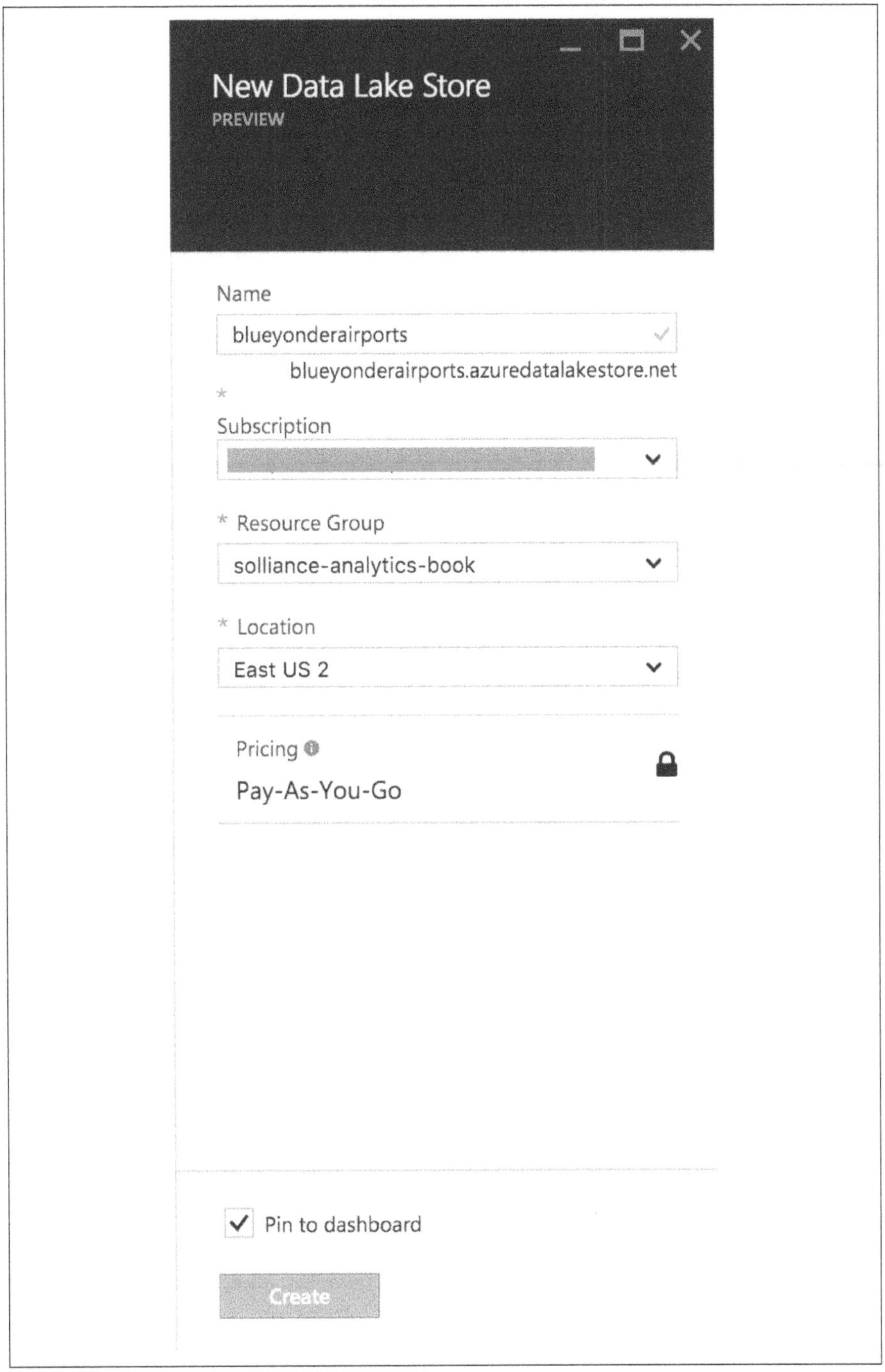

New Data Lake Store
PREVIEW

Name

blueyonderairports

blueyonderairports.azuredatalakestore.net

Subscription

* Resource Group

solliance-analytics-book

* Location

East US 2

Pricing ⓘ

Pay-As-You-Go

☑ Pin to dashboard

Create

Figure 3-6. Configuring the new Data Lake Store.

Transferring the data

If you followed the previous steps on uploading your data to Azure Blob Storage, you already have your data in Azure. Now we can perform a lateral copy of the data in your Azure Data Lake Store. As we indicated in Chapter 2, this can be accomplished using the AdlCopy command-line program.

To do this, load up the command prompt and navigate to the directory to which you downloaded AdlCopy. Build your command to copy from Blob Storage to a folder named *FlightDelays* in your Data Lake Store:

```
adlcopy /Source https://<StorageAccountName>.blob.core.windows.net/
<path>/<to>/<flights>/
/Dest adl://adlmvp.azuredatalakestore.net/FlightDelays/
/SourceKey <StorageAccountKey>
```

In the previous command, replace *<StorageAccountName>* with the name of the source Storage account and *<StorageAccountKey>* with the key to that Storage account. Also replace *<path>/<to>/<flights>* with the actual path to your uploaded flight delay CSVs. Be sure to keep the last / after *<flights>* because this is what indicates to AdlCopy that it is copying a directory and not an individual blob.

When you run AdlCopy, and after it has prompted you to log in with your credentials to your Azure Data Lake Store (which are likely the same credentials you use to access the Azure Portal), the copy should take only a few minutes. When the copy is finished, the output will look something like Figure 3-7.

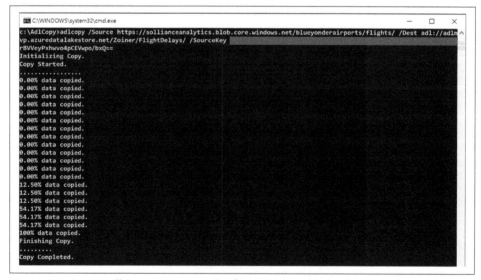

Figure 3-7. Using AdlCopy.exe to copy the flight delay CSV files from Blob Storage to Azure Data Lake Store.

Exploring the data via the portal

Now that you have your historical flight delay data uploaded, let's examine it via the Azure Portal.

Open the portal and navigate to your Azure Data Lake Store. At the top of the blade, click Data Explorer (Figure 3-8).

Figure 3-8. The Azure Data Lake Store command bar, showing the Data Explorer button.

Click on the folder to which your files were uploaded and notice the listing shows the uploaded CSV files (Figure 3-9).

Figure 3-9. The Data Explorer blade showing the folders and files present in the Data Lake Store.

Click on any one of the CSV files to preview the file contents. The File Preview blade will open to let you view the first 25 rows of data (Figure 3-10).

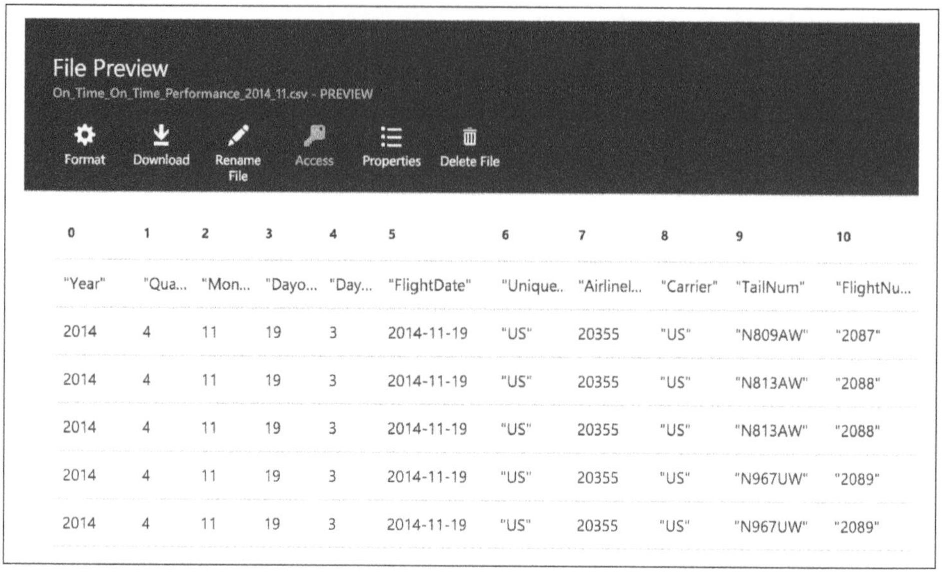
File Preview
On_Time_On_Time_Performance_2014_11.csv - PREVIEW
Format
Download
Rename File
Access
Properties
Delete File
0 1 2 3 4 5 6 7 8 9 10
"Year" "Qua... "Mon... "Dayo... "Day... "FlightDate" "Unique.. "Airlinel... "Carrier" "TailNum" "FlightNu...
2014 4 11 19 3 2014-11-19 "US" 20355 "US" "N809AW" "2087"
2014 4 11 19 3 2014-11-19 "US" 20355 "US" "N813AW" "2088"
2014 4 11 19 3 2014-11-19 "US" 20355 "US" "N813AW" "2088"
2014 4 11 19 3 2014-11-19 "US" 20355 "US" "N967UW" "2089"
2014 4 11 19 3 2014-11-19 "US" 20355 "US" "N967UW" "2089"

Figure 3-10. The File Preview blade showing a preview of the contents of a CSV file uploaded to the Data Lake Store.

Congratulations, you now have the historical flight delay data stored in Azure Data Lake Store and ready for analysis (which we will return to in the upcoming chapters).

HDFS

The Hadoop File System (HDFS) has become the de facto filesystem for storing data used in big data and analytics scenarios. The value proposition is that HDFS can scale its storage linearly by adding more compute nodes to provide storage to the cluster; with the latest versions, it can support upward of 10,000 compute nodes. As a simple example, if each node you provide has 24 disks attached with each disk being 4 TB in size, you can reach 960 PB of capacity—in other words, almost an exabyte of storage! Increase the size of the disks, and you can get to multiple exabytes of storage.

The design of HDFS is primarily focused on supporting analytics workloads; it is optimized for write once, read many (WORM) workloads where files can be appended to but not modified. At its core, the architecture of HDFS is fairly straightforward. Name nodes manage the metadata about what directories and files (which are broken up into blocks typically of 128 MB in size) are available and where the blocks of data that make up those files is stored. Data nodes actually store the blocks of data. When a block of data is stored, it is replicated, by default, to three different disks across the cluster. This provides availability in the case of failure, but also supports parallel compute as more copies of the data are available for simultaneous reads (Figure 3-11).

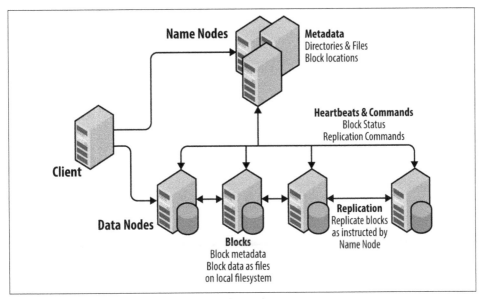

Figure 3-11. A high-level view of the topology of HDFS.

With this topology in mind, let's cover the key points of how a client application reads from and writes to HDFS.

When reading from HDFS, a client application using the HDFS API makes a request to the name node for the file and in response receives a list of data nodes and blocks from which to read the file. The client then requests the appropriate blocks from each data node (Figure 3-12).

When writing to HDFS, a client application first communicates with the name node and retrieves a list of data nodes to write to. The client then receives a list of blocks from the first data node in the list, and uses those blocks to begin writing the file (Figure 3-13).

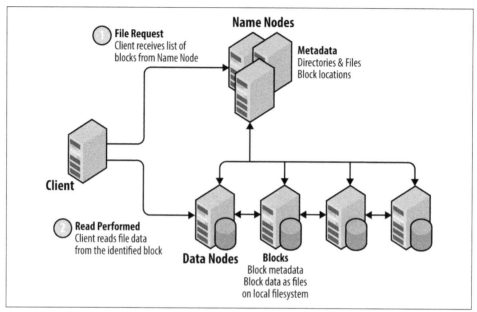

Figure 3-12. Reading a file from HDFS.

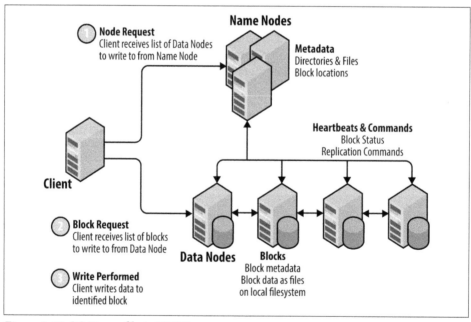

Figure 3-13. Writing a file to HDFS.

While not meant to turn you into an HDFS professional administrator, hopefully this description helps you understand how HDFS operates under the covers and clarifies how important benefits such as linear scale, parallel reads, and high availability are achieved. As you will find in the following sections, in Azure you are less concerned with managing HDFS than you are with the various services that build upon it.

How do you use HDFS in Azure?

Within Azure you can use HDFS in a few different ways. The most obvious is you could provision an HDInsight cluster and use the HDFS that is provisioned with it (Figure 3-14). In this case the disks attached to the cluster virtual machines provide the actual storage. The downside to this approach is the requirement to have the cluster running before you can access your data; in order to simply provide storage, you are paying for running compute (both in terms of money and in the time it takes to spin up a cluster). This is because if the cluster is shut down, the name nodes and data nodes created with the cluster are shut down as well, and without those there is no access to the data stored by HDFS locally. By externalizing the storage from the cluster, you enable multiple clusters and applications to simultaneously access the data. For this reason, the use of cluster local storage is rarely the approach taken.

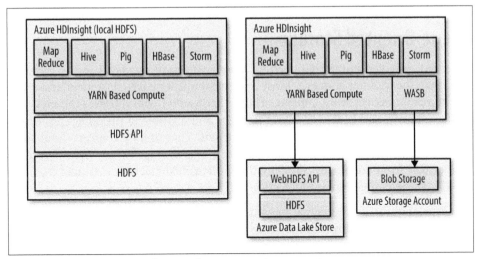

Figure 3-14. Where HDFS "appears" in various Azure services.

The options that externalize storage are to use HDFS-compatible storage such as that offered by Azure Blob Storage or Azure Data Lake Store. Within an HDInsight cluster, for example, your applications can use the *wasb:* scheme to access files that are actually stored in Azure Blob Storage via the HDFS API. Windows Azure Storage Blobs (*wasb:*) is an extension built upon HDFS APIs; more technically it's provided via the hadoop-azure module, which is a part of the Hadoop distribution.

Similarly, your applications can access files that are stored in Azure Data Lake Store via the *adls:* scheme.

The key takeaway is that by using either the Azure Data Lake Store or Azure Blob Storage, you gain the ability to leverage HDFS for your HDFS-compatible applications while still being able to shut down any compute clusters without fear of losing access to your data.

ASV

If you search around the internet for other schemes, you may come across the *asv:* scheme. ASV, which stood for Azure Storage Vault, is a now-deprecated scheme and approach that was used to access Azure Blob Storage from HDInsight. You should be using the *wasb:* scheme moving forward.

How do we use HDFS in the scenario?

At this point in the Blue Yonder scenario, you already have stored your files in both Azure Blob Storage and Azure Data Lake Store, so you are all ready to perform processing on this data.

Queue-Oriented Storage

The queue-oriented storage designed for massive ingest of events takes on a different form than the traditional queue. Most traditional queues have consumers who compete to read messages from a queue. The first consumer who retrieves the messages "wins"—the message is deleted from the queue and invisible to the other consumers. The queues we cover in this section are different. They are, by contrast, "multiconsumer" queues. In other words, the processing of a message by any consumer does not delete it from the queue. The only thing that actually deletes messages from the queue is the retention policy, which effectively ages out old messages.

This type of queuing expects that messages will be processed by downstream components in a specific window of time. It is very common in the Event Sourcing pattern, and surfaces time and again with event log analytics. In this chapter we will examine sending messages to the "multiconsumer" queues exposed by Event Hubs and IoT Hub. In the subsequent chapters, we will get into the details about how messages are actually consumed and how progress through a given queue is managed.

Before we do that, let's add a little more detail to our Blue Yonder Airports scenario to put the usage of these queues in context.

Blue Yonder Scenario: Smart Buildings

The medium and large hub airports served by BYA have between 12 and 22 gates per terminal, and anywhere from 2 to 9 terminals. Most airports they serve have between 50 and 207 gates in total.

Blue Yonder Airports installs a sensor package at each gate consisting of four temperature sensors (one sensor in the center of the gate area, one by the gate doorway, and two on the outskirts of the gate area). They also install one motion sensor in the area. In addition, the climate control units report when the heat or air conditioning is activated or deactivates. All of this telemetry is emitted in the form of time series data.

In the case of temperature sensors, the average temperature over the reporting window is reported 6 times per minute (every 10 seconds, the average for that 10 seconds is transmitted). In the case of the motion sensors, activity or lack of activity is reported within each 10-second window (so if there was any activity within the 10-second window, it's reported as activity). Finally, in the case of the climate control activation, this telemetry is transmitted per occurrence, and can be tied back to one or more gates (since in many airports a given control unit may affect the temperature in more than one gate).

In summary, let's assume that a large hub airport has the following characteristics:

- 200 gates
- 800 temperature sensors
- 200 motion sensors
- 100 climate control units

A medium hub airport has the following characteristics:

- 50 gates
- 200 temperature sensors
- 50 motion sensors
- 25 climate control units

The sensors each emit telemetry of a slightly different shape. Table 3-3 documents the shape of the telemetry emitted from the temperature sensors.

Table 3-3. Temperature sensor telemetry

Field	Type
temp	double
createDate	timestamp
deviceId	string

Table 3-4 represents the telemetry emitted from the motion sensors.

Table 3-4. Motion sensor telemetry

Field	Type
activityDetected	bool
createDate	timestamp
deviceId	string

Finally, the HVAC activation telemetry has the shape shown in Table 3-5.

Table 3-5. HVAC activation telemetry

Field	Type
state	int (noChange = 0, heatActivated=1, coolingActivated=2, heatDeactivated=3,coolingDeactivated=4)
createDate	timestamp
deviceId	string

Event Hubs

We briefly introduced Event Hubs in Chapter 2, noting that it provides for message storage and supports a variety of protocols (HTTP, AMQP, and AMQP over Web Sockets) for sending messages from the sender to the event hub. In this chapter we dive one layer further into the ingest storage aspects of the highly scalable, multiconsumer queue that is Event Hubs. In subsequent chapters we will examine the other side of ingest, which is the consumption and processing of messages pulled from Event Hubs.

Ingest and storage with Event Hubs

Let's address ingest storage with the client of the event hub. The sender can use any of a multitude of software development kits (SDKs) to communicate with Event Hubs. At the time of this writing there are client SDKs for .NET, C, Node.js, and Java. Alternately, the REST API can be used directly from any platform that supports making RESTful calls.

The sender creates an event, which represents the "message" that is sent to the service bus. In the .NET SDK for Event Hubs, a sender creates an instance of the EventData class, which has the structure shown in Figure 3-15.

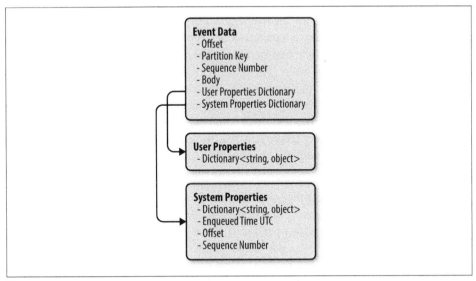

Figure 3-15. The structure of an event sent to Event Hubs.

From a high level, there are three types of properties that are the most important: user, system, and body. System properties are set by Event Hubs itself, while user properties can include key/value pairs that contain string data that is useful for downstream message processing (identifying the importance of a message, capturing the ID of the sender, etc.). Body properties are ultimately always serialized to a binary payload. When you are sending from the .NET SDK, the body is represented as a byte[]. However, when you are sending using the REST API, it could prove challenging to prepare a binary payload, so Event Hubs accepts JSON as the payload format. The most common format is to have the body contain binary serialized JSON (which we will show in code shortly).

The Offset, Enqueued Time, and Sequence Number properties are set by Event Hubs upon event ingest. We will return to defining these properties in subsequent chapters, as they have a more important role to play with consumers of the Event Hub.

What's the capacity?

Each event instance can be at most 256 KB in size. For improved sending performance, senders can batch a list of events to send in a single go so long as the total size of all events in the batch does not exceed 256 KB.

Event Hubs supports partitioning the ingested events into partitions—in other words, spreading messages across different "buckets" for storage. When an Event Hub is provisioned, the number of partitions, which can be 1–32, is specified. The number of partitions cannot be changed after provisioning. When you send events to Event Hubs, the default approach is for the messages to be distributed among partitions in a round-robin fashion. However, if a partition key is provided, this value can be used to influence the selection of the actual partition instead. The partition key is a string, and any events sent to Event Hubs that share the same partition key value (or more precisely, whose hash of the partition key is the same) are delivered in order to the same partition. From the sender's perspective, beyond using the partition key (which does not identify a partition directly), individual partitions are not usually targeted by a sender. Partitions play a very important role for consumers of Event Hubs, and we will return to this role in subsequent chapters.

The scale of an Event Hub is controlled via throughput units (TUs), as shown in Figure 3-16. Each TU controls the volume of data ingress and egress that can be handled by the Event Hubs instance. For the senders, the event ingress throughput scales at 1 MB/s per TU or 1,000 events/s per TU. If either limit is triggered, message ingress is throttled. By default, there is a per-subscription quota of 20 TUs, but this is a soft limit that can be raised via a request to Azure support. When requesting additional TUs, you can request them in batches of 20 up to a total of 100 TUs. Beyond 100 TUs, you can request additional TUs in batches of 100. Note that TUs apply at the level of the service bus namespace (a scoping container for a set of service bus messaging entities like Event Hubs), meaning that your allocated TUs can be shared among multiple Event Hubs.

There is also an ingress limit that applies to each partition. Each partition within an Event Hub can utilize at most 1 TU, so if you had an Event Hubs instance with 32 partitions, and had allocated 32 TUs to the service bus namespace that contains the Event Hubs instance, you are basically ensuring that each partition has access to its full potential of 1 MB/s ingress. By way of example, if you allocated 33 TUs, this would not benefit the partitions any further (albeit the extra capacity would benefit other Event Hubs instances in the service bus namespace).

Now that you understand the throughput of message ingress, let's turn to message storage. The total storage capacity for an Event Hubs instance is not limited. Out of the box, 84 GB of storage per TU is included free of charge. Any storage you consume beyond 84 GB is billed at the rates for using Azure Storage in the locally redundant storage (LRS) mode. The way Event Hubs manages storage (since events are not deleted by the consumer when they are retrieved) is by applying a retention policy. Event Hubs has a configurable retention policy where messages older than the retention period are automatically purged. The retention period can be set in units of days, between 1 and 7 days.

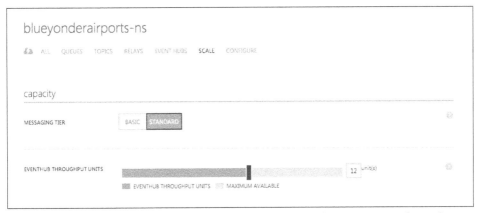

Figure 3-16. Scaling TUs using a slider. Notice that this configuration is performed upon the service bus namespace and not an individual Event Hubs instance.

There's one final important consideration for message ingest: the number of concurrent connections has limitations depending on how the senders are communicating with Event Hubs. If you are using HTTPS, there is no limit on the number of concurrent connections; however, if you are using AMQP, then there is a service bus namespace–wide limit of 5,000 concurrent connections.

Table 3-6 summarizes the important quotas and limits having to do with Event Hubs message ingest.

Table 3-6. Event Hubs ingress quotas and limits

Item	Limits
Throughput units	Default soft limit of 20 TUs per subscription
Ingress throughput	1 MB/s per TU and 1,000 events/s per TU
Total storage capacity	No limit (~500 TB)
Message retention	Min 1 day, max 7 days
Partitions	Between 1 and 32 partitions
Max event size	256 KB
Max batch size	256 KB

How do we use Event Hubs in the scenario?

Now that we have some background on Event Hubs ingest and storage, let's look at how Blue Yonder Airports might apply it. Per the scenario, telemetry is being received from three different sources—temperature sensors, motion sensors, and HVAC devices—into an Event Hub.

Exploring the sensor simulators

To illustrate the approach with code, we have provided a C# .NET-based simulator that shows each of the three sensor types transmitting telemetry for an entire day according to a schedule that simulates planes arriving/departing from a single gate in a terminal.

You can download the source code from *http://bit.ly/2bgsfHa*.

Extract this solution and open it using Visual Studio.

This solution contains a few projects. For this chapter, we will focus on the Simple-SensorConsole and Sensors projects. The former provides the command-line UI for simulating sensor data and emitting it to Event Hubs or IoT Hub. The latter project provides the logic for building up a virtual schedule of events and emitting them, where the logic that handles the emitted event is pluggable (so it can target either Event Hubs or IoT Hub).

Introducing the Sensors and SimpleSensorConsole projects. The Sensors project provides a base class for the simulated sensors in *SensorBase.cs*. At a high level `SensorBase` looks as shown in Example 3-1.

Example 3-1. SensorBase provides the base class for our simulated sensors

```
public class SensorBase
{
    protected string deviceId;
    protected Action<string> transmitHandler;
    protected List<string> datapoints;
    protected int reportingIntervalSeconds;

    public int CountOfDataPoints{}

    protected SensorBase(string deviceId, Action<string> transmitHandler){}

    public virtual void InitSchedule(int reportingIntervalSeconds){}

    public Task Start(){}

    private Task RunAsync(){}

    private void InternalEmitEvents(){}
}
```

The implementation details are not super important (feel free to peruse the code!), but there are a few things to point out. First, the purpose of each sensor is to populate a list of data points. Each data point represents a telemetry event, where the data for the event is JSON serialized to a string. Second, each sensor implementation, which derives from `SensorBase`, needs to implement its own `InitSchedule` method. This method is what creates the time series data by generating a list of data points according to whatever logic is appropriate for the sensor. Once `InitSchedule` executes, the data points for a single day at the gate are created. Third, the `Start` method invokes an asynchronous execution of `InternalEmitEvents`, which simply loops over each data point in the data points list and invokes the `transmitHandler` (that was passed in as a parameter to the constructor). The `transmitHandler` is an action that takes as a parameter the string data point (Example 3-2).

Example 3-2. InternalEmitEvents invokes the pluggable action provided in transmitHandler, passing it one data point at a time

```
private void InternalEmitEvents()
{
    for (int i = 0; i < datapoints.Count; i++)
    {
        transmitHandler.Invoke(datapoints[i]);
    }
}
```

Now let's take a look at a single, concrete sensor implementation. Since all sensor implementations work the same way, if you understand one, you will understand the others. We'll look at `TemperatureSensor` (defined in *TemperatureSensor.cs*), shown in Example 3-3.

Example 3-3. The TemperatureSensor class simulates the fluctuations in temperature such a device might experience during the course of a day at a single gate in an airport

```
public class TemperatureSensor: SensorBase
{
    public TemperatureSensor(string deviceId, Action<string> transmitHandler)
    : base(deviceId, transmitHandler) [...]

    public override void InitSchedule(int reportingIntervalSeconds) [...]

    private bool IsWithinPreFlightWindow(int intervalNumber,
    int reportingInterval, int departureIntervalNumber) [...]

    private bool IsWithinPostFlightWindow(int intervalNumber,
    int reportingInterval, int departureIntervalNumber) [...]

    private bool HasPlaneDeparted(int intervalNumber,
    int reportingInterval, int departureIntervalNumber) [...]

    private class TempDataPoint
    {
        public double temp;
        public DateTime createDate;
```

```
        public string deviceId;
    }

}
```

Notice that it defines its own private data structure called `TempDataPoint` that contains the temperature, the date the data point was created, and the ID of the device that took the temperature reading. This structure ultimately gets serialized to a JSON string that looks like the following:

```
{"temp":65.0,"createDate":"2016-04-11T07:00:00Z","deviceId":"1"}
```

The first method the harness (implemented within the SimpleSensorConsole project) of the simulated sensor needs to call is the constructor, to provide the instance of the `TemperatureSensor` a device ID and an action to use as a callback when processing each data point for transmission. After that, the harness invokes the `InitSchedule` method, passing it a reporting interval in seconds. This interval defines the maximum reporting granularity of the device—in other words, how often it generates events if it always has an event to transmit. By default the harness sets the reporting interval to 10 seconds.

Within the SimpleSensorConsole project, examining *EventHubLoadSimulator.cs* shows just how this sensor is set up and executed (see Example 3-4).

Example 3-4. Setting up and executing a simulated sensor

```
public void SimulateTemperatureEvents()
{
    stopWatch.Restart();
    numEventsSent = 0;
    LogStatus("Sending Temperature Events...");
    SensorBase sensor = new TemperatureSensor("1", TransmitEvent);
    sensor.InitSchedule(10);
    Console.WriteLine("Generated {0:###,###,###} Events", sensor.CountOfDataPoints);
    sensor.Start().Wait();
    FlushEventHubBuffer();
    stopWatch.Stop();
    Console.WriteLine(
    "Completed transmission in {0} seconds. Sent {1:###,###,###} events.",
        stopWatch.Elapsed.TotalSeconds, numEventsSent);
}
```

To use the sensor, we begin by restarting a `StopWatch` instance that we use to track the execution time of the sensor. We also track the number of events that have been sent (`numEventSent`), which is used to report on the number of events generated versus the number of events actually sent to Event Hubs. Then we create an instance of `TemperatureSensor`, passing it an arbitrary device ID as a string, and the method name of our `transmitHandler` function will be responsible for actually sending the events to Event Hubs (we will show the details shortly). Next, we pregenerate the events for the day by calling InitSchedule. Then we kick off the sending of the generated events by calling Start on the sensor. We call Wait on the sensor to ensure we have transmitted all of the day's events before moving on. Then we flush any remaining unsent events using FlushEventHubBuffer. We conclude the run by displaying the time it took to send the events to Event Hubs and the actual number of events that were sent. When we run the SimpleSensorConsole, the output looks like Figure 3-17.

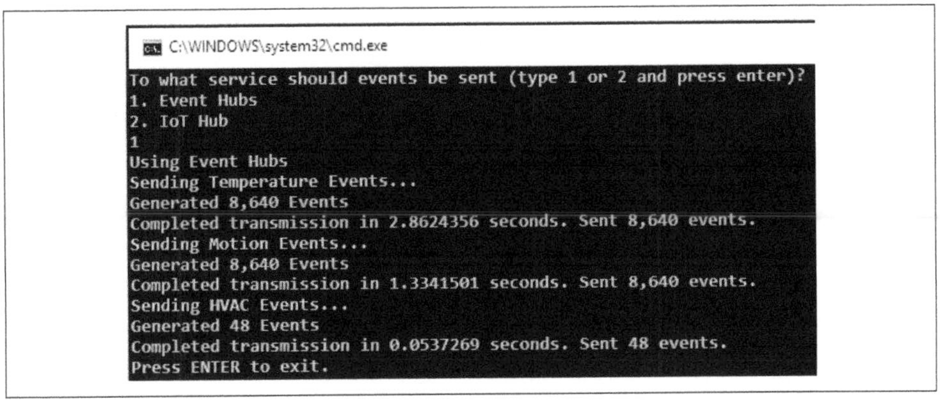

Figure 3-17. Output from running the three different sensors in the SimpleSensorConsole harness application.

The SimpleSensorConsole harness is able to transmit events to Event Hubs either one event at a time or in a batched (hundreds of events at a time) fashion, so that you can understand how transmission works in both scenarios (Example 3-5). This is accomplished by the TransmitEvent method in *EventHubLoadSimulator.cs*. The TransmitE vent method takes the string data point, converts the string to a UTF8-encoded byte array, and passes it to the constructor of the EventData class (which will stash this byte array as the body of the EventData instance).

Example 3-5. The load simulator can transmit sensor events one at a time or in a batch

```
void TransmitEvent(string datapoint)
{
    EventData eventData;
    try
    {
        eventData = new EventData(Encoding.UTF8.GetBytes(datapoint));

        if (sendAsBatch)
        {
            SendToEventHubAsBatch(eventData);
        }
        else
```

```
    {
        SendToEventHubDirect(eventData);
    }

    //NOTE: Fastest execution time happens without console output.
    //LogStatus(datapoint);
    }
    catch (Exception ex)
    {
        LogError(ex.Message);
    }
}
```

Let's begin by examining how events are emitted one at a time to Event Hubs using the Event Hubs .NET SDK. The load simulator has an `Init` method that reads the Event Hubs connection string from the *app.config* file (see Example 3-6).

Example 3-6. Initializing the EventHubClient instance

```
public void Init()
{
    try
    {
        eventHubsConnectionString =
        System.Configuration.ConfigurationManager.AppSettings[
        "EventHubsSenderConnectionString"];
        eventHubClient =
        EventHubClient.CreateFromConnectionString(eventHubsConnectionString);
        sendAsBatch =
        bool.Parse(System.Configuration.ConfigurationManager.AppSettings[
        "SendEventsAsBatch"]);
    }
    catch (Exception ex)
    {
        LogError(ex.Message);
        throw;
    }

}
```

The `Init` method uses this connection string to create an instance of `EventHub Client`, which is used for communicating with the Event Hubs instance. With an `EventHubClient` instance in hand, we are now ready to send events. This is as simple as calling `Send` on the `EventHubClient` instance and passing it the `EventData` object (see Example 3-7).

Example 3-7. Sending a single event to an Event Hubs instance

```
void SendToEventHubDirect(EventData eventData)
{
    eventHubClient.Send(eventData);
}
```

Sending events as a batch, such that one call to Event Hubs includes multiple messages, is not much more difficult: you invoke EventHubClient.SendBatch, passing it a list of EventData objects (see Example 3-8). It does come with a caveat, however: the total size for all messages must be less than 256 KB.

Example 3-8. Sending a batch of events to Event Hubs

```
void SendToEventHubAsBatch(EventData eventData)
{
    long currEventSizeInBytes = eventData.SerializedSizeInBytes;

    if (bufferedSizeInBytes + currEventSizeInBytes >= maxBatchSizeInBytes)
    {
        FlushEventHubBuffer();
    }

    sendBuffer.Add(eventData);
    bufferedSizeInBytes += currEventSizeInBytes;
}

void FlushEventHubBuffer()
{
    if (sendBuffer.Count > 0)
    {
        eventHubClient.SendBatch(sendBuffer);

        numEventsSent += sendBuffer.Count;
        sendBuffer.Clear();
        bufferedSizeInBytes = 0;
    }
}
```

In the snippet shown in Example 3-8, SendToEventHubAsBatch typically just collects events and adds them to a list acting as a buffer. Only when the maximum batch size is exceeded does it actually send out the list and clear the buffer. You may recall from the implementation of SimulateTemperatureEvents in Example 3-4 that we also call FlushEventHubBuffer once after all messages have been processed by our transmitHandler. This is done to handle any of the few events that were buffered up before reaching the end of all the simulator generated events, in case they didn't trigger a flush.

For completeness, Example 3-9 shows the Main method of the SimpleSensorConsole application. Here, we interview the user (to ask if she wants to use Event Hubs or IoT Hub). Assuming she selects Event Hubs, we create an instance of the EventHubsLoad Simulator, which has helper methods to generate one day's worth of events from each of three sensors.

Example 3-9. The Main method of the load generating console harness

```
static void Main(string[] args)
{
    InterviewUser();

    if (useEventHub)
    {
        EventHubLoadSimulator simulator = new EventHubLoadSimulator();
        simulator.Init();
        simulator.SimulateTemperatureEvents();
        simulator.SimulateMotionEvents();
        simulator.SimulateHVACEvents();
    }
    else
    {
        IoTHubLoadSimulator simulator = new IoTHubLoadSimulator();
        simulator.Init();
        simulator.SimulateTemperatureEvents().Wait();
        simulator.SimulateMotionEvents().Wait();
        simulator.SimulateHVACEvents().Wait();
    }

    Console.WriteLine("Press ENTER to exit.");
    Console.ReadLine();
}
```

Running the Event Hubs load simulator.   Now that you have had a walkthrough of the code, you probably want to give it a run. You need to do two things. First, you need to provision an Event Hubs instance. Second, you'll need to update the configuration of SimpleSensorConsole with the connection string to that Event Hubs instance.

Creating an Event Hubs instance.   We'll walk through the steps to create an Event Hubs instance.

1. Log in to the Management Portal (*https://manage.windowsazure.com/*).

2. Click New and select App Services→Service Bus→Event Hub (Figure 3-18).

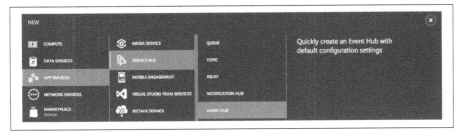

Figure 3-18. Creating a new Event Hub in the Management Portal.

3. Click Custom Create (Figure 3-19)

Figure 3-19. The Custom Create option to select.

4. Enter a name for your Event Hub instance.

5. Choose the region.

6. For namespace, select "Create a new namespace."

7. Optionally modify the namespace name as desired.

8. Click the right arrow. See Figure 3-20.

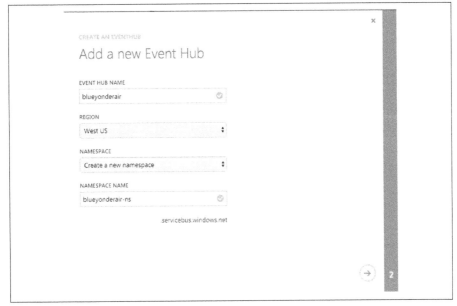

Figure 3-20. Basic Event Hub configuration.

9. On the Configure Event Hub dialog, set the partition count to 4. We will guide you on how to properly determine the number of partitions when we cover Event Hub consumers later in the book.

10. For message retention, set it to 1 day.

11. Click the checkmark to create it. See Figure 3-21.

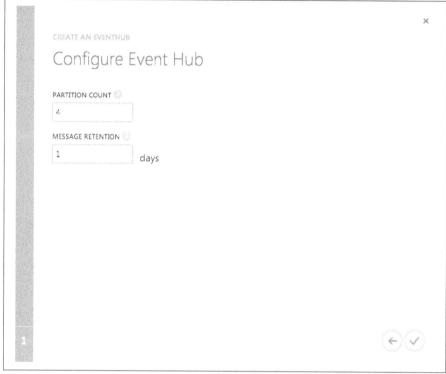

Figure 3-21. Configuring the number of partitions and the duration of message retention for an Event Hub.

Within a minute, your new namespace and constituent Event Hubs instance should be ready. Now you need create some connection credentials.

1. In the Service Bus list of namespaces, click on the name of the namespace you just created. This should take you to its details.

2. Click on the Event Hubs tab at the top (Figure 3-22).

Figure 3-22. The Event Hubs tab shown in the Management Portal.

3. Your Event Hubs instance should appear selected. Click on its name.

4. Click the Configure tab at the top (Figure 3-23).

Figure 3-23. The Configure tab in the Management Portal.

5. Under Shared Access Policies, under the Name column, type a name for this first policy (e.g., SendPolicy).

6. Click on the Permissions cell to expand the drop-down and check only the checkbox for Send (Figure 3-24).

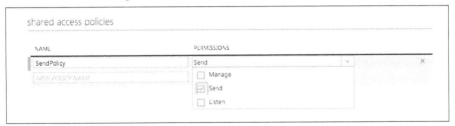

Figure 3-24. Selecting permissions for a shared access policy assigned to an Event Hub.

7. Click the Save button at the bottom to apply the new policy.

8. Now click the big left arrow above your Event Hubs instance name to return to the list of Event Hubs in the namespace (Figure 3-25).

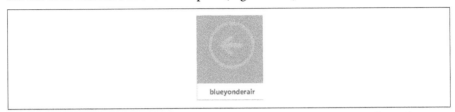

Figure 3-25. The arrow to select in moving back to the list of Event Hubs in the namespace.

9. With your Event Hubs instance selected in the list, click Connection Information.

10. Hover over the Connection String field, you should see a button to copy the connection string to your clipboard. Click it (Figure 3-26).

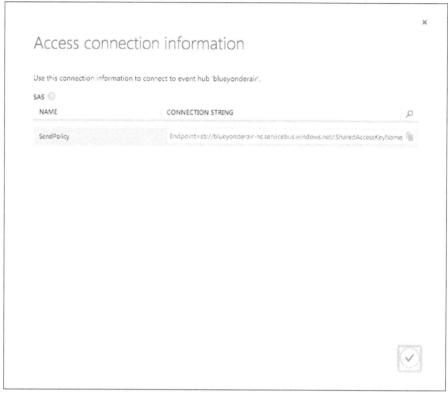

Figure 3-26. Copying the connection string for the Event Hub that uses the newly created policy.

11. Next, return to Visual Studio.

12. In Solution Explorer, expand the SimpleSensorConsole and open *app.config*.

13. Paste the value in between the double quotes of the value attribute for the setting with the key EventHubsSenderConnectionString:

```
<appSettings>
        <add key="EventHubsSenderConnectionString" value="" />
</appSettings>
```

14. Save your *app.config*.

15. Run the SimpleSensorConsole project. When it starts, enter **1** to select to simulate Event Hubs events and watch it run to completion (Figure 3-27).

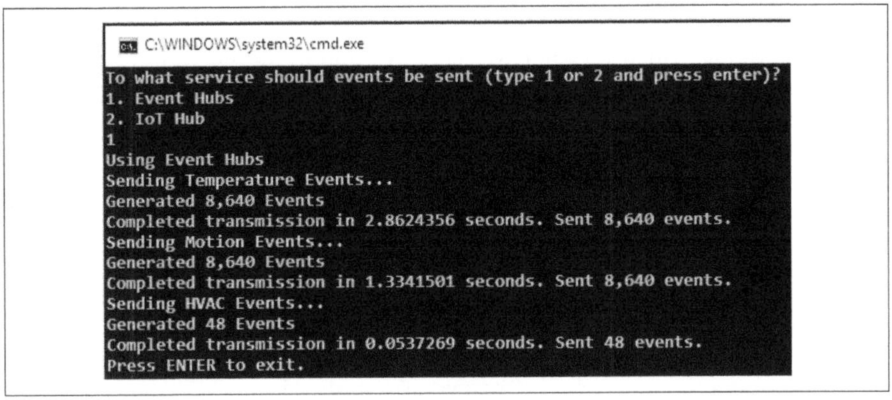

Figure 3-27. Output shown after running the SimpleSensorConsole application.

By default it runs by sending messages in batch mode. To see the difference in the time it takes to send the same messages event by event, open *app.config* for Simple-SensorConsole and change the value of the SendEventsAsBatch setting to false. Then save *app.config* and rerun the project.

To recap, at this point you have created an Event Hubs instance, run a simulator that creates some sample data, and transmitted those events to your Event Hubs instance.

IoT Hub

We briefly introduced IoT Hub in Chapter 2. As a reminder, IoT Hub enables reliable bidirectional communication between millions of Internet of Things devices and applications. From a message ingest standpoint (i.e., messages from devices to cloud), you can think of it as encapsulating an Event Hub, and providing richer functionality tailored to the needs of an IoT scenario. These extra features include support for additional protocols, such as MQTT, as well as a device registry that provides per-device access control functionality. In this chapter we will delve a little deeper into IoT Hub, focusing on the device-to-cloud message ingest flow.

Ingest and storage with IoT Hub

From an ingest standpoint, the IoT Hub behaves very similarly to Event Hubs. It provides client SDKs for .NET, C, Node.js, and Python. Clients built with these SDKs are used to send device-to-cloud messages. Just as for Event Hubs, a REST API can be used directly from any platform that supports making RESTful calls. One notable difference from Event Hubs is the shift in terminology from *events* to *messages*.

The core set of properties in the message (in .NET this has the type Micro soft.Azure.Devices.Client) includes the body (which is a binary stream created from a byte[]) as well as the user and system dictionaries (Figure 3-28). There are many other properties that this type supports, but they are geared toward cloud-to-device messaging, which we will cover later. An important omission is the Partition Key field—in IoT Hub messages, the partition for a message is always based upon the device ID of the source.

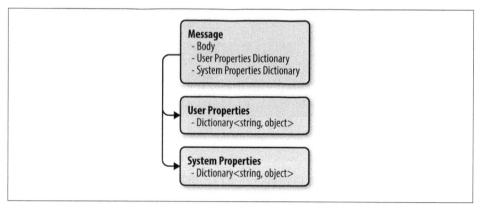

Figure 3-28. The simplest form of an IoT Hub client message.

What's the capacity?

Each device-to-cloud message instance can be at most 256 KB in size. For improved sending performance, senders can batch a list of events to send in a single go as long as the total size of all events in the batch does not exceed 256 KB, and as long as there are no more than 500 messages total in the batch.

IoT Hub supports partitioning the ingested events into partitions—in other words, spreading messages across different "buckets" for storage. When an IoT Hub is provisioned, the number of partitions, which can be 1–32, is specified. The number of partitions cannot be changed after provisioning. When you are sending events to IoT Hub, the default approach is for the messages to be distributed among partitions according to the hash of the originating device ID. Partitions play a very important role for consumers of IoT Hub, and we will return to this role in subsequent chapters.

The scale of an IoT Hub is controlled via IoT Hub units. Each unit controls the volume of messages that can be handled by the IoT Hub instance. Ingest throughput is separated into S1 and S2 tiers. The S1 tier provides about 1.1 MB/s/unit and 400k messages/day/unit, while the S2 tier provides 16 MB/s/unit and 6M messages/day/unit. Ingest throughput is throttled to 12 messages/second/unit for the S1 tier and 120 messages/second/unit for the S2 tier, with the caveat that 100 messages/second is the minimum performance you will see regardless of tier or unit quantity.

You can raise the number of IoT Hub units at any time by adjusting the setting for your IoT Hub in the Azure Portal. By default, there is a per-subscription quota of 200 units per subscription, but this is a soft limit that can be raised via a request to Azure support (Figure 3-29).

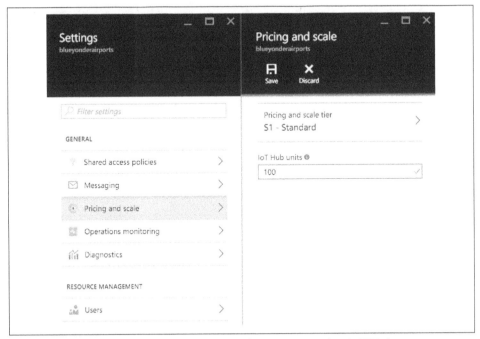

Figure 3-29. Adjusting the number of IoT Hub units assigned to IoT Hubs.

Just as for Event Hubs, the way IoT Hub manages storage (since messages are not deleted by the consumer when they are retrieved) is by applying a retention policy. IoT Hub has a configurable retention policy where messages older than the retention period are automatically purged. The retention period can be set in units of days, between 1 and 7 days.

There's one final important difference for message ingest between IoT Hub and Event Hubs: the number of concurrent connections has no limitation. In other words, there is no hard limit or no unit-based limit on the number of devices you can have communicating with your IoT Hub. That said, the service will throttle requests to connect to your IoT Hub. It throttles connections requests per second by tier, where the S1 tier supports 12 requests/s/unit and the S2 tier supports a 120 requests/s/unit.

Table 3-7 summarizes the important quotas and limits having to do with IoT Hub message ingest.

Table 3-7. IoT Hub ingress quotas and limits

Item	Limits
IoT Hub units	Default soft limit of 200 units per subscription
Ingress throughput	S1: ~1.1MB/min/unit, S2: 16MB/min/unit S1: 400k messages/day/unit, S2: 6M messages/day/unit S1: 12 messages/sec/unit and S2: 120 messages/sec/unit, starting at 100 messages/sec
Total storage capacity	No limit (~500 TB)
Message retention	Min 1 day, max 7 days
Partitions	Between 1 and 32 partitions
Max message size	256 KB
Max batch size	256 KB
Max # of connected devices	No limit
Max # of connection requests	S1: 12 requests/sec/unit, S2: 120 requests/sec/unit

How do we use IoT Hub in the BYA scenario?

For the purposes of ingesting telemetry from the various airport sensors, we can apply IoT Hub in almost the same fashion as we demonstrated for Event Hubs.

Revisiting the Sensors project

Return to Visual Studio and the sample solution. Since we already covered a lot of the infrastructure for generating the telemetry in the SimpleSensorConsole and Sensors projects, we will focus just on the components that handle sending the sensor telemetry to IoT Hub.

From a high level, the biggest difference is that before our simulated devices can begin transmitting data to the IoT Hub, they need to be added to the IoT Hub registry, which tracks the devices, their authentication keys, and whether or not they are allowed to connect (enabled versus disabled).

We begin by looking at the `Init` method in *IoTHubLoadSimulator.cs* (Example 3-10).

Example 3-10. Creating an instance of RegistryManager that is used to manage devices allowed to communicate with IoT Hub

```
public void Init()
{
    try
    {
        iotHubSenderConnectionString =
        System.Configuration.ConfigurationManager.AppSettings[
        "IoTHubSenderConnectionsString"];
        iotHubManagerConnectionString =
        System.Configuration.ConfigurationManager.AppSettings[
```

```
        "IoTHubManagerConnectionsString"];
        sendAsBatch =
        bool.Parse(System.Configuration.ConfigurationManager.AppSettings[
        "SendEventsAsBatch"]);

        registryManager =
        RegistryManager.CreateFromConnectionString(iotHubManagerConnectionString);

    }
    catch (Exception ex)
    {
        LogError(ex.Message);
        throw;
    }

}
```

Within the `Init` method, we load two different connection strings to our single IoT Hub instance: one will be used by the devices to send their telemetry, while the other has different permissions and is allowed to add new devices to the IoT Hub registry. Once we have the latter connection string, we create an instance of `RegistryManager` from the factory class, providing it this connection string.

Our pattern for creating the device and sending the messages is very similar to how we approached it with Event Hubs, with the key difference that first we need to register and activate the device (Example 3-11).

Example 3-11. Simulating a temperature sensor sending to IoT Hub

```
public async Task SimulateTemperatureEvents()
{
    deviceId = "1";

    RegisterDeviceAsync().Wait();
    bool deviceActivated = await ActivateDeviceAsync();

    if (deviceActivated)
    {
        InitDeviceClient();

        stopWatch.Restart();
        numEventsSent = 0;
        LogStatus("Sending Temperature Events...");

        SensorBase sensor = new TemperatureSensor(deviceId, TransmitEvent);
        sensor.InitSchedule(10);
        Console.WriteLine("Generated {0:###,###,###} Events",
        sensor.CountOfDataPoints);
        sensor.Start().Wait();
        FlushIoTHubBuffer();
```

```
        stopWatch.Stop();

        Console.WriteLine(
        "Completed transmission in {0} seconds. Sent {1:###,###,###} events.",
            stopWatch.Elapsed.TotalSeconds, numEventsSent);
    }
    else
    {
        LogError("Device Not Activated.");
    }
}
```

Let's take a look at `RegisterDeviceAsync` in greater detail (Example 3-12).

Example 3-12. Adding a device to the registry is performed via RegistryManager

```
async Task RegisterDeviceAsync()
{
    Device device = new Device(deviceId);
    device.Status = DeviceStatus.Disabled;

    try
    {
        device = await registryManager.AddDeviceAsync(device);
    }
    catch (Microsoft.Azure.Devices.Common.Exceptions.DeviceAlreadyExistsException)
    {
        //Device already exists, get the registered device
        device = await registryManager.GetDeviceAsync(deviceId);

        //Ensure the device is disabled until Activated later
        device.Status = DeviceStatus.Disabled;

        //Update IoT Hubs with the device status change
        await registryManager.UpdateDeviceAsync(device);
    }

    deviceKey = device.Authentication.SymmetricKey.PrimaryKey;
}
```

In Example 3-12, we create a new instance of `Device`, passing it the string device ID. By convention, we set the device's status to `Disabled` (and we will set this status to `Enabled` when we later activate the device). For many situations in the real world, this is a convention that enables you to register a device, ship it, and activate it only once it has been received by the trusted party installing the device. Notice in Example 3-12 that we have special case handling of the `DeviceAlreadyExistsException`. This handles the situation where if you try to run the simulator multiple times, you are allowed to reuse devices with the same device ID. Finally, take note of the last line, which collects the primary key for the device. This secret is effectively the password the device needs to provide to authenticate with IoT Hub before it can begin transmitting.

ActivateDevice uses RegistryManager in a similar fashion, by getting the existing device, changing its status to Enabled, and then updating the registry, as shown in Example 3-13.

Example 3-13. Activating a device by setting its status to enabled in the IoT Hub registry

```
async Task<bool> ActivateDeviceAsync()
{
    bool success = false;
    Device device;

    try
    {
        //Fetch the device
        device = await registryManager.GetDeviceAsync(deviceId);

        //Verify the device keys match
        if (deviceKey == device.Authentication.SymmetricKey.PrimaryKey)
        {
            //Enable the device
            device.Status = DeviceStatus.Enabled;

            //Update IoT Hubs
            await registryManager.UpdateDeviceAsync(device);

            success = true;
        }
    }
    catch (Exception)
    {
        success = false;
    }

    return success;
}
```

The next step is to instantiate a DeviceClient instance that we use to communicate with the IoT Hub (Example 3-14). Notice we need to provide it the IoT Hub hostname (which we parse from the sender connection string), device ID, and device key (which we acquired when we registered the device).

Example 3-14. Creating an instance of DeviceClient

```
void InitDeviceClient()
{
    var builder = Microsoft.Azure.Devices.
    IotHubConnectionStringBuilder.Create(iotHubSenderConnectionString);
    string iotHubName = builder.HostName;

    deviceClient = DeviceClient.Create(iotHubName,
        new DeviceAuthenticationWithRegistrySymmetricKey(deviceId, deviceKey));
}
```

Now that we have our device registered, we can send messages to the IoT Hub using either the batch approach or one-message-at-a-time approach, just as we did for Event Hubs. See Example 3-15.

Example 3-15. Sending messages in a batch and a message at a time

```
void FlushIoTHubBuffer()
{
    if (sendBuffer.Count > 0)
    {
        deviceClient.SendEventBatchAsync(sendBuffer);

        numEventsSent += sendBuffer.Count;
        sendBuffer.Clear();
        bufferedSizeInBytes = 0;
    }
}

void SendToIoTHubDirect(Microsoft.Azure.Devices.Client.Message message)
{
    deviceClient.SendEventAsync(message);
}
```

Now that you've gotten a tour of the IoT Hub load simulator, it's time to run it.

Running the IoT Hub load simulator. In order to run the IoT Hub load simulator you will need an existing IoT Hub instance and two connection strings, one for sending and one with manage registry permissions. Once you have those connection strings, you can update *app.config* and run the project.

Creating an IoT Hub instance. In this section we will walk through creating the IoT Hub instance.

1. Navigate to the Azure Portal (*https://portal.azure.com*).

2. Click New, and select Internet of Things and then Azure IoT Hub (Figure 3-30).

Figure 3-30. Creating a new Azure IoT Hub in the Azure Portal.

3. In the IoT Hub blade, provide a name for your new IoT Hub instance.

4. Choose a resource group.

5. Verify the desired subscription is selected.

6. Choose a location nearest you. See Figure 3-31.

Figure 3-31. Configuring a new IoT Hub.

7. Click Create.

Your new IoT Hub instance should be ready within a few minutes. When it is ready, navigate to the Settings blade of your IoT Hub instance and follow these steps to get your connection strings.

1. Click "Shared access policies" (Figure 3-32).

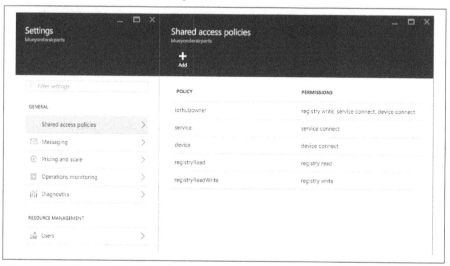

Figure 3-32. Viewing the Shared access policies for an IoT Hub.

2. Click on the policy named "device."

3. On the blade that appears, click the copy button for "Connection string—primary key" (Figure 3-33). This connection string will be used by the devices to send their telemetry.

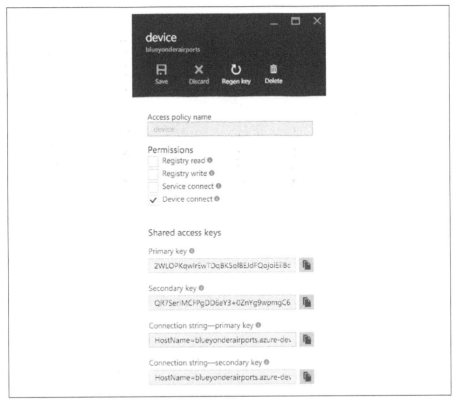

Figure 3-33. Viewing the device shared access policy.

4. Return to Visual Studio, open the *app.config* file within the SimpleConsoleSimulator project, and for the setting with the key IoTHubConnectionString, paste this value.

5. Go back to the portal, close the device blade, and click on the registryRead Write policy.

6. Copy the "Connection string—primary" for that policy.

7. Return to the *app.config* file in Visual Studio, and paste the value for the setting with the key IoTHubManagerConnectionString.

8. Save the *app.config* file.

Build and run the project. This time, when console starts up, choose option 2 to send your messages to your IoT Hub (Figure 3-34).

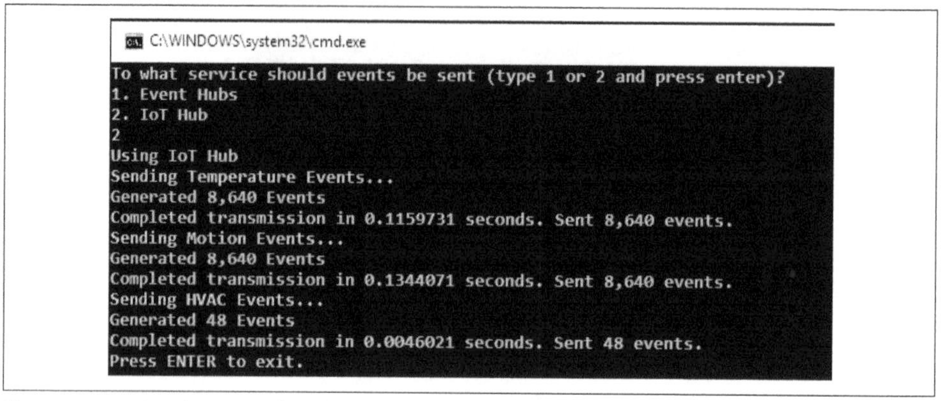

Figure 3-34. Sending simulated messages to IoT Hub.

Summary

In this chapter we focused on the telemetry ingest, targeting files and queues for storage. With respect to file-based storage, we looked at Azure Data Lake Store, Azure Blob Storage, and HDFS. With respect to storage of messages or events in a queue, we examined ingest for both Event Hubs and IoT Hub.

CHAPTER 4

Real-Time Processing in Azure

Real-time processing is defined as the processing of a typically infinite stream of input data, whose time until results ready is short—measured in milliseconds or seconds in the longest of cases. In this first chapter on real-time processing, we will examine various methods for quickly processing input data ingested from queueing services like Event Hubs and IoT Hub (Figure 4-1).

Stream Processing

When it comes to stream processing, there are generally two approaches to working through the infinite stream of input data (or tuples): you can process one tuple at a time with downstream processing applications, or you can create small batches (consisting of a few hundred or a few thousand tuples) and process these *micro-batches* with your downstream applications. In this chapter we will focus on the tuple-at-a-time approach, and in the next we will examine the micro-batch approach.

For our purposes in this book, the source of streamed data processed by an analytics pipeline is either Event Hubs or IoT Hub. The options consolidate further when you consider that when it comes to the services side of IoT Hub (i.e., the side that consumes and processes ingested telemetry), it is exposing an Event Hubs–compatible endpoint. In other words, regardless of whether we ingest via Event Hubs or IoT Hub, we process the messages by pulling from Event Hubs (see Figure 4-2).

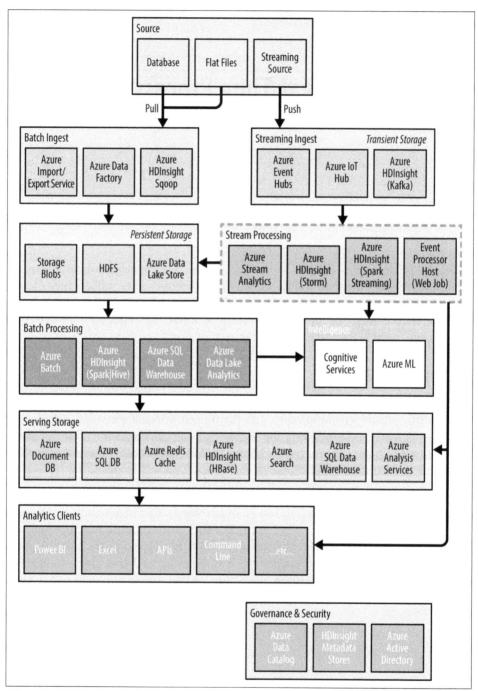

Figure 4-1. This chapter focuses on a subset of the listed stream processing components that process data in a tuple-at-a-time fashion.

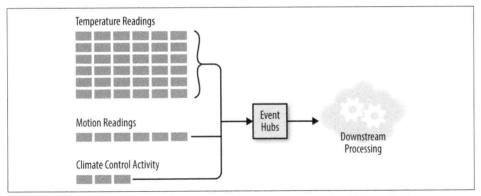

Figure 4-2. High-level view of the ingest and consumptions side of Event Hubs.

Consuming Messages from Event Hubs

We covered how Event Hubs ingest data from clients into Event Hub partitions in depth in the previous chapter.In this chapter we focus on the path that pulls event data from Event Hub partitions: the event consumer applications. There are SDKs to build consumers in .NET, Java, and Node.js. However, be aware that not all SDKs provide support for both sending to and receiving from Event Hubs. An example of this is the Azure Event Hub client for C, which is intended for embedded devices to utilize in transmitting their data to Event Hubs (and not for these devices to consume Event Hub events).

Regardless of the implementation used for the consumer, there are some cross-cutting concepts that apply. We will address those here and demonstrate the SDK specifics in sample implementations.

The consumer (also referred to as the receiver) of the Event Hub draws events from a single partition within an Event Hub. Therefore, an Event Hub with four partitions will have four consumers—one assigned to consume from each partition. The consumers communicate with Event Hubs via the AMQP protocol, and the payload retrieved is an `EventData` instance (having both event properties and a binary serialized body).

The logical group of consumers that receive messages from each Event Hub partition is called a *consumer group*. The intention of a consumer group is to represent a single downstream processing application, where that application consists of multiple parallel processes, each consuming and processing messages from a partition. All consumers must belong to a consumer group. The consumer group also acts to limit concurrent access to a given partition by multiple consumers, which is desired for most applications, because two consumers could mean data is being redundantly processed by downstream components and could have unintended consequences.

Creating Consumer Groups

By default every Event Hub starts with one consumer group named $Default. Consumer groups can be created through the Azure Portal. Navigate to your deployed Event Hub in the Management Portal and click Create New Consumer Group. The only configuration a consumer group accepts is a string name. To view the list of consumer groups for your Event Hub, drill into your Event Hub from the namespace view and click the Consumer Groups tab.

In the situation where multiple processes need to consume events from a partition, there are two options. First, consider if the parallel processing required should belong in a new consumer group. Event Hubs has a soft limit that allows you to create up to 20 consumer groups. Second, if the parallel processing makes sense within the context of a single consumer group, then note that Event Hubs will allow up to five such processes within the same consumer group to process events concurrently from a single partition.

On the event consumer side, Event Hubs works differently from traditional queues. In the traditional queue, you typically see a pattern called *competing consumers*. It is so named because each consumer targeting a queue is effectively competing against all other consumers targeting the same queue for the next message: the first consumer to get the message wins, and the other consumers will not get that message (Figure 4-3).

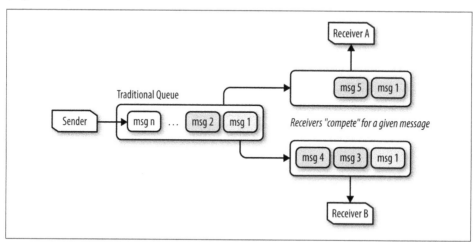

Figure 4-3. Two receivers dequeueing messages in a competing consumer pattern; notice that Receiver A and Receiver B never receive the same message.

By contrast, you can look at Event Hubs (or more precisely, the partitions within an Event Hubs instance) as following a multiconsumer (or broadcast) pattern where every consumer can receive every message (Figure 4-4).

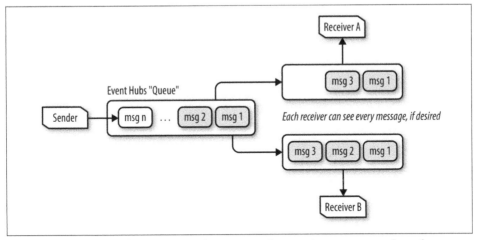

Figure 4-4. Example of two Event Hubs receivers dequeueing messages, where the messages Receiver A gets are not affected by messages acquired by Receiver B.

The critical difference between the two dequeuing patterns amounts to state management. In competing consumers, the queue system itself keeps track of the delivery state of every message. In Event Hubs, no such state is tracked, so managing the state of progress through the queue becomes the responsibility of the individual consumer.

So what is this state that the consumers manage? It boils down to byte offsets and message sequence numbers in a process called *checkpointing*. If you think of the underlying storage for a partition as a file, then you can think of the byte offset as a way of describing a location in the file. Anything before the byte offset represents messages you have already consumed, and anything after the byte offset represents messages awaiting consumption. Sequence number is similar, except instead of measuring an offset in bytes, it is an ordinal based on the message position (so you might have a sequence number of 10, indicating you had consumed 10 messages and your next message will be the 11th). Both the byte offset and sequence number increase as messages are added to the partition.

Consumers checkpoint their sequence number and an offset to some form of durable storage, such as Azure Blob Storage or Apache Zookeeper, which enables new consumer instances to be started and resume from the checkpoint location should the consumer process fail.

An important side effect of outsourcing this state management to the consumer is that messages are no longer deleted from the queue when processed (as in the competing consumers pattern). Instead, Event Hubs queues have a retention period of 1 to 7 days, and it is the expiration of that retention period that effectively ages out and deletes messages. With that retention period in mind, each partition tracks a begin sequence number and an end sequence number that represents the current range of available events. You can observe these values using the SDKs or with tools like Service Bus Explorer (*http://bit.ly/servicebusexplorer*), pictured in Figure 4-5.

Figure 4-5. Service Bus Explorer showing the begin and end sequence numbers for a partition in Event Hubs.

When consumers process events from a partition, they can typically choose to indicate either a byte offset or a start date/time. They can begin consuming messages anywhere in the stream of events within the retention period.

Consumer groups manage one final value, which has to do with the versioning of the consumer application: the *epoch*. For a given partition, the epoch represents the numeric "version" or "phase" of the consumer and can be used to ensure that only the latest is allowed to pull events. When a higher-valued epoch receiver is launched, the lower-valued one is disconnected.

It is possible to create a receiver without an epoch, in which case the epochs are not enforced, but it is here that you are limited to five concurrent consumers per partition/consumer group combination. The epoch value is typically supplied when the consumer is created (at the same time where it might indicate an offset).

Table 4-1 summarizes the egress limits applicable to Event Hubs consumers.

Table 4-1. Event Hubs egress quotas and limits

Item	Limits
Consumer groups	Max of 20 consumer groups per Event Hub
Consumers per partition	Max of 1 consumer per partition per consumer group when consumer created with epoch; up to 5 consumers per partition per consumer group when consumer created without epoch
Egress throughput	2 MB/s per TU; no limit on # of events per second

We will show many examples of clients that consume messages from Event Hubs using the preceding concepts. That said, many of the SDKs abstract away some of these details and make the consumer application easier to implement. It's important to recognize that these concepts are still taking effect "under the covers."

Tuple-at-a-Time Processing in Azure

This chapter focuses on tuple-at-a-time processing options including Storm on HDInsight (in Java and .NET) and the Event Processor Host API for use in .NET.

Introducing HDInsight

HDInsight provides Hadoop ecosystem components in the form of a managed service. It takes the burden off of you from having to create, configure, and deploy individual virtual machines in order to build a cluster, keep it operational, and scale it by adding or removing nodes. HDInsight uses the Hortonworks Data Platform (HDP) to provide a consistent set of Hadoop ecosystem components, where the versions of each have been tested to work well together. HDInsight lets you provision clusters for major components such as Apache Spark, Apache Storm, Apache HBase, Apache Hive, Apache Pig, and, of course, Apache Hadoop.

HDInsight Hadoop Components

For a complete listing of all the Hadoop ecosystem components available and their versions in each release of HDInsight, see the Microsoft Azure documentation (*http://bit.ly/2nSoIUi*).

Storm on HDInsight

HDInsight enables you to easily provision clusters that run Apache Storm, and tooling from Microsoft makes it easy to manage Storm using the Azure Portal and Visual Studio.

Apache Storm provides a scalable, fault-tolerant platform for implementing real-time data processing applications. From a physical view a Storm application runs in perpetuity across a cluster of nodes with separate responsibilities. Zookeeper nodes run

Apache Zookeeper and are used to maintain state. Supervisor nodes run worker processes, which in turn spawn threads called *executors*. These executors provide the compute cycles to run tasks, which are instances of Storm components that contain the processing logic. Nimbus nodes keep tabs on the supervisors and the tasks they are running, restarting them in the face of failures.

From a logical perspective, what you actually implement—a Storm application—is built by defining a *topology*. A topology describes a directed acyclic graph, meaning looping is not permitted.

Storm takes the approach that input data is viewed as a continuous stream, where each datum in the stream is called a *tuple*. In this graph, the entry point of the data stream is the spout, and it is responsible for consuming the input data stream, such as reading from a filesystem or a queue, and emitting tuples for downstream processing. Bolts receive a stream of tuples from the spout, process the tuples one at a time, and either emit them for further processing by another layer of bolts or complete the processing (such as by writing the result to a data store).

The way in which a tuple is assigned to a downstream bolt is controlled by stream grouping. For a given downstream bolt, the stream grouping identifies the source and parent component (spout or bolt) by name, and indicates how tuples should be distributed among the instances of the bolt. These stream groupings include:

Shuffle grouping
    Randomly distributes tuples among all of the bolt's tasks.

None grouping
    Effectively the same as shuffle grouping.

Local or shuffle grouping
    If the target bolt shares a worker process with the source task, then that bolt task is preferred for receiving the tuple. Otherwise, the tuple is randomly distributed to one of the bolt's tasks (as done by shuffle grouping). The idea is to keep the tuple within the same worker process and avoid an interprocess or network transfer.

Fields grouping
    Partitions the stream so that fields of the tuple having the same value are assigned to the same bolt task.

Partial key grouping
    Performs the same grouping as fields grouping, but instead of having a single task for any given group, there are always two bolt tasks between which the tuples are distributed.

All grouping
    The task is broadcast to all bolt tasks.

Direct grouping

Allows the producer of the tuple to specifically indicate which bolt task will receive the tuple.

Global grouping

This is the opposite of all grouping; it indicates that all upstream tuples should flow to one bolt task.

Out of the box, Storm includes prebuilt spouts for consuming from queueing systems such as Azure Event Hubs, Apache Kafka, and RabbitMQ. It also includes bolts that are capable of writing to filesystems, like HDFS, and interacting with data stores, such as Hive, HBase, Redis, and databases accessible by JDBC.

While a given tuple is flowing through the directed acyclic graph described by the topology, Storm is able to keep track of its progress. It can provide three different processing guarantees:

No guarantee

Not all situations require guarantees that an incoming tuple not be lost or fail to be processed.

At-least-once guarantee

Ensures that any given tuple will never fail to be processed, even if it means it must be processed multiple times because previous attempts encountered a failure.

Exactly-once guarantee

Ensures that any tuple running in the topology is processed to completion by the topology, with mechanisms to ensure resiliency of processing in the face of failure without reprocessing.

In the context of tuple-at-a-time processing in this section, we will focus on topologies that offer at-least-once tuple processing guarantees.

Let's briefly explore at a high level how Storm provides an at-least-once guarantee. Assume we have tuple input into the topology. Storm keeps track of the success or failure status of this tuple at every step in the topology. It does so by requiring each spout or bolt component that receives the tuple to do two things: it must acknowledge the tuple was processed successfully (or fail it outright), and when the component emits a new tuple in response to this original tuple, it must "anchor" the new tuple to the original. By relating all derived tuples to the original tuple sourced at the spout using this anchoring technique, Storm is able to establish a lineage for tuples processed by a topology. By having this lineage, Storm can compute if a given input tuple was fully processed by all components. It can also detect if a tuple failed to process, by checking at the end of a window of time if it has been successfully processed by all components. If not, the processing can be retried.

Applying Storm to Blue Yonder Airports

To understand how tuple-at-a-time processing works with Storm, let's apply it to a situation within the Blue Yonder Airports scenario. When it comes to the ambient temperature around a gate, BYA would like to keep the temperatures within a fairly narrow range throughout the course of the day. If the temperature is outside of the range, then either the thermostat is malfunctioning or there is actually a problem at the gate. They would like the system to call attention to it by raising an alert. The overall Storm topology looks like Figure 4-6.

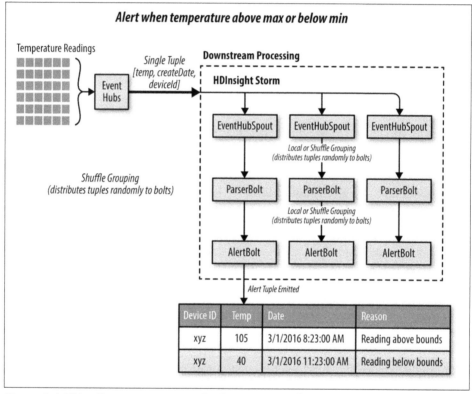

Figure 4-6. Using Storm to process tuples from Event Hubs in a tuple-at-a-time fashion in order to raise alerts about exception conditions.

In the approach, we collect the temperature telemetry into Event Hubs (or IoT Hub) as we have shown previously. HDInsight runs a Storm topology that reads tuples from Event Hubs. There is one instance of an EventHubSpout for each partition present in Event Hubs. The EventHubSpout also checkpoints its progress through the Event Hub partitions, maintaining this state in Zookeeper. This enables the topology to be restarted (such as in the case of supervisor node failure) and the reading of events to be resumed where the EventHubSpout left off. The topology uses the Local

OrShuffleGrouping to randomly distribute the tuples received by the EventHubSpout to a ParserBolt instance, which has the effect of preferring to send the tuple to a ParserBolt instance that is running within the same worker as the EventHubSpout. This eliminates a network transfer between separate worker processes and can dramatically improve topology throughput. If there is no local ParserBolt available, the LocalOrShuffleGrouping sends the tuple to a randomly selected ParserBolt.

The ParserBolt deserializes the telemetry string, and parses the JSON it contains. If the tuple object has a temperature field, then the ParserBolt emits a new tuple (consisting of the three fields: temperature, date created, and device ID) for downstream processing by the AlertBolt. If the telemetry lacks a temperature field, then the logic assumes it is not a temperature reading and no tuple is emitted—effectively ignoring the telemetry input.

The AlertBolt receives the tuple, and checks if the value of the temperature field is greater or less than a configured value. If either is true, then it emits a new tuple that contains the original three fields, plus a new field that provides the reason for emitting this alert tuple. On the other hand, if the tuple is within range, then no tuple is emitted.

The assumption is this alert tuple could then be handled by downstream components, either by storing it in a data store or by invoking an API. We will show examples of consuming this alert later in the book.

Alerting with Storm on HDInsight (Java + Linux Cluster)

Storm topologies can be implemented on HDInsight in two ways: they can be implemented in Java and run on either a Windows or Linux HDInsight cluster, or they can be implemented in C#, which requires a Windows HDInsight cluster.

In this section we will explore the Storm implementation in Java and run it on a Linux HDInsight cluster.

Dev environment setup.   While there are many IDEs you can choose from to develop in Java, for the following section we choose IntelliJ IDEA. If you are new to Java development, this allows us to give a simple from-zero-to-sixty option that gets you productive with Storm quickly. If you are established with Java, feel free to modify the following to the IDE of your choice.

For our purposes, you only need IntelliJ IDEA Community Edition, which you can download for the platform (Windows, macOS, and Linux) of your choice from *https://www.jetbrains.com/idea/#chooseYourEdition*.

Once you've downloaded the installer and completed the guided installation with the default settings, you are ready to go. The next step is to download and open the Blue Yonder Airports sample in IntelliJ IDEA.

You can download the Storm sample from *http://bit.ly/2beutHQ*.

The download includes the Alerts Topology sample, and when opened in IntelliJ IDEA will automatically download all dependencies, including Storm.

Once you have downloaded the sample, open IntelliJ IDEA and follow these steps:

1. Select File→Open.

2. In the "Open File or Project" dialog, navigate to the folder that contains the sample, and select that folder.

3. Click OK.

4. If you are prompted to import dependencies, do so.

You should now be ready to explore the project. In the project tree view, expand source→main→java→net.solliance.storm. You should see the three classes that define the topology, the parser bolt, and the alert bolt, respectively, as shown in Figure 4-7.

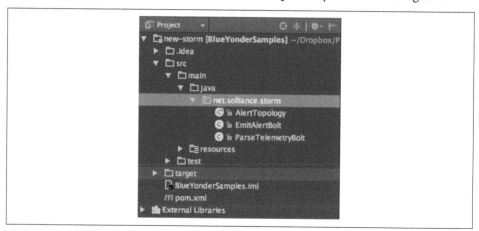

Figure 4-7. The three classes that make up the alerting solution.

Next, expand source→main→resources. This folder contains the *config.properties* file that holds the settings used to connect to your previously created Event Hubs instance (Figure 4-8).

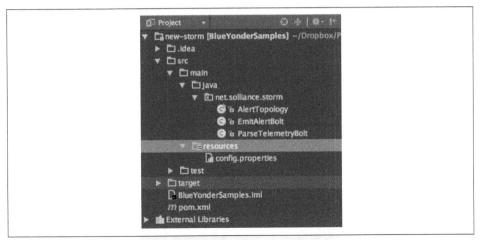

Figure 4-8. The config.properties file holds the connection information to Event Hubs.

Open *config.properties* and specify the following settings (Example 4-1):

`eventhubspout.username`
    The policy name with read permissions to Event Hubs

`eventhubspout.password`
    The primary key for the aforementioned policy

`eventhubspout.namespace`
    The service bus namespace containing your Event Hubs instance

`eventhubspout.entitypath`
    The name of your Event Hubs instance

`eventhubspout.partitions.count`
    The number of partitions your Event Hubs instance contains

Example 4-1. Example configuration settings for the Event Hub Spout in config.properties

```
eventhubspout.username = reader

eventhubspout.password = zotQvVFyStprcSe4LZ8Spp3umStfwC9ejvpVSoJFLlU=

eventhubspout.namespace = blueyonderairports-ns

eventhubspout.entitypath = blueyonderairports

eventhubspout.partitions.count = 4
```

The rest of the settings should already have reasonable defaults and are described by the comments within the file, should you desire to understand the other "knobs" you can adjust.

Now you are ready to build the project. Storm projects are built with Maven, a build manager that is the recommended way to manage dependencies and define build steps for Storm projects. At its core is the Project Object Model, an XML document that describes the project structure, repositories (from which to acquire dependencies), the dependencies themselves, and any components needed during the build. You can view the *pom.xml* document in the project tree view, in the root of the project directory (Figure 4-9).

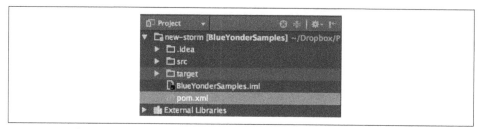

Figure 4-9. The pom.xml file, which configures dependencies and build settings.

IntelliJ IDEA provides a window that can execute the build steps as described in *pom.xml*. To view this window, select View→Tool Windows→Maven Projects. When you display this dialog, it should appear as shown in Figure 4-10.

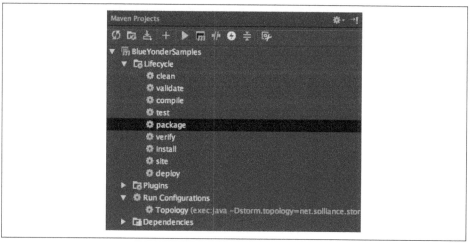

Figure 4-10. The Maven Projects window showing the actions that can be run on the project.

Double-click on "compile" to build the project, and make sure you do not have any build errors (which would appear in the window docked to the bottom of IntelliJ IDEA).

Topology implementation.   Before we get to running the topology, let's explore the implementation. We'll start at the top, the topology, and then drill into the spouts and bolts.

If you open *AlertTopology.java*, you should notice the AlertTopology class consists of one static method, main; an empty constructor; and a few protected helper functions. The purpose of this class is to instantiate the various bolts and spouts needed by the topology and wire them together into a directed acyclic graph. The main method takes as its only input argument an array of strings, which will contain any command-line parameters used to launch the topology using the Storm command-line client. When the topology is run, this main method is invoked first.

```
public static void main(String[] args) throws Exception {
    AlertTopology scenario = new AlertTopology();

    String topologyName;
    String configPropertiesPath;
    if (args != null && args.length >0){
        topologyName = args[0];
        configPropertiesPath = args[1];
    }
    else
    {
        topologyName = "AlertTopology";
        configPropertiesPath = null;
    }


    scenario.loadAndApplyConfig(configPropertiesPath, topologyName);
    StormTopology topology = scenario.buildTopology();
    scenario.submitTopology(args, topology);
}
```

The main method implementation follows a typical pattern for Storm topologies: load configuration properties, build the topology, and submit the topology to run it.

Let's look at each of these steps in detail, starting with the loading of configuration properties. Within AlertTopology.loadAndApplyConfig we have the following:

```
protected void loadAndApplyConfig(String configFilePath, String topologyName)
    throws Exception {

    Properties properties = loadConfigurationProperties(configFilePath);

    String username = properties.getProperty("eventhubspout.username");
    String password = properties.getProperty("eventhubspout.password");
```

```java
String namespaceName = properties.getProperty("eventhubspout.namespace");
String entityPath = properties.getProperty("eventhubspout.entitypath");
String targetFqnAddress =
  properties.getProperty("eventhubspout.targetfqnaddress");
String zkEndpointAddress =
  properties.getProperty("zookeeper.connectionstring");
int partitionCount =
  Integer.parseInt(properties.getProperty("eventhubspout.partitions.count"));
int checkpointIntervalInSeconds =
  Integer.parseInt(properties.getProperty("eventhubspout.checkpoint.interval"));
int receiverCredits =
  Integer.parseInt(properties.getProperty("eventhub.receiver.credits"));
String maxPendingMsgsPerPartitionStr =
  properties.getProperty("eventhubspout.max.pending.messages.per.partition");
if(maxPendingMsgsPerPartitionStr == null) {
   maxPendingMsgsPerPartitionStr = "1024";
}
int maxPendingMsgsPerPartition =
  Integer.parseInt(maxPendingMsgsPerPartitionStr);
String enqueueTimeDiffStr =
  properties.getProperty("eventhub.receiver.filter.timediff");
if(enqueueTimeDiffStr == null) {
   enqueueTimeDiffStr = "0";
}
int enqueueTimeDiff = Integer.parseInt(enqueueTimeDiffStr);
long enqueueTimeFilter = 0;
if(enqueueTimeDiff != 0) {
   enqueueTimeFilter = System.currentTimeMillis() - enqueueTimeDiff*1000;
}
String consumerGroupName =
  properties.getProperty("eventhubspout.consumer.group.name");

System.out.println("Eventhub spout config: ");
System.out.println("  partition count: " + partitionCount);
System.out.println("  checkpoint interval: " + checkpointIntervalInSeconds);
System.out.println("  receiver credits: " + receiverCredits);

spoutConfig = new EventHubSpoutConfig(username, password,
        namespaceName, entityPath, partitionCount, zkEndpointAddress,
        checkpointIntervalInSeconds, receiverCredits,
        maxPendingMsgsPerPartition,
        enqueueTimeFilter);

if(targetFqnAddress != null)
{
    spoutConfig.setTargetAddress(targetFqnAddress);
}
spoutConfig.setConsumerGroupName(consumerGroupName);

//set the number of workers to be the same as partition number.
//the idea is to have a spout and a partial count bolt co-exist in one
//worker to avoid shuffling messages across workers in storm cluster.
```

```
        numWorkers = spoutConfig.getPartitionCount();

        spoutConfig.setTopologyName(topologyName);

        minAlertTemp = Double.parseDouble(properties.getProperty("alerts.mintemp"));
        maxAlertTemp = Double.parseDouble(properties.getProperty("alerts.maxtemp"));
    }
```

As you can see, the gist of this method is to use the properties collection to retrieve string properties from the *config.properties* file and store the result either in a method local variable or a global instance variable. Take particular note of the creation of the `spoutConfig` variable, which is one such global variable. This instance of `EventHub SpoutConfig` represents all the settings the `EventHubSpout` will need in order to retrieve events from Events Hubs. Also, it is worth pointing out `numWorkers`. Recall that in Storm, workers represent threads running within an executor. This setting will be used when we build the topology. The last two lines in the method load the temperature below which an alert should be raised (`minAlertTemp`) and the temperature above which an alert should be raised (`maxAlertTemp`).

The `loadConfigurationProperties` method invoked at the beginning of `loadAndAp plyConfig` is responsible for doing the actual loading of the properties collection— drawing the values either from a *config.properties* file indicated via a command-line argument (such as when running the topology using the Storm client) or defaulting to the copy of it embedded as a resource (which is needed when you're running the topology locally in the debugger).

```
    protected Properties loadConfigurationProperties(String configFilePath)
      throws Exception{
        Properties properties = new Properties();
        if(configFilePath != null) {
            properties.load(new FileReader(configFilePath));
        }
        else {
            properties.load(AlertTopology.class.getClassLoader().getResourceAsStream(
                    "config.properties"));
        }
        return properties;
    }
```

The next method to be called, from `main`, is `buildTopology`. This method creates an instance of the `EventHubSpout`, passing in the `spoutConfig` previously created. Then an instance of `TopologyBuilder` is used to tie each of the topology components together.

The call to `builder.setSpout` is how the spout for the topology is added. The first parameter provides the name of the spout (as well as names the stream of tuples it emits), the second parameter provides the instance of the spout constructed, and the third sets the initial parallelism that configures the initial number of executor threads allocated to the spout. The intent of setting the initial parallelism is to have one thread available for each partition in Event Hubs.

The chained call to setNumTasks controls the number of task instances. The value for the call to setNumTasks is also set to the number of partitions. Together, the initial parallelism and declaration of the number of tasks ensure that when the topology runs, there will always be one EventHubSpout instance actively running per partition in Event Hubs.

This warrants a little explanation. While the initial parallelism controls the number of threads allocated to a spout, the number of tasks controls how many instances of the spout are run across the topology. If the number of tasks equals the initial parallelism —for example, if you have four tasks and an initial parallelism of 4, then each spout instance will run on its own thread. You can "double up" tasks on a thread, running multiple spout instances per thread if the number of tasks is greater than the initial parallelism. When it comes to consuming from Event Hubs, the best practice to achieve the highest throughput is to have one consuming thread dedicated to a spout instance that is able to retrieve messages from one partition without interruption.

```
protected StormTopology buildTopology() {
    TopologyBuilder builder = new TopologyBuilder();

    EventHubSpout eventHubSpout = new EventHubSpout(spoutConfig);

    builder.setSpout("EventHubSpout",
      eventHubSpout, spoutConfig.getPartitionCount())
            .setNumTasks(spoutConfig.getPartitionCount());

    builder.setBolt("ParseTelemetryBolt",
      new ParseTelemetryBolt(), 4).localOrShuffleGrouping("EventHubSpout")
            .setNumTasks(spoutConfig.getPartitionCount());

    builder.setBolt("EmitAlertBolt",
      new EmitAlertBolt(minAlertTemp, maxAlertTemp), 4).localOrShuffleGrouping(
      "ParseTelemetryBolt")
            .setNumTasks(spoutConfig.getPartitionCount());

    return builder.createTopology();
}
```

The next line is the first call to builder.setBolt. Here we configure the number of tasks and the initial parallelism as before, but we don't have the requirement of having as many executor threads initially, so we can set it to a different value than the number of partitions. This line creates an instance of the ParseTelemetryBolt.

To configure the ParseTelemetryBolt so it gets its input tuples from the EventHubSp out, we reference the latter by name in the localOrShuffleGrouping chained method. The localOrShuffleGrouping provides an optimization in selecting the instance of the bolt that will receive tuples from the instance of a spout. If a spout and an instance of the bolt are running within the same worker process, then this localOr ShuffleGrouping prefers to use that bolt instance rather than any of the other instances running within other worker processes. This avoids having to send the tuple over the network to a remote bolt. However, if no local bolt is available, then the tuple is sent to a randomly selected bolt.

The final call to builder.setBolt creates an instance of the EmitAlertBolt, which takes in its constructor the minimum and maximum values used to control the range outside of which an alert tuple is created. The EmitAlertBolt is configured to receive its input tuples from the ParseTelemetryBolt, again using a localOrShuffleGroup ing.

The final line creates the actual instance of the topology, which we can submit to Storm to execute. This execution happens in the last line of main, which calls sce nario.submitTopology, passing it any command-line arguments and the instance of the topology constructed. The implementation of submitTopology is as follows:

```
protected void submitTopology(String[] args, StormTopology topology)
  throws Exception {
    Config config = new Config();
    config.setDebug(false);

    if (args != null && args.length > 0) {
        StormSubmitter.submitTopology(args[0], config, topology);
    } else {
        config.setMaxTaskParallelism(2);

        LocalCluster localCluster = new LocalCluster();
        localCluster.submitTopology("test", config, topology);
        Thread.sleep(600000);
        localCluster.shutdown();
    }
}
```

The goal of the submitTopology method is to support another common Storm pattern—to enable you to run the topology locally or against a Storm cluster. An instance of Config is created that wraps the settings Storm will use when running the topology. Next, we pass false to the call config.setDebug to minimize the logging (setting it to true would mean Storm logs details every time a tuple is received or emitted). After that, we examine the args array of command-line parameters. If we have command-line parameters, then by convention we know we want to run it against a Storm cluster. To do so, we use the submitTopology method of the Storm class, passing it the first argument (the name of the topology), the Config instance, and the topology we built. If we do not have any args, we create an instance of Local Cluster, call submitTopology against that, and wait for 10 minutes (600,000 ms) in the `Thread.sleep` before automatically shutting down the local cluster (without the sleep call, the cluster would shut down before the topology even gets going).

Since we are processing telemetry from Event Hubs, we do not need to implement a spout for that. The `EventHubsSpout` is a part of the Storm core libraries. So we will jump into the implementation of the bolts.

Let's take a look at the `ParseTelemetryBolt`. Recall that the objective of this bolt is to take the input tuple, which contains the telemetry data in the form of a JSON serialized string, and turn it into a tuple with fields for each property (temperature, create date, and device ID). This class overrides the two key methods of `BaseBasicBolt`: execute and `declareOutputFields`.

The `declareOutputFields` method is called before the bolt begins executing, and its purpose is to indicate the names of the fields that will be emitted in the tuples created by this bolt. Think of it as declaring the schema of the output of the bolt, without explicitly describing the types of the fields, just the names. In our case, the output bolt from this will be a tuple that contains three fields: `temp`, `createDate`, and `deviceId`.

The `execute` method is called by Storm whenever there is a tuple to process by the bolt. The collector parameter is used to emit the bolt after this method has finished its processing. In the implementation, we use the Jackson library to parse the JSON string into an object, and we check if it has a temp field. If it does, we assume this a temperature reading tuple (as opposed to a motion sensor or HVAC reading) and we create a new tuple using the `Values` class, passing into its constructor the value for each field in the same order as the fields were declared in `declareOutputFields`. Finally, we emit the tuple for processing by downstream bolts via the call to `collector.emit`.

Observe that this class extends `BaseBasicBolt`. This is the class to use when you want Storm to automatically acknowledge successful processing of an input tuple when the execute method completes without error.

```
public class ParseTelemetryBolt extends BaseBasicBolt{

    private static final long serialVersionUID = 1L;

    public void execute(Tuple input, BasicOutputCollector collector) {

        String value = input.getString(0);
        ObjectMapper mapper = new ObjectMapper();
        try {
            JsonNode telemetryObj = mapper.readTree(value);

            if (telemetryObj.has("temp")) //assume must be a temperature reading
            {
                Values values = new Values(
                        telemetryObj.get("temp").asDouble(),
```

```
                        telemetryObj.get("createDate").asText(),
                        telemetryObj.get("deviceId").asText()
            );

            collector.emit(values);
        }
    } catch (IOException e) {
        System.out.println(e.getMessage());
    }
}

public void declareOutputFields(OutputFieldsDeclarer declarer) {
    declarer.declare(new Fields("temp","createDate", "deviceId"));
}
}
```

Now let's turn our attention to the implementation of the EmitAlert bolt. We follow the same basic pattern as before. In this case we declare the schema of our output tuples to have one additional field, reason, in addition to the fields we have in a temperature tuple. Within the execute method, we look at the value of the temperature received from the incoming tuple, and if it's outside of the bounds we emit a new tuple with the reading's value and the reason.

```
public class EmitAlertBolt extends BaseBasicBolt{

    private static final long serialVersionUID = 1L;

    protected double minAlertTemp;
    protected double maxAlertTemp;

    public EmitAlertBolt(double minTemp, double maxTemp) {
        minAlertTemp = minTemp;
        maxAlertTemp = maxTemp;
    }

    public void execute(Tuple input, BasicOutputCollector collector) {

        double tempReading = input.getDouble(0);
        String createDate = input.getString(1);
        String deviceId = input.getString(2);

        if (tempReading > maxAlertTemp )
        {

            collector.emit(new Values (
                    "reading above bounds",
                    tempReading,
                    createDate,
                    deviceId
            ));
            System.out.println("Emitting above bounds: " + tempReading);
        } else if (tempReading < minAlertTemp)
```

```
            {
                collector.emit(new Values (
                        "reading below bounds",
                        tempReading,
                        createDate,
                        deviceId
                ));
                System.out.println("Emitting below bounds: " + tempReading);
            }
        }

        public void declareOutputFields(OutputFieldsDeclarer declarer) {
            declarer.declare(new Fields("reason","temp","createDate", "deviceId"));
        }
    }
```

With the tour of the code artifacts behind us, let's turn to running the topology locally using IntelliJ IDEA. We will show two approaches: running the topology without the debugger, and running the topology with the debugger.

To run the topology without the debugger, use the Maven Projects window and under Run Configurations, double-click Topology (Figure 4-11).

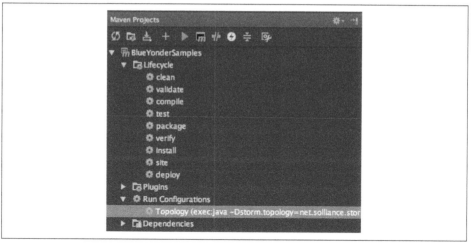

Figure 4-11. Double-click on Topology to run the topology without the debugger.

The output of any diagnostic information, including the out-of-bound messages produced by the EmitAlertBolt, will be shown in the bottom window (Figure 4-12).

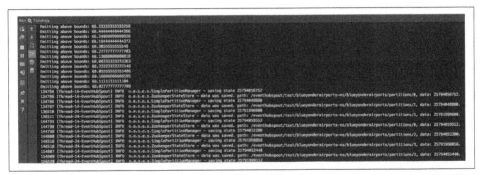

Figure 4-12. Example of the output that will scroll by when you run the topology locally.

The process will automatically terminate, or you can press the "Stop process" button in the output dialog (the red square) to terminate on demand.

To run the topology with the debugger attached—and thereby stop at any breakpoints, allowing you to inspect variables and step through the code—from the Run menu choose Debug "Topology." When it is running you can use the controls in the Debug window to step into, step over, and step out of code, as well as examine frames, threads, and variables when you have hit a breakpoint (Figure 4-13).

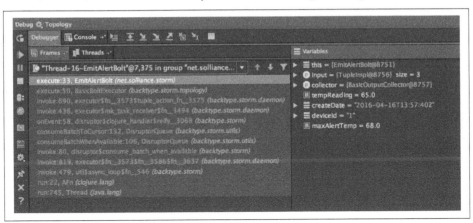

Figure 4-13. The Debug window.

This sample project has been provided with the configuration topology. It is useful to understand how this build configuration was created so that you can apply it in your own Storm projects. From the Run menu, select Edit Configurations.

Notice in the tree that a Maven configuration was added (traditionally you'd do this by clicking the + and choosing Maven in the Add New Configuration dialog). In the tree, select the Topology entry. The working directory should be set to the root of your Storm project directory. The command line should be set to use the Maven exec plugin to run the `java` command, passing it the fully qualified name of your Storm topology via the `Dstorm.topology` parameter (Figure 4-14). To be able to run another topology you create in the future, alter this parameter to have a value of the class name of your new topology.

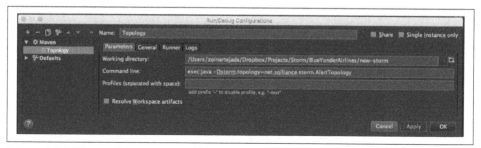

Figure 4-14. The configuration needed to run topologies locally.

Now that we have run the topology locally, we'll turn to running it in a production cluster. Naturally, in order to do that, we first need a Storm cluster, which we will achieve by provisioning an HDInsight cluster that is running Storm on Linux.

Provisioning the Linux HDI cluster.   To provision a minimal Linux HDInsight Cluster with Storm, follow these steps:

1. Log in to the Azure Portal (*https://portal.azure.com*).
2. Select New→Intelligence + Analytics→HDInsight.
3. On the New HDInsight blade, provide a unique name for your cluster.
4. Choose your Azure subscription.
5. Click "Select Cluster configuration."
6. On the "Cluster type configuration" blade, set the cluster type to Storm, operating system to Linux, version to Storm 0.10.0 (you can use any version of HDP, so long as it uses this version of Storm for compatibility with the sample), and leave cluster tier to Standard. Click Select.
7. Click "credentials."
8. Set the admin login username and password, then the SSH username and password, and click Select (Figure 4-15).

Figure 4-15. Configuring authentication to HDInsight cluster.

9. Click Data Source.

10. Select an existing Azure Storage account or create a new one as desired (Figure 4-16).

11. Modify the container name as desired. This container name will act as the root folder for your HDInsight cluster.

Figure 4-16. Configuring storage for the cluster.

12. Choose the location nearest you.

13. Click Select.

14. Click Node Pricing Tiers.

15. Set the number of supervisor nodes to 1 (you do not need more to run the sample), as shown in Figure 4-17.

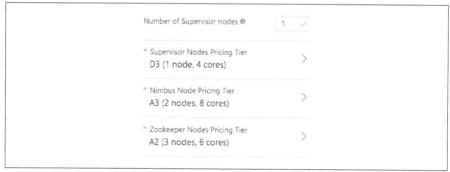

Figure 4-17. Configuring the cluster size.

16. Click on Zookeeper Nodes Pricing Tier.

17. Click View All.

18. Click A2 and click Select to change the tier to A2 (you will not need a more powerful Zookeeper host for this sample).

19. Click Select on the Node Pricing Tiers blade.

20. Click resource group and select an existing resource group or create a new one as desired. You should now have all the settings specified (Figure 4-18).

21. Click Create to begin creating the HDInsight cluster. It will take about 25 minutes to complete. When it's ready, continue with the next section to run the topology.

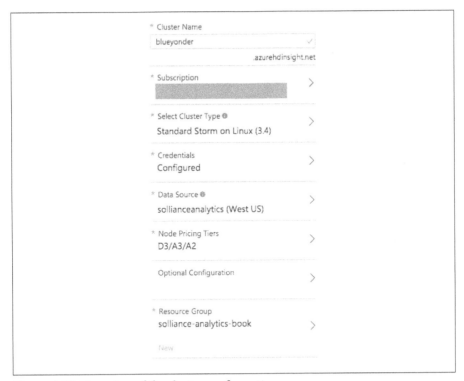

Figure 4-18. Overview of the cluster configuration.

Running the topology on HDI.   In order to run a topology on HDInsight, you need to package the topology and all of its dependencies (excepting Storm) into an uber (aka fat) JAR. Then you will need to use the SCP utility to upload the JAR and its *config.properties* file to the cluster head node. You run the topology by using SSH to connect to the cluster head node, and then use the Storm client to run the topology. You can monitor the status and view logs of the running topology via the Storm UI, which is accessed by a web browser.

Let's walk through each of these steps, starting with packaging the uber JAR. To build the uber JAR, with the project open in IntelliJ IDEA, use the Maven Projects window and double-click on the package node (Figure 4-19). This will compile the project and create the uber JAR, with a name ending in "*-jar-with-dependencies.jar.*"

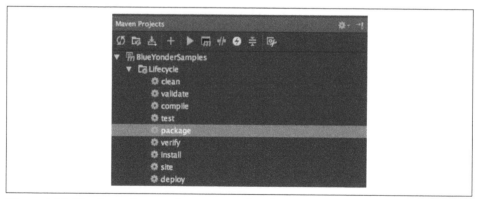

Figure 4-19. Use the package action to create the uber JAR.

Next, to upload the uber JAR and config file, you will need to use Secure Copy (SCP), which effectively copies files over SSH. The SCP utility is included with most Linux distributions in the bash shell. The syntax to upload any file via SCP to your HDInsight head node is as follows:

```
scp <localFileName> <userName>@<clusterName>-ssh.azurehdinsight.net:.
```

localFileName refers to the path on your local filesystem to the file you wish to upload. userName refers to the SSH user you created when provisioning the cluster. clusterName refers to the unique name you provided for your HDInsight cluster. Note there are a few subtle characters in the command as well. Right after the clusterName is a dash (-), and at the end after .net there is a colon (:) followed by a period (.).

When you run the SCP command, you will be prompted for the password associated with the SSH username. Enter that, and your upload will commence. In the context of the sample, to upload the uber JAR and the *config.properties* file, we could run the following two commands:

```
scp ./target/BlueYonderSamples-1.0.0-jar-with-dependencies.jar
zoinertejada@solstorm0-10-0-ssh.azurehdinsight.net:.
scp ./target/config.properties
zoinertejada@solstorm0-10-0-ssh.azurehdinsight.net:.
```

Now that you have your topology JAR and its config uploaded to the head node, you need to run it using the Storm client, which is run from bash when you are connected to the head node via SSH.

To SSH into the head node of your HDInsight cluster, the command looks as follows:

```
ssh <userName>@<clusterName>-ssh.azurehdinsight.net
```

The parameters enclosed in angle brackets have the same meaning as for the SCP command. For example, here is what we used to SSH into our cluster:

```
ssh zoinertejada@solstorm0-10-0-ssh.azurehdinsight.net
```

When you connect, you will be prompted for the password associated with the SSH username. With the SSH connection established, you use the Storm client as follows:

```
storm jar <uber.jar> <className> <topologyName> <…topology specific params…>
```

The `uber.jar` parameter should have as its value the name of the uber JAR you uploaded via SCP. The `className` parameter should be set to the fully qualified name of the class that defines your topology. The `topologyName` is the name of the topology as it will appear when Storm runs it (i.e., in the monitoring UIs and when you want to manage a topology, you provide this name). Finally, each topology implementation can require its own set of additional command-line parameters after the `topology Name`. In our `AlertTopology`, we require the name of the file that contains the configuration properties, as follows:

```
storm jar BlueYonderSamples-1.0.0-jar-with-dependencies.jar
    net.solliance.storm.AlertTopology alerts config.properties
```

When the `storm` command is run, it will kick off the topology and then return. To monitor the status of the topology, you can used the browser-based Storm UI.

Running SSH and SCP in Windows

If you are developing your solution on Windows, you will need to download and install the PuTTY Windows client to use SSH, and the PSCP command-line client to use SCP. For instructions on setting up SSH to target your HDInsight cluster, see the Microsoft Azure documentation (*http://bit.ly/2nJWXQN*).

You can download both PuTTY and PSCP from the same location: *http://bitly.com/XSB88p*.

To access the Storm UI, open your favorite web browser and navigate to *https://<clusterName>.azurehdinsight.net/stormui*.

When you first do so, you will be prompted to enter the admin username and password you established when you created the cluster. Note that you should not use the SSH username and password in this case.

The first view that loads provides you with a high-level summary of the Storm cluster (Figure 4-20).

Figure 4-20. The top-level view of the Storm UI.

The view provides five sections:

Cluster Summary

Describes the top-level layout of the cluster, the version of Storm being run, the number of supervisor virtual machines (Supervisors column), the number of worker processes deployed (Total slots), the number of worker processes used (Used slots) and unused (Free slots), the number of executor threads (Executors), and the number of tasks across the cluster (Tasks).

Nimbus Summary

Provides a listing of all of the virtual machine nodes, indicating which nodes in the cluster are providing Nimbus primary (Status is Leader) and secondary (Status is Not a Leader) functionality.

Topology Summary

Lists all the topologies currently deployed to the cluster, whether they are actively running (Status), and their consumption of the cluster resources (Num workers, Num tasks).

Supervisor Summary

Lists the virtual machine nodes that are running as supervisor nodes.

Nimbus Configuration

Provides a read-only view into the Nimbus settings that are in effect.

To view the status for a topology, click on its name in the Topology Summary (Figure 4-21).

Figure 4-21. The topology view of the Storm UI.

The topology view has seven sections:

Topology summary
Shows the same values as on the top-level, cluster-wide view.

Topology actions
These buttons enable you to deactivate (pause) a running topology or activate (resume) a previously deactivated topology. You can click Rebalance to have

Storm reallocate available executors and tasks to the topology. You click Kill to terminate the topology, which will also remove it from being listed in the Storm UI.

Topology stats

These stats give the counts on the number of tuples emitted in total across all spouts and bolts (the Emitted column) and the number of tuples actually transferred between spouts and bolts or bolts and bolts (the Transferred column). These values may be different, for example, when a bolt emits a tuple, but there is not a downstream bolt to consume it. Acked indicates the number of tuples that were succesfully processed across all spouts and bolts, whereas Failed is the count of those that failed (typically where the spout or bolt threw an exception).

Spouts

Provides the stats for each spout in the topology.

Bolts

Provides the stats for each bolt in the topology.

Topology Visualization

This should show a graph of the directed acyclic graph form of the topology, but is currently disabled in HDInsight.

Topology Configuration

This is a read-only listing of the config properties provided when the topology was submitted.

If you click on the ID of a spout (in the Spouts listing) or a bolt (in the Bolts listing) you are taken to a detailed view for just that spout or bolt (Figure 4-22).

This provides similar statistics as the other views, with two interesting additions:

Executors

Lists the executor threads in which instances of this bolt or spout are running.

Errors

Lists the text of any runtime errors encountered across all instances of the spout or bolt.

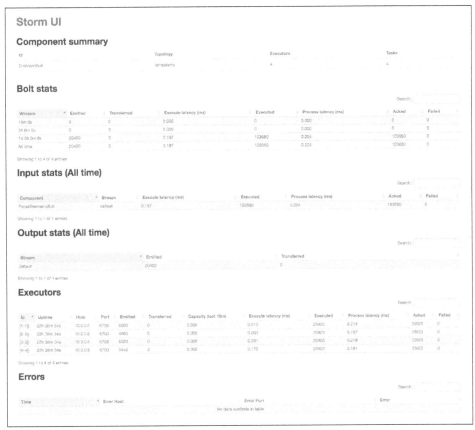

Figure 4-22. Viewing the details for the EmitAlertsBolt.

There is a subtlety to this UI that is worth understanding. If you want to view the log output from any instance of the spout or bolt, under the Executors listing click the hyperlinked port number. This will take you to a new screen where you can view the logs captured for any instance of the spout or bolt being run by the executor (Figure 4-23).

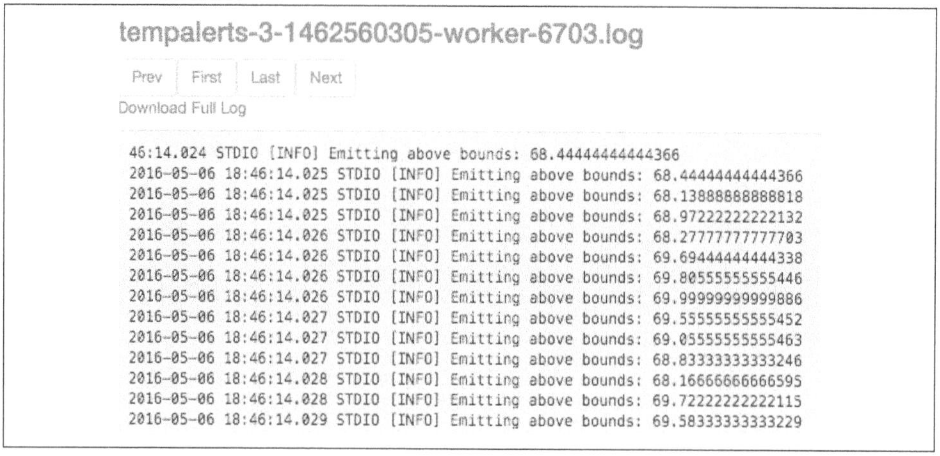
tempalerts-3-1462560305-worker-6703.log
Prev
First
Last
Next
Download Full Log
46:14.024 STDIO [INFO] Emitting above bounds: 68.44444444444366
2016-05-06 18:46:14.025 STDIO [INFO] Emitting above bounds: 68.44444444444366
2016-05-06 18:46:14.025 STDIO [INFO] Emitting above bounds: 68.13888888888818
2016-05-06 18:46:14.025 STDIO [INFO] Emitting above bounds: 68.97222222222132
2016-05-06 18:46:14.026 STDIO [INFO] Emitting above bounds: 68.27777777777703
2016-05-06 18:46:14.026 STDIO [INFO] Emitting above bounds: 69.69444444444338
2016-05-06 18:46:14.026 STDIO [INFO] Emitting above bounds: 69.80555555555446
2016-05-06 18:46:14.026 STDIO [INFO] Emitting above bounds: 69.99999999999886
2016-05-06 18:46:14.027 STDIO [INFO] Emitting above bounds: 69.55555555555452
2016-05-06 18:46:14.027 STDIO [INFO] Emitting above bounds: 69.05555555555463
2016-05-06 18:46:14.027 STDIO [INFO] Emitting above bounds: 68.83333333333246
2016-05-06 18:46:14.028 STDIO [INFO] Emitting above bounds: 68.16666666666595
2016-05-06 18:46:14.028 STDIO [INFO] Emitting above bounds: 69.72222222222115
2016-05-06 18:46:14.029 STDIO [INFO] Emitting above bounds: 69.58333333333229

Figure 4-23. Viewing the logs for a bolt.

Alerting with Storm on HDInsight (C# + Windows cluster)

In addition to the Java implementation we demonstrated, Storm topologies can also be implemented in C#. In fact, in this approach, you can build hybrid topologies that are a mix of components written in C# and Java—effectively allowing you to get the best from both worlds. The primary requirement is that topologies implemented in C# can run only on Storm on HDInsight clusters running Windows.

In this section we will look at implementing the same alerting topology we showed previously in Java. Here we will use the Java EventHubSpout that is included with Storm, but implement our `ParserBolt` and `EmitAlertBolt` using C#. The topology itself will also be defined using C#.

Let's begin by setting up your development environment.

Dev environment setup. Building Storm topologies with C# requires Visual Studio 2015. However, you can use any edition of VS 2015, from the free Community edition to the premium Enterprise edition.

You will also want to ensure you have the Microsoft Azure HDInsight Tools for Visual Studio installed, which provide you with projects ranging from empty Storm projects to hybrid topologies that read from Event Hubs.

Installing the HDInsight Tools for Visual Studio

Currently, the Microsoft Azure HDInsight Tools for Visual Studio are installed along with Azure SDK 2.9. You can always find the latest Azure SDK at *https://azure.microsoft.com/en-us/downloads/*.

On this page, look for the title ".NET" and click the link labeled "VS 2015." This will download the Web Platform Installer, which will guide you through the simple SDK installation process.

With Visual Studio properly updated, the next step is to download and open the Blue Yonder Airports sample in Visual Studio.

You can download the Storm sample from *http://bit.ly/2buuAwT*.

The download includes the `AlertTopology` sample as a Visual Studio solution with a single project that contains the topology, spouts, and bolts.

Once you have downloaded the sample, open the solution in Visual Studio. You should now be ready to explore the project. In Solution Explorer, expand the `ManagedAlertTopology` project. You should see the three classes that define the topology (*AlertTopology.cs*), the parser bolt (*ParserBolt.cs*), and the alert bolt (*EmitAlertBolt.cs*), as shown in Figure 4-24.

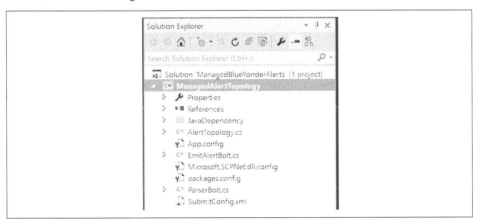

Figure 4-24. The files contained in the managed Storm project.

Next, expand *JavaDependency*. This is your first peek into how hybrid C# plus Java projects are structured. The *JavaDependency* folder contains a single JAR file that contains the Java-based `EventHubSpout` (Figure 4-25).

Figure 4-25. The JAR containing the EventHubSpout implementation.

We will walk through the implementation shortly, but first let's finish preparing the solution for build and deployment. Open *app.config* and set the values in appSettings as follows to enable the EventHubSpout to connect your instance of Event Hubs:

EventHubNamespace
> The service bus namespace containing your Event Hubs instance

EventHubEntityPath
> The name of your Event Hubs instance

EventHubSharedAccessKeyName
> The policy name with read permissions to Event Hubs

EventHubPartitions
> The number of partitions your Event Hubs instance contains

Save *app.config* and from the Build menu, select "Build solution." Verify that you do not get any build errors.

Topology implementation.   C# topologies are enabled via the Stream Computing Platform for .NET (SCP.NET). This platform provides both the plumbing to interact with Storm's native Java runtime, as well as classes for implementing topologies, spouts, and bolts. If you are comfortable with our previous illustration of the AlertTopology implemented with Java, then you should find most of the implementation in C# very familiar. There are a few differences, and we will call them out as we proceed.

Let's begin by examining *AlertTopology.cs*:

```
[Active(true)]
public class AlertTopology : TopologyDescriptor
{
    public ITopologyBuilder GetTopologyBuilder()
    {
        TopologyBuilder topologyBuilder = new TopologyBuilder("AlertTopology");

        var eventHubPartitions =
        int.Parse(ConfigurationManager.AppSettings["EventHubPartitions"]);

        topologyBuilder.SetEventHubSpout(
            "EventHubSpout",
            new EventHubSpoutConfig(
```

```
            ConfigurationManager.AppSettings["EventHubSharedAccessKeyName"],
            ConfigurationManager.AppSettings["EventHubSharedAccessKey"],
            ConfigurationManager.AppSettings["EventHubNamespace"],
            ConfigurationManager.AppSettings["EventHubEntityPath"],
            eventHubPartitions),
        eventHubPartitions);

    List<string> javaSerializerInfo = new List<string>() {
    "microsoft.scp.storm.multilang.CustomizedInteropJSONSerializer" };

    var boltConfig = new StormConfig();

    topologyBuilder.SetBolt(
        typeof(ParserBolt).Name,
        ParserBolt.Get,
        new Dictionary<string, List<string>>()
        {
            {Constants.DEFAULT_STREAM_ID, new List<string>(){ "temp",
            "createDate", "deviceId" } }
        },
        eventHubPartitions,
        true
        ).
        DeclareCustomizedJavaSerializer(javaSerializerInfo).
        shuffleGrouping("EventHubSpout").
        addConfigurations(boltConfig);

    topologyBuilder.SetBolt(
        typeof(EmitAlertBolt).Name,
        EmitAlertBolt.Get,
        new Dictionary<string, List<string>>()
        {
            {Constants.DEFAULT_STREAM_ID, new List<string>(){ "reason",
            "temp", "createDate", "deviceId" } }
        },
        eventHubPartitions,
        true
        ).
        shuffleGrouping(typeof(ParserBolt).Name).
        addConfigurations(boltConfig);

    var topologyConfig = new StormConfig();
    topologyConfig.setMaxSpoutPending(8192);
    topologyConfig.setNumWorkers(eventHubPartitions);

    topologyBuilder.SetTopologyConfig(topologyConfig);
    return topologyBuilder;
    }
}
```

The first thing that might jump out at you is the use of the Active attribute atop the class declaration. In the Java approach, we provided a static Main method that kicked off the topology construction, and we selected which class's Main method to invoke when we actually ran the topology using the Storm client. With SCP.NET, the Active attribute (when set to true) indicates that this is the one and only class within the assembly that should be used to build the topology.

The topology class derives from TopologyDescriptor and implements only a single public method: GetTopologyBuilder. This method takes the place of the Main method we used in Java. Within it, we create an instance of TopologyBuilder, give it a name, and then attach spouts and bolts, via the SetSpout, SetBolt, and more specialized SetEventHubSpout methods.

In the constructor of TopologyBuilder, we provide the runtime name of the topology. This can have almost whatever value you desire, but there is an important caveat when you are working with the EventHubSpout. Recall that when reading from the Event Hub partition, the spout tasks periodically checkpoint their progress with Zookeeper. Their progress is effectively grouped underneath the name of the topology provided to the constructor of TopologyBuilder. This means that if you resubmit a Storm topology with the same name, the EventHubSpouts will resume where they left off. If you want the spouts to start from the beginning of each Event Hubs partition, then be sure to provide a unique name that has not been used before.

In building the EventHubSpout, we load from the *app.config* the settings needed for the Event Hub and use them to populate an instance of EventHubSpoutConfig. The call to setEventHubSpout takes three arguments: a name for the component, the EventHubSpoutConfig, and the initial parallelism hint (i.e., the initial number of threads to allocate, which should be one thread per partition).

Moving to the call to topologyBuilder.setBolt, we provide the method the name for the component, a reference to the method for constructing instances of the bolt, a dictionary that lists the names of the fields emitted by the bolt, the initial parallelism hint, and a boolean that enables or disables tuple ack. This latter property must be set to true for topologies that consume from the EventHubSpout, since the spout itself will keep in memory (for the purposes of resiliency) any tuples that have not been acknowledged and will error out after a certain threshold is reached of unacknowledged tuples. This setting means that downstream bolts must also ack all the tuples with a lineage tracing back to the EventHubSpout. In the Java implementation, this was done automatically for us via the implementation of BasicBolt. In SCP.NET we have a little extra work to do, which we will demonstrate shortly.

Right after the closing parenthesis of topologyBuilder.setBolt, we chain on a call to DeclareCustomizedJavaSerializer and pass it the dictionary that names the Java-based type of the serializer to use. The purpose of this call is to take the tuples that are traditionally serialized using Java, and instead serialize them as JSON so our .NET bolts can properly deserialize them.

Finally, observe that in this chain that follows setEventHubSpout, we invoke shuffle Grouping and reference the name of the EventHubSpout component to flow tuples from the EventHubSpout to this ParserBolt.

The second call to topologyBuilder.setBolt works in an almost identical fashion, but with one exception. In this case, we are flowing tuples from the ParserBolt to the EmitAlertBolt—both of which are C# components. In this case we do not need to inject a serializer.

Next, let's look at the implementation for *ParserBolt.cs*. Bolts need to implement the ISCPBolt interface, which only defines the Execute method that takes a tuple as input. In reality, you will commonly also implement a constructor that defines the input and output schema as well as any serializer or deserializer required, and a Get method that acts as a factory method to construct instances of the bolt.

```
public class ParserBolt : ISCPBolt
{
    Context _context;

    public ParserBolt(Context ctx)
    {
        this._context = ctx;

        // set input schemas
        Dictionary<string, List<Type>> inputSchema = new Dictionary<string,
        List<Type>>();
        inputSchema.Add(Constants.DEFAULT_STREAM_ID, new List<Type>() {
        typeof(string) });

        // set output schemas
        Dictionary<string, List<Type>> outputSchema = new Dictionary<string,
        List<Type>>();
        outputSchema.Add(Constants.DEFAULT_STREAM_ID, new List<Type>() {
        typeof(double), typeof(string), typeof(string) });

        // Declare input and output schemas
        _context.DeclareComponentSchema(new ComponentStreamSchema(inputSchema,
        outputSchema));

        _context.DeclareCustomizedDeserializer(
        new CustomizedInteropJSONDeserializer());
    }

    public void Execute(SCPTuple tuple)
    {
        string json = tuple.GetString(0);

        var node = JObject.Parse(json);
        var temp = node.GetValue("temp");
        JToken tempVal;
```

```
    if (node.TryGetValue("temp", out tempVal)) //assume must be a
                                               //temperature reading
    {
        Context.Logger.Info("temp:" + temp.Value<double>());
        JToken createDate = node.GetValue("createDate");
        JToken deviceId = node.GetValue("deviceId");
        _context.Emit(Constants.DEFAULT_STREAM_ID, new List<SCPTuple>() {
        tuple }, new List<object> { tempVal.Value<double>(),
        createDate.Value<string>(),
        deviceId.Value<string>() });
    }

    _context.Ack(tuple);
}

public static ParserBolt Get(Context ctx, Dictionary<string, Object> parms)
{
    return new ParserBolt(ctx);
}
}
```

Finally, let's examine *EmitAlertBolt.cs*. It is very similar structurally to `ParserBolt`. Note that in this case the constructor does not define a deserializer because one is not needed in the C# object to C# object pipeline.

```
public class EmitAlertBolt : ISCPBolt
{
    Context _context;

    double _minAlertTemp;
    double _maxAlertTemp;

    public EmitAlertBolt(Context ctx)
    {
        this._context = ctx;

        Context.Logger.Info("EmitAlertBolt: Constructor called");

        try
        {
            // set input schemas
            Dictionary<string, List<Type>> inputSchema = new Dictionary<string,
            List<Type>>();
            inputSchema.Add(Constants.DEFAULT_STREAM_ID, new List<Type>() {
            typeof(double), typeof(string), typeof(string) });

            // set output schemas
            Dictionary<string, List<Type>> outputSchema = new Dictionary<string,
            List<Type>>();
            outputSchema.Add(Constants.DEFAULT_STREAM_ID, new List<Type>() {
            typeof(string), typeof(double), typeof(string), typeof(string) });
```

```
        // Declare input and output schemas
        _context.DeclareComponentSchema(new ComponentStreamSchema(inputSchema,
        outputSchema));

        _minAlertTemp = 65;
        _maxAlertTemp = 68;

        Context.Logger.Info("EmitAlertBolt: Constructor completed");
    }
    catch (Exception ex)
    {
        Context.Logger.Error(ex.ToString());
    }
}

public void Execute(SCPTuple tuple)
{
    try
    {
        double tempReading = tuple.GetDouble(0);
        String createDate = tuple.GetString(1);
        String deviceId = tuple.GetString(2);

        if (tempReading > _maxAlertTemp)
        {
            _context.Emit(new Values(
                    "reading above bounds",
                    tempReading,
                    createDate,
                    deviceId
                ));
            Context.Logger.Info("Emitting above bounds: " + tempReading);
        }
        else if (tempReading < _minAlertTemp)
        {
            _context.Emit(new Values(
                    "reading below bounds",
                    tempReading,
                    createDate,
                    deviceId
                ));
            Context.Logger.Info("Emitting below bounds: " + tempReading);
        }

        _context.Ack(tuple);
    }
    catch (Exception ex)
    {
        Context.Logger.Error(ex.ToString());
    }
}
```

```
    public static EmitAlertBolt Get(Context ctx, Dictionary<string, Object> parms)
    {
        return new EmitAlertBolt(ctx);
    }
}
```

With an understanding of the managed topology in place, we'll turn our attention to running the topology in HDInsight.

Provisioning the Windows HDI cluster.   Provisioning an HDInsight cluster that runs Storm on Windows follows a similar process to that used for provisioning a Linux cluster. Follow these steps:

1. Log in to the Azure Portal (*https://portal.azure.com*).

2. Select New→Intelligence + Analytics→HDInsight.

3. On the New HDInsight blade, provide a unique name for your cluster.

4. Choose your Azure subscription.

5. Select "Cluster configuration."

6. On the "Cluster type configuration" blade, set the cluster type to Storm, operating system to Windows, version to Storm 0.10.0, and the cluster tier to Standard. Click Select.

7. Click "credentials."

8. Set the cluster login username and password, enable Remote Desktop (if desired) and set the Remote Desktop username and password, and click Select (Figure 4-26).

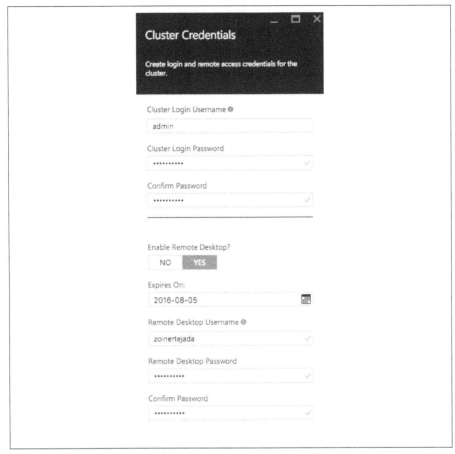

Figure 4-26. Setting the Windows-based cluster credentials.

9. Click Data Source.

10. Select an existing Azure Storage account or create a new one as desired.

11. Modify the container name as desired. This container name will act as the root folder for your HDInsight cluster.

12. Choose the location nearest you.

13. Click Select.

14. Click Node Pricing Tiers.

15. Set the number of supervisor nodes to 1 (you do not need more to run the sample).

16. Click on Zookeeper Nodes Pricing Tier.

17. Click View All.

18. Click A2 and click Select to change the tier to A2 (you will not need a more powerful Zookeeper host for this sample).

19. Click Select on the Node Pricing Tiers blade.

20. Click Resource Group and select an existing resource group or create a new one as desired. You should now have all the settings specified (Figure 4-27).

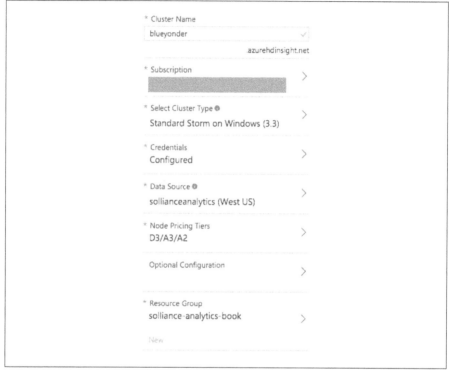

Figure 4-27. Overview of the cluster configuration.

21. Click Create to begin creating the HDInsight cluster. It will take about 25 minutes to complete. When it's ready, continue with the next section to run the topology.

Running the topology on HDI.   Thanks to the integration provided by the HDInsight Tools for Visual Studio, deploying and running a topology (even a hybrid one like we demonstrate here) can be done completely within Visual Studio 2015.

To begin, in Solution Explorer, right-click on your project and select "Submit to Storm on HDInsight" (Figure 4-28).

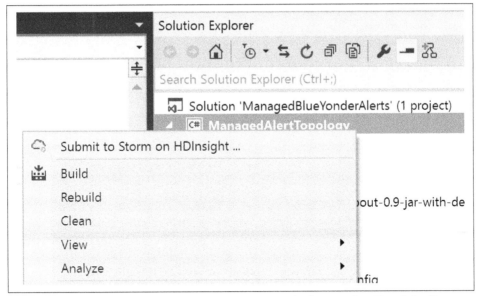

Figure 4-28. Submitting a topology project to HDInsight from within Visual Studio.

You will be prompted to log in with the credentials to your Azure subscription. When you have logged in, you will see the Submit Topology dialog (Figure 4-29).

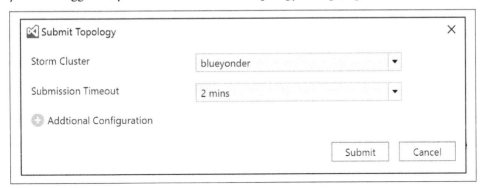

Figure 4-29. The Submit Topology dialog within Visual Studio.

This dialog may take a few seconds to load the list of HDInsight clusters. You can see the progress in the background by looking at the HDInsight Task List, which will have an entry labeled "Get storm clusters list."

When the list has loaded, select your HDInsight cluster from the Storm Cluster dropdown. Next, expand the Additional Configuration section. When creating a hybrid topology, this is where you indicate the folder containing any JARs to include with your Storm topology (Figure 4-30).

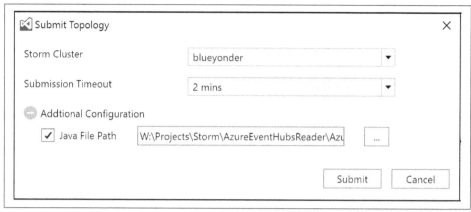

Figure 4-30. The Submit Topology dialog showing where to specify the folder containing JAR files used by a hybrid topology.

Click Submit to deploy and run your topology on your HDInsight cluster.

Once it has deployed, a new document named Storm Topologies View will appear. The lefthand pane will list all topologies deployed to the cluster (Figure 4-31).

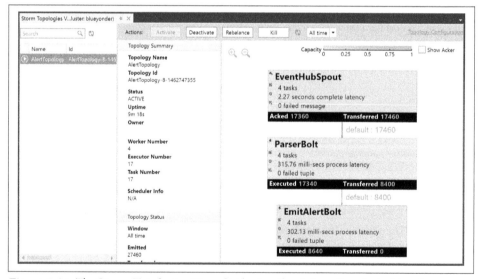

Figure 4-31. The Storm Topologies View displaying the status of a selected topology.

If you click on any one topology, you will get the visualization that summarizes the status.

On the visualization, if you double-click any of the components (e.g., the box repre-senting a spout or bolt), you will be taken to a new document that is very similar to the Storm UI and presents the same statistics (Figure 4-32).

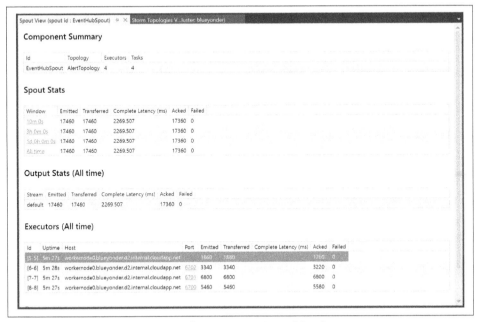

Figure 4-32. Viewing the statistics for a spout in Visual Studio.

In fact, if you click on the hyperlinked port for an executor, you can view the logs directly within Visual Studio (Figure 4-33).

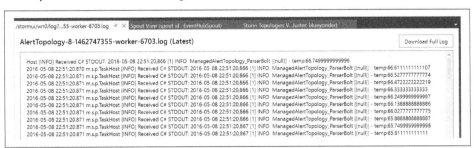

Figure 4-33. Viewing the logs for an executor within Visual Studio.

You can always return to the Storm Topologies View by using Server Explorer, expanding the Azure and HDInsight nodes, and then right-clicking on the HDInsight cluster and selecting View Storm Topologies (Figure 4-34).

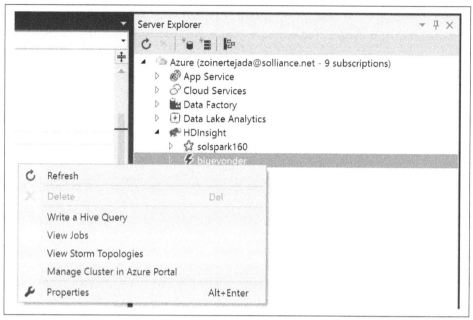

Figure 4-34. Using Server Explorer to access the Storm Topologies View.

EventProcessorHost

When you are developing with .NET and Visual Studio 2015, the recommended way to build scalable, fault-resilient consuming applications for Event Hubs is to use the EventProcessorHost class. EventProcessorHost takes care of:

- Spawning a consumer for each partition in the Event Hubs instance
- Checkpointing the state of each consumer periodically to Azure Blob Storage
- Ensuring that there is always exactly one consumer per partition, and re-creating a new consumer should one fail
- Managing epochs to enable updating of event processing logic

The EventProcessorHost class is available with the Azure Service Bus SDK, and can be found within the Microsoft.ServiceBus.Messaging.EventProcessorHost assembly. It can be hosted in a console application, a cloud service web or worker role, and even an Azure function, but the easiest place to host it is within a Web Job, which we demonstrate next.

EventProcessorHost API

For other examples that leverage the `EventProcessorHost` API at a lower level than Web Jobs (such as if you wanted to self-host in a console or in a cloud service worker role), see the Microsoft Azure documentation (*http://bit.ly/2nSjZ4S*).

EventProcessorHost in Web Jobs

Azure Web Jobs (a feature of Azure App Services) provide the compute environment for running many forms of tasks, from command-line applications to methods within a .NET assembly in response to triggers that can include messages in a queue and blobs being added to Blob Storage. Web Jobs also provide a tailored hosting environment for the `EventProcessorHost`, where new events can trigger the invocation of a processing method.

You can download the sample from *http://bit.ly/2bJDLOi*.

In this sample, we show how to accomplish the alert processing we have demonstrated throughout the chapter. Let's begin with the implementation for the program that creates the Web Job host in *Program.cs*:

```
class Program
{
    private static void Main()
    {
        var eventHubConnectionString =
        ConfigurationManager.AppSettings["eventHubConnectionString"];
        var eventHubName = ConfigurationManager.AppSettings["eventHubName"];
        var storageAccountName =
        ConfigurationManager.AppSettings["storageAccountName"];
        var storageAccountKey =
        ConfigurationManager.AppSettings["storageAccountKey"];

        var storageConnectionString =
            $"DefaultEndpointsProtocol=https;AccountName={storageAccountName};
            AccountKey={storageAccountKey}";

        var eventHubConfig = new EventHubConfiguration();
        eventHubConfig.AddReceiver(eventHubName, eventHubConnectionString);

        var config = new JobHostConfiguration(storageConnectionString);
        config.NameResolver = new EventHubNameResolver();
        config.UseEventHub(eventHubConfig);

        var host = new JobHost(config);
        host.RunAndBlock();
    }
}
```

This is a common pattern for authoring Web Jobs. The code begins with the loading of the Event Hub connection string, the Event Hub name, and the Azure Storage account name and key from the `appSettings` contained within *app.config*.

Next, we create an instance of `EventHubConfiguration` and invoke the `AddReceiver` method to register that we want to listen for events at the Event Hub indicated by the parameters.

After that, we create an instance of `JobHostConfiguration` that takes in its constructor the connection string for an Azure Storage account. This account will be used to checkpoint the state of the consumers managed by this `EventProcessorHost`. We set the `NameResolver` property to an instance of `EventHubNameResolver`, a small utility class that helps us load the Event Hub name from `appSettings`, and provide it to the attribute we use to decorate the methods that respond to new events appearing in the Event Hub (we will show this attribute shortly). Finally, we invoke the `UseEventHub` method on the `JobHostConfiguration` instance to provide the Event Hub configuration.

Finally, we use the `JobHostConfiguration` as a parameter to the Web Job's `JobHost` and then kick off the Web Job by the blocking call to `host.RunAndBlock`.

Let's look at the implementation that actually handles the processing of events, in *AlertsProcessor.cs*:

```
public class AlertsProcessor
{
    double _maxAlertTemp = 68;
    double _minAlertTemp = 65;

    public void ProcessEvents(
    [EventHubTrigger("%eventhubname%")] EventData[] events)
    {
        foreach (var eventData in events)
        {
            try
            {
                var eventBytes = eventData.GetBytes();
                var jsonMessage = Encoding.UTF8.GetString(eventBytes);
                var evt = JObject.Parse(jsonMessage);

                JToken temp;
                double tempReading;

                if (evt.TryGetValue("temp", out temp))
                {
                    tempReading = temp.Value<double>();

                    if (tempReading > _maxAlertTemp)
                    {
```

```
                    Console.WriteLine("Emitting above bounds: " +
                        tempReading);
                }
                else if (tempReading < _minAlertTemp)
                {
                    Console.WriteLine("Emitting below bounds: " +
                        tempReading);
                }
            }


        }
        catch (Exception ex)
        {
            LogError(ex.Message);
        }
    }
}

private static void LogError(string message)
{
    Console.ForegroundColor = ConsoleColor.Red;
    Console.WriteLine("{0} > Exception {1}", DateTime.Now, message);
    Console.ResetColor();
}
}
```

The attribute that ensures the `ProcessEvents` method is invoked when new events arrive at the Event Hub is the `EventHubTriggerAttribute`, applied to the first parameter of `ProcessEvents`. This attribute typically takes a string that is the name of the Event Hub:

```
public void ProcessEvents([EventHubTrigger("%eventhubname%")] EventData[] events)
```

To avoid hardcoding the name of the Event Hub, you can register a `NameResolver` as we did. We implement our `NameResolver` in the `EventHubNameResolver` class, whose `Resolve` method takes as input the name of the `appSetting` and returns the value. `Resolve` is invoked and the actual name of the Event Hub stored in configuration is passed to the `EventHubTrigger` constructor:

```
public class EventHubNameResolver : INameResolver
{
    public string Resolve(string name)
    {
        return ConfigurationManager.AppSettings[name].ToString();
    }
}
```

Returning to `ProcessEvents`, once the method is invoked, we are provided with an array of events that we can process in the usual way. In this case we check if the JSON string contains a temp field. If so, we check if it is out of bounds and write a console message if it is. When `ProcessEvents` completes successfully (without throwing an exception), the `EventProcessorHost` running under the covers makes a checkpoint, persisting the progress through the partition to Azure Blob Storage. The Storage account used in this case to store checkpoints is the same account used by the Web Job. That's all there is to it! This Web Job can be published to Azure and when it starts it will begin processing messages from the Event Hub.

Deploying to Azure

If you have never deployed a Web Job to Azure App Services before, a detailed step-by-step explanation is available in the Microsoft Azure documentation (*http://bit.ly/ 2nJRnhe*).

Azure Machine Learning

While we have an upcoming chapter dedicated to Machine Learning and applying Cortana Intelligence components, it is worth mentioning how you might leverage Azure Machine Learning in the context of tuple-at-a-time processing. All the solutions in this chapter have shown how to process one tuple at a time. When you build a service using Azure Machine Learning and then operationalize it, you expose that Machine Learning model as a RESTful web service. All of the examples we have shown could be extended to invoke this web service to make predictions, using the fields from the tuple as input. Of course, keep in mind this adds extra latency to the processing (on account of the time added due to the network hop added).

Summary

In this chapter we dug deeper into how consumers from Event Hubs can be implemented that process events in a tuple-at-a-time fashion. We introduced the way consumer groups define applications that collectively process events from all partitions in the Event Hub. Then we looked at implementing processing applications in Apache Storm using both Java- and C#-based topologies. Finally, we looked at how we can host a consumer application in Azure Web Jobs and implement a consumer application using C# by leveraging the infrastructure provided by the `EventProcessorHost` API.

In the next chapter, we will look at the options for building real-time processing applications that take a micro-batch approach.

CHAPTER 5

Real-Time Micro-Batch Processing in Azure

In the previous chapter, we explored the tuple-at-a-time options in Azure for processing real-time, streaming data. In this chapter we focus on the options that take a micro-batch approach to data processing (see Figure 5-1).

Micro-Batch Processing in Azure

In Azure, there are three approaches that process telemetry streams, such as those coming from an Event Hub or IoT Hub, in small batches. Two of these options (Spark Streaming and Storm) run on managed HDInsight clusters and one of them (Azure Stream Analytics) is purely a managed service with no infrastructure you have to manage at all.

Spark Streaming on HDInsight

Apache Spark provides a fast and general-purpose solution for in-memory and distributed computing, providing APIs that are programmable with the Scala, Java, Python, and R languages. The unique value of Spark is that it provides a set of higher-level frameworks above the main functionality (referred to as Spark Core) for performing structured and SQL-based data processing (Spark SQL), machine learning (MLlib and SparkML), graph processing (GraphX), and stream processing (Spark Streaming). While there are many solutions in the wild that perform each of these functions individually, Spark is unique in how it lets you combine the frameworks to achieve your goals. For example, you can write a single streaming application that uses Spark Streaming as the data processing framework that internally uses SQL queries (supported by Spark SQL) to implement your data processing logic.

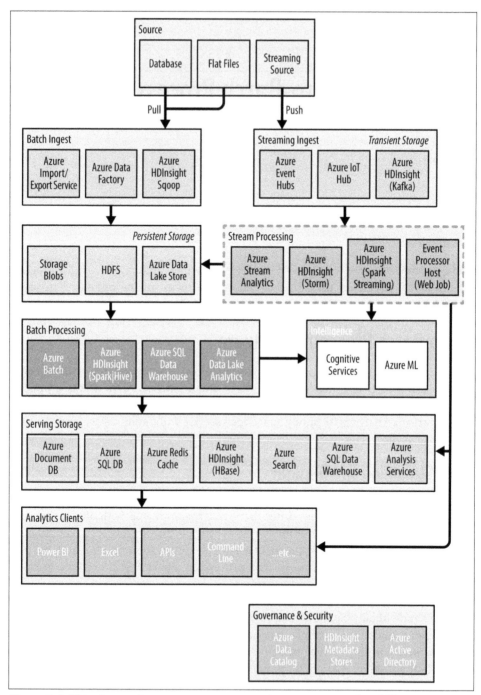

Figure 5-1. This chapter focuses on stream processing components that follow a micro-batch approach.

Spark is most commonly deployed to a Hadoop cluster that is running the YARN resource manager, but can also be deployed locally for development purposes to a cluster running Apache Mesos, or to a standalone cluster in which Spark itself provides the resource management. In Azure you can provision an HDInsight cluster preconfigured to run Spark on a Hadoop cluster using the YARN resource manager, with a few clicks in the Azure Portal.

In this section, we will focus on applying Spark Streaming to the challenge of processing streaming data. Spark Streaming provides scalable, high-throughput, and fault-tolerant processing of live data streams where data can be ingested from a multitude of sources, including Azure Event Hubs (and by extension IoT Hub), Kafka, Flume, Twitter, ZeroMQ, raw TCP sockets, and filesystems like HDFS. Data can be processed using high-level functions like map, reduce, join, and window. The processed data can then be pushed out to filesystems, databases, and dashboards. As you will see, Spark Streaming takes a micro-batch approach to processing data streams.

To best understand Spark Streaming, it's useful to understand the flow of data through a streaming application. From a high level, Spark Streaming receives live input data streams and divides the data into batches, which are then processed by the Spark engine to generate the final stream of batched results.

Spark Streaming represents a continuous stream of data using a high-level abstraction called a *discretized stream*, or *DStream*. The DStream is created either from input data streams from sources like Event Hubs, or by applying other high-level operations on an existing DStream. Internally, a DStream is represented by a sequence of *resilient distributed datasets (RDDs)*, which is Spark's core data structure that distributes partitioned data across multiple nodes in the cluster, and is generally maintained in cluster memory for best performance. Each input source has a specialized client called a *receiver* that understands the source, reads the data from the source, and emits batches of data at a configurable interval that are themselves made up of a set of RDDs. The DStream provides an abstraction on top of this endless stream of batches (and by extension stream of RDDs). This process is shown in Figure 5-2.

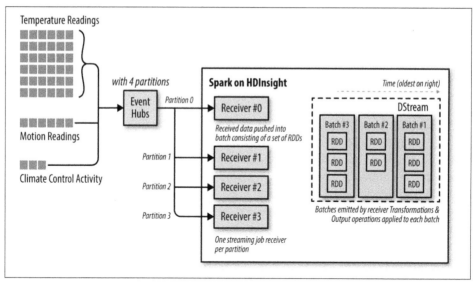

Figure 5-2. How events are consumed from Event Hubs and processed by Spark Streaming in the form of DStreams.

A Spark Streaming application is basically a long-running application that continues to receive data from input sources, processes them, and pushes them out to one or more destinations. Every Spark Streaming application has the following steps:

1. Create a `SparkContext` that points to your Spark cluster.

2. Create a `StreamingContext` from the `SparkContext`, and define the batch interval (e.g., 2 seconds, 10 minutes).

3. Using the `StreamingContext`, create an input `DStream` from the input source.

4. Implement the streaming computations by applying *transformations* to the input `DStream`.

5. Push the processed results out to target systems by applying *output operations*.

6. Start the long-running application by invoking `StreamingContext.start`.

7. Wait for the processing to be stopped (mannually or due to an error) using `StreamingContext.awaitTermination()`. You can also manually stop processing using `StreamingContext.stop()`.

Once you've built your streaming application, you can run it locally on your machine or in an Azure HDInsight Spark cluster.

In the sections that follow, we will look in greater detail at the steps to implement, deploy, and run a Spark Streaming application.

Implementing a Spark Streaming application

Let's build the same alerting application we have shown previously on temperature telemetry data that is streaming into an Event Hub, but this time using Spark Streaming.

You can download the Spark Streaming sample from *http://bit.ly/2bzr05J*.

Open the project using IntelliJ IDEA. In the project, open *EventHubsEmitAlerts.scala* (which is located underneath *src\main\scala\net.solliance.spark.streaming.examples \workloads*).

The entry point for this application is the `main` method, which effectively controls the lifecycle of the streaming application:

```scala
def main(inputArguments: Array[String]): Unit = {

  val inputOptions: ArgumentMap = EventhubsArgumentParser.parseArguments(Map(),
  inputArguments.toList)

  //Create or recreate (from checkpoint storage) streaming context
  val streamingContext = StreamingContext
    .getOrCreate(inputOptions(Symbol(EventhubsArgumentKeys.CheckpointDirectory))
    .asInstanceOf[String],
    () => createStreamingContext(inputOptions))

  streamingContext.start()

  if(inputOptions.contains(
    Symbol(EventhubsArgumentKeys.TimeoutInMinutes))) {

    streamingContext.awaitTerminationOrTimeout(inputOptions(
    Symbol(EventhubsArgumentKeys.TimeoutInMinutes))
      .asInstanceOf[Long] * 60 * 1000)
  }
  else {

    streamingContext.awaitTermination()
  }
}
```

In the first line, the `inputOptions` `ArgumentMap` includes all of the following configuration, passed in as command-line parameters:

`eventhubs.namespace`
  The service bus namespace containing the Event Hub

`eventhubs.name`
  The name of the Event Hub

`eventhubs.policyname`
> The name of the Event Hub policy used for access

`eventhubs.policykey`
> The key associated with the Event Hub policy

`eventhubs.consumergroup`
> The consumer group assumed by the application

`eventhubs.partition.count`
> The number of partitions in the Event Hub

`eventhubs.checkpoint.interval`
> The interval in seconds between the checkpointing of progress through an Event Hub partition to Azure Storage

`eventhubs.checkpoint.dir`
> The path, relative to the Azure Storage container deployed with the cluster, under which to store checkpoint metadata

In the next line, we instantiate a `StreamingContext`. The `getOrCreate` method is used in two ways. When the streaming application is first run, the "create" aspect takes effect and the `createStreamingContext` method is invoked, which creates a new, "from-scratch" instance of the `streamingContext` that will read all the `EventHub` `Partitions` from the beginning. However, if a checkpoint directory is found to exist at the configured path, then the "get" aspect takes effect to resume reading from the Event Hub partitions based on where the checkpoint indicates reading left off. The `createStreamingContext` is ultimately where the streaming application is defined, and we will return to it momentarily.

After we have a `streamingContext` instance in hand, we invoke the `start` method to effectively run the long-running application. The logic that keeps the application alive sits in the following lines with the call to `awaitTerminationOrTimeout` or `awaitTermination`. Both methods respond to termination events caused by the user cancelling the application or terminating due to an error. However, `awaitTerminationOrTimeout` will also terminate the application once the configured interval has elapsed.

The `createStreamingContext` method is where a new `StreamingContext` is created from a `SparkContext`, and the batch interval is specified:

```
def createStreamingContext(inputOptions: ArgumentMap): StreamingContext = {

  val eventHubsParameters = Map[String, String](
    "eventhubs.namespace" -> inputOptions(
    Symbol(EventhubsArgumentKeys.EventhubsNamespace)).asInstanceOf[String],
    "eventhubs.name" -> inputOptions(
    Symbol(EventhubsArgumentKeys.EventhubsName)).asInstanceOf[String],
```

```
"eventhubs.policyname" -> inputOptions(
Symbol(EventhubsArgumentKeys.PolicyName)).asInstanceOf[String],
"eventhubs.policykey" -> inputOptions(
Symbol(EventhubsArgumentKeys.PolicyKey)).asInstanceOf[String],
"eventhubs.consumergroup" -> inputOptions(
Symbol(EventhubsArgumentKeys.ConsumerGroup)).asInstanceOf[String],
"eventhubs.partition.count" -> inputOptions(
Symbol(EventhubsArgumentKeys.PartitionCount))
.asInstanceOf[Int].toString,
"eventhubs.checkpoint.interval" -> inputOptions(
Symbol(EventhubsArgumentKeys.BatchIntervalInSeconds))
.asInstanceOf[Int].toString,
"eventhubs.checkpoint.dir" -> inputOptions(
Symbol(EventhubsArgumentKeys.CheckpointDirectory)).asInstanceOf[String]
)

val sparkConfiguration = new SparkConf().setAppName(
this.getClass.getSimpleName)

sparkConfiguration
.set("spark.streaming.receiver.writeAheadLog.enable", "true")
sparkConfiguration
.set("spark.streaming.driver.writeAheadLog.closeFileAfterWrite", "true")
sparkConfiguration
.set("spark.streaming.receiver.writeAheadLog.closeFileAfterWrite", "true")
sparkConfiguration
.set("spark.streaming.stopGracefullyOnShutdown", "true")

val sparkContext = new SparkContext(sparkConfiguration)

val streamingContext = new StreamingContext(sparkContext,
  Seconds(inputOptions(
  Symbol(EventhubsArgumentKeys.BatchIntervalInSeconds)).asInstanceOf[Int]))
streamingContext.checkpoint(inputOptions(
  Symbol(EventhubsArgumentKeys.CheckpointDirectory)).asInstanceOf[String])

val eventHubsStream = EventHubsUtils.createUnionStream(streamingContext,
eventHubsParameters)

val eventHubsWindowedStream = eventHubsStream
  .window(Seconds(inputOptions(
  Symbol(EventhubsArgumentKeys.BatchIntervalInSeconds)).asInstanceOf[Int]))

defineComputations(streamingContext, eventHubsWindowedStream, inputOptions)

streamingContext

}
```

We begin by creating a Map that loads in all of the configuration values from the command line. After that, we create an instance of SparkConf that allows us to set the name of the long-running application that will appear in Spark's monitoring UIs.

The next four lines control the reliability and restartability of the receiver by configuring the write ahead log (we won't cover these settings in detail here).

Then we get to the constructor of the SparkContext, which takes in our sparkConfi guration object and provides us the baseline settings we need to reach the Spark cluster.

This SparkContext instance is used to create a new StreamingContext instance. As a part of the call to the StreamingContext constructor, we provide the all-important batch interval. We invoke the checkpoint method on the StreamingContext instance to configure the checkpoint directory that it will use.

We create our input DStream, assigned to the variable eventHubsStream, by using the createUnionStream method of EventHubUtils, which is a library provided by Microsoft to simplify the process.

With our input DStream ready, we can overlay tumbling or sliding windows that define the set of batches to be used in each computation. In our example, and to illustrate the point while keeping it simple, we create a sliding window with the same duration as the batch size, meaning that each window effectively contains one batch of RDDs.

In the penultimate line, we invoke the defineComputations method, which we use to declare our transformations and output operations. In the last line, we return the constructed StreamingContext.

Let's look in more detail at how we actually provide the logic for the streaming application, by way of our defineComputations method:

```
def defineComputations(streamingContext : StreamingContext,
    windowedStream : DStream[Array[Byte]],
    inputOptions: ArgumentMap) = {

// Simulate detecting an alert condition
windowedStream.map(x => EventContent(new String(x)))
  .foreachRDD { rdd =>
    rdd.foreachPartition { partition =>
    //...Create/open connection to destination...

      partition.foreach {record =>
        // examine alert status
        val json = parse(record.EventDetails)
        val dataPoint = json.extract[TempDataPoint]

        if (dataPoint.temp > maxAlertTemp)
          {
            println(s"=== reading ABOVE bounds.
            DeviceId: ${dataPoint.deviceId}, Temp: ${dataPoint.temp} ===")
            //...push alert out ...
```

```
        }
      else if (dataPoint.temp < minAlertTemp)
        {
          println(s"=== reading BELOW bounds.
          DeviceId: ${dataPoint.deviceId}, Temp: ${dataPoint.temp} ===")
          //...push alert out ...
        }
    }
  //...Close connection ...
  }
 }


}
```

We begin by using the map operation to convert each record in the stream into an instance of EventContent (which is a simple type that contains a property called Even tDetails that represents the record as a string).

In the nested steps that follow, we set up a series of loops that ultimately allows us to examine the temperature reported in each record, and emit an alert if the value is out of bounds. The pattern we take—first iterating over each RDD (the DStream.fore achRDD transformation), followed by iterating over each partition within each RDD (rdd.foreachPartition), and ending in processing each record (partition.fore ach)—has a specific purpose. If you are going to emit your alerts to an external system, such as a SQL database or alerting service where you need to open up a connection before sending data, then you likely want to minimize the overhead of opening the connection repeatedly. We accomplish this by opening the connection only once per partition and using that open connection for transmitting details about any records that the partition contains.

Within the innermost foreach, we deserialize the string payload of the record (now contained in EventDetails) using the Lift library. We invoke Lift's parse method to create a JValue object, and on that object use the extract method to retrieve the deserialized record value as an instance of TempDataPoint, which has the following case definition:

```
case class TempDataPoint(temp: Double,
                         createDate : java.util.Date,
                         deviceId : String)
```

With an instance of our record as a TempDataPoint in hand, we can examine the temp property to see if it is out of bounds and react accordingly.

Running the Spark Streaming application locally

Assuming you have downloaded Spark and unzipped it on your local machine, you can run a Spark Streaming application in local mode on your machine to verify it works before deploying it to a cluster. You would implement the aforementioned application in Scala as shown earlier and then compile it into a JAR file. Then, from the bash shell or command line you run `spark-submit`, providing all the settings needed by your application as command-line switches, to launch the application locally.

Let's look at the steps required to run our `EventHubsEmitAlerts` application locally. First things first: within IntelliJ IDEA, select Build→Make the Project. This should provide you a JAR file located underneath *out\artifacts\spark-streaming-data-persistence-examples*.

Copy this JAR into the root directory of your Spark installation. Using bash or the command prompt, navigate to your Spark installation. The following command illustrates, using bash syntax, how to invoke `spark-submit` to run this streaming application (be sure to remove the line breaks and substitute in the values for your Event Hub instance):

```
./bin/spark-submit --master local[*]
--class net.solliance.spark.streaming.examples.workloads.EventhubsEmitAlerts
spark-streaming-data-persistence-examples.jar
--eventhubs-namespace 'blueyonderairports-ns'
--eventhubs-name 'blueyonderairports'
--policy-name 'receivePermissions'
--policy-key 'ZRapZ4N8GI9tgkOyO/OTLlj/ZFSX4f8sOAMjj/X4Fh8='
--consumer-group '$default'
--partition-count 4
--batch-interval-in-seconds 2
--checkpoint-directory './eventCheckpoints'
--event-count-folder 'eventCount/data'
--job-timeout-in-minutes 5
```

The syntax `--master local[*]` enables us to run Spark locally using all available cores. The remainder of the settings should be pretty self-explanatory at this point.

When the application runs, you will see an *eventCheckpoints* directory created in the root of your Spark installation directory, which will be used in the case when you terminate the application and later submit again. If you run the `SimpleSensorConsole` application (the application included with this book's source code to generate sample telemetry) and use the option to transmit telemetry to Event Hub, you will eventually see output like Figure 5-3 in the bash shell.

Figure 5-3. Sample output showing simulated alerts from the streaming application.

While you have the streaming application running, you can navigate to Spark's Web UI (located by default at *http://localhost:4040/*) to view the status of the application. Once your streaming application has started, you should see a Streaming tab appear as shown in Figure 5-4.

Figure 5-4. The Streaming tab that appears when Spark is running streaming applications.

This UI provides you with graphical representations of your streaming application's performance (as well as insights into possible causes affecting performance), its active batches, and its completed batches (Figure 5-5).

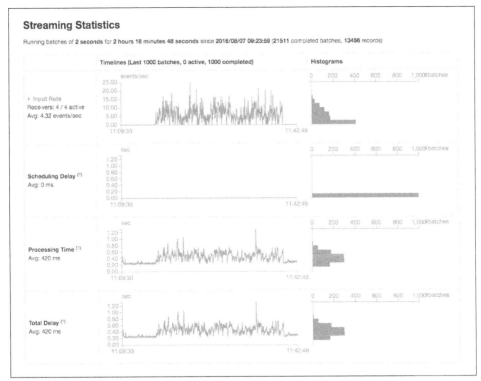

Figure 5-5. Example of the statistics displayed for a running streaming application in the Spark Web UI.

Now that you have verified your streaming application runs locally, let's turn our attention to running it on HDInsight.

Provisioning the Spark Streaming application on an HDInsight cluster

Before you can run your streaming application on an HDInsight cluster, you will need to provision one. The following steps walk you through the process.

Spark on HDInsight is supported only with Linux-based clusters. To provision a minimal HDInsight cluster with Spark, follow these steps:

1. Log in to the Azure Portal.
2. Select New→Intelligence + Analytics→HDInsight.
3. On the New HDInsight blade, provide a unique name for your cluster.
4. Choose your Azure subscription.
5. Select "Cluster configuration."
6. On the "Cluster type configuration" blade, set the cluster type to Spark, operating system to Linux, version to Spark 1.6.1, and cluster tier to Standard. Click Select.
7. Click "credentials."
8. Set the admin login username and password, then the SSH username and password, and click Select. See Figure 5-6.

Figure 5-6. Configuring the cluster security.

9. Click Data Source.

10. Select an existing Azure Storage account or create a new one as desired.

11. Modify the container name as desired (Figure 5-7). This container name will act as the root folder for your HDInsight cluster.

Figure 5-7. Configuring cluster storage.

12. Choose the location nearest you.

13. Click Select.

14. Click Pricing.

15. Set the number of worker nodes to 4 (you do not need more to run the sample), and adjust the worker node size and head node size as desired (any of the smaller available options will work). See Figure 5-8.

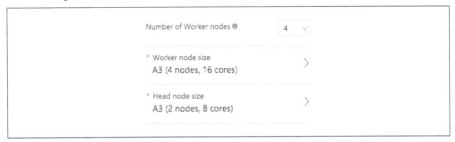

Figure 5-8. Configure cluster mode sizes.

16. Click Select on the pricing blade.

17. Click Resource Group and select an existing one or create a new resource group as desired. You should now have all the settings specified (see Figure 5-9).

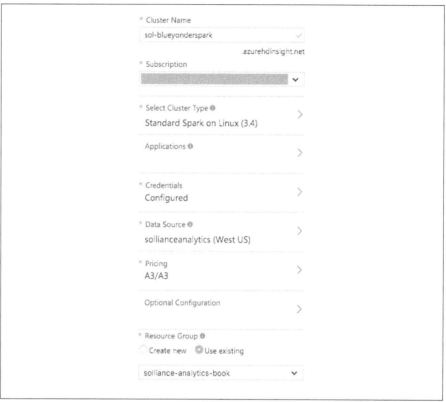

Figure 5-9. Cluster configuration overview.

18. Click Create to begin creating the HDInsight cluster. It will take about 25 minutes to complete. When it's ready, continue with the next section to run the streaming application.

Running the Spark Streaming application on HDInsight

So how do you run your application on a Spark cluster? Taking the aforementioned application in Scala you upload its resultant JAR file to the Azure Blob Storage container associated with your HDInsight cluster. You launch the application using the Livy REST API's submit batch operation. The submit batch operation is a POST operation that expects a JSON document in the body that identifies the application to run and contains all the settings needed by your application (it requires your cluster's admin username and password in the authorization header, in case you were wondering about security).

Let's examine these steps in more detail. First, copy the JAR for your application up to the container in Azure Blob Storage that is associated with your HDInsight cluster.

You can use your Azure Storage Explorer tool of choice, or if you like a bash approach you can take the following two steps.

First, upload your JAR file to the HDInsight head node using SCP:

```
scp ./spark-streaming-data-persistence-examples.jar
<username>@<yourclustername>-ssh.azurehdinsight.net:.
```

Second, SSH into the head node and copy the JAR file from local storage on the head node to HDFS (which means it will appear in Azure Blob Storage):

```
hdfs dfs -copyFromLocal -f
./spark-streaming-data-persistence-examples.jar /example/jars/
```

Now you are ready to run your streaming application. To do this, you should use the Livy API. You can use any tool that can execute REST requests. I tend to prefer the Chrome application Postman (*https://www.getpostman.com/*) for this.

Launching a new job with Livy requires you to perform a POST against the */livy/ batches* endpoint on your HDInsight cluster (this endpoint is automatically exposed to the Internet). So, for example, you would construct a POST against a URL of the format *https://<yourclustername>.azurehdinsight.net/livy/batches*.

You need to configure an authorization header, where the username is the name of administrative user you provided when provisioning the cluster and the password is the password you provided to the same. In Postman, this looks as shown in Figure 5-10.

Figure 5-10. Configuring authorization for submitting a new streaming application via Livy.

Then you will need to provide a text file for the body that contains all the settings you would have previously provided to `spark-submit` on the command line, plus a few other Spark-specific settings that define the number of executors, number of cores, and amount of memory used to run the application. Here is the template (be sure to substitute in your own values):

```
{ "file":"wasbs:///example/jars/spark-streaming-data-persistence-examples.jar",
"className":"net.solliance.spark.streaming.examples.workloads.EventhubsEventCount",
"args":[
    "--eventhubs-namespace", "blueyonderairports-ns",
    "--eventhubs-name", "blueyonderairports",
    "--policy-name", "receivePermissions",
    "--policy-key", "8XzdjasMdApl7caNk8hQn2RPJNsSxkmCVrPKvjytcHo=",
    "--consumer-group", "$default",
    "--partition-count", 4,
    "--batch-interval-in-seconds", 2,
    "--checkpoint-directory",
    "/EventCheckpoint", "--event-count-folder",
    "/EventCount/EventCount10"
],
"numExecutors":8,
"executorMemory":"1G", "executorCores":1, "driverMemory":"2G" }
```

Using Postman, use this file as the binary body for the post (see Figure 5-11).

Figure 5-11. Configuring the body of the POST to include the settings file within Postman.

Finally, click Send to schedule the execution of your application. You should see output similar to the following in response. Take note of the `id`; you can use this value later to check on the status of your application or to terminate it using Livy (Figure 5-12).

You can check the status of all applications (referred to as *batches* in Livy) by sending a GET request of the form *https://sol-spark161.azurehdinsight.net/livy/batches/*.

```
 1 ▾ {
 2     "id": 8,
 3     "state": "running",
 4     "appId": null,
 5 ▾   "appInfo": {
 6         "driverLogUrl": null,
 7         "sparkUiUrl": null
 8     },
 9     "log": []
10 }
```

Figure 5-12. Response for a newly submitted application.

Alternately, you can get the status for a single application by using its batch id in a URL of the form *https://sol-spark161.azurehdinsight.net/livy/batches/<id>*.

For example, the previously started batch is queried in Postman as shown in Figure 5-13.

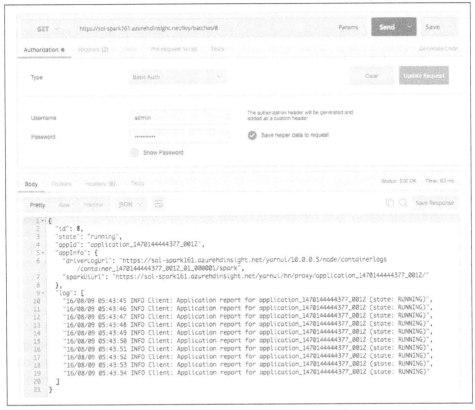

Figure 5-13. Examining the status of a particular streaming application using Livy.

If you want to terminate the application, you can send a DELETE request to the same URL as that used to inspect a particular batch's details (Figure 5-14).

Figure 5-14. Terminating a streaming application using Livy.

With these steps in mind, you are now fully equipped to build, deploy, and manage your Spark Streaming application on HDInsight.

Storm on HDInsight

Storm on HDInsight provides two approaches for micro-batch processing. The first is the Trident framework and the second is by using tick tuples. We cover both in the sections that follow.

Storm with Trident

Trident provides an alternative approach to implementing Storm topologies that adds exactly-once processing and transactional support to persisting data in a data store.

The underlying stream is also different. Unlike for classic Storm topologies, where the stream consists of a unbounded collection of tuples (that are processed in a tuple-at-a-time fashion), Trident streams consist of batches of tuples (whose size is controlled by the spout), where this processing happens in a micro-batch fashion.

Syntactically, if you are familiar with LINQ to objects from .NET, the approach Trident takes to defining a topology should be familiar. Instead of explicitly building a topology adding spouts and bolts, you chain together operations on a stream that can process, filter, aggregate, and store state for micro-batches of tuples. The biggest change in defining a topology is that you no longer define bolts; instead, you build much simpler logic in the form of:

Functions
  Take a set of fields as input, apply the function you define, and output new fields that are appended to the original input tuple.

Filters
> Take in a tuple and apply a function you define that decides whether a tuple should continue to flow downstream or not.

Aggregates
> Apply an aggregation function (either a built-in one like `count` or one you define) against the micro-batch or globally across the entire stream of micro-batches, where the output tuple(s) replace the input in the stream.

Repartitioning
> Repartition the tuples contained within each batch, ranging from the shuffle to evenly redistribute tuples across all partitions, to operations that let you control how the repartitioning happens programmatically.

Stream merges and joins
> Enable you to combine multiple, separate streams into a single stream.

Trident topologies are compiled into an optimized, classic Storm topology that uses spouts, but the bolts are generated automatically based on the operations present in your Trident topology.

Trident Window Computations

At the time of writing this chapter, the current version of Storm supported on HDInsight is 0.10.0, which only begins to hint at the true power that Trident can unlock. Version 1.0.0 of Storm adds the much-needed support for built-in windowing semantics. With this capability, you can add processing such as sliding or tumbling windows that look at batches of tuples where the batch size is controlled either by a count of tuples or by an interval of time.

By way of comparison, let's build the `AlertTopology` using Trident.

You can download the Trident sample from *http://bit.ly/2bzd62J*.

The project is structured in the same way as the classic Storm topology shown previously, except instead of bolts we implement much simpler functions, and the way in which we define the topology takes on a different syntax.

Open *AlertTopology.java*. The only change in this file from the classic Storm topology can be seen in the `buildTopology` method:

```
protected StormTopology buildTopology() {

    TridentTopology topology = new TridentTopology();

    OpaqueTridentEventHubSpout spout =
    new OpaqueTridentEventHubSpout(spoutConfig);
```

```
topology.newStream("stream-" + spoutConfig.getTopologyName(), spout)
        .each(new Fields("message"), new ParseTelemetry(),
        new Fields("temp", "createDate", "deviceId"))
        .each(new Fields("message", "temp", "createDate", "deviceId"),
        new EmitAlert(65, 68), new Fields("reason"))
        .parallelismHint(spoutConfig.getPartitionCount());

    return topology.build();
}
```

Notice that in this case we create an instance of `TridentTopology` and then a Trident-specific instance of the `EventHubSpout`. The line starting with `topology.newStream` is where it gets interesting. The call to `newStream` does exactly as it describes, creating a new, named stream using the `OpaqueTridentEventHubSpout`.

After that we chain on a call to the `each` operation. It takes as its first parameter, via the `Fields` constructor, a comma-separated list of the fields coming from the spout that we want to process by the function, which is provided in the second parameter. In other words, the first parameter to `each` lets you project only the fields you want to pass to the function. The third parameter lists the additional fields the `ParseTeleme try` function will tack on to the tuple when it returns its result. So for the first line, the input tuple just has the `"message"` field, and that is the only field that will be passed as an input to `ParseTelemetry`. When `ParseTelemetry` has completed and it has emitted a tuple, the tuple will be emitted with the fields `"message"`, `"temp"`, `"crea teDate"`, and `"deviceId"`.

Let's look at the complete implementation of the `ParseTelemetry` function:

```
public class ParseTelemetry extends BaseFunction {

    public void execute(TridentTuple tuple, TridentCollector collector) {

        String value = tuple.getString(0);

        ObjectMapper mapper = new ObjectMapper();
        try {
            JsonNode telemetryObj = mapper.readTree(value);

            if (telemetryObj.has("temp")) //assume must be a temperature reading
            {
                Values values = new Values(
                        telemetryObj.get("temp").asDouble(),
                        telemetryObj.get("createDate").asText(),
                        telemetryObj.get("deviceId").asText()
                );

                collector.emit(values);
            }
        } catch (IOException e) {
```

```
        System.out.println(e.getMessage());
    }
}
}
```

Notice how much simpler and more focused this code is than the equivalent bolt. To declare a function, we create a class that extends `BaseFunction` and then implement the `execute` method. If the function will emit a tuple as a result of its execution, it uses the `TridentCollector` provided and calls the `emit` method. If it does not emit a tuple, then effectively the input tuple is removed from any downstream processing.

Returning to `AlertTopology`, the next call to `each` applies the `EmitAlert` function to each tuple in the stream:

```
topology.newStream("stream-" + spoutConfig.getTopologyName(), spout)
    .each(new Fields("message"), new ParseTelemetry(), new Fields("temp",
    "createDate", "deviceId"))
    .each(new Fields("message", "temp", "createDate", "deviceId"),
    new EmitAlert(65, 68), new Fields("reason"))
    .parallelismHint(spoutConfig.getPartitionCount());
```

The implementation of `EmitAlert` is equally straightforward, with the notable difference that in this case the function has a constructor we use to pass in the minimum and maximum temperatures used for alerting:

```
public class EmitAlert extends BaseFunction {

    protected double minAlertTemp;
    protected double maxAlertTemp;

    public EmitAlert(double minTemp, double maxTemp) {
        minAlertTemp = minTemp;
        maxAlertTemp = maxTemp;
    }

    public void execute(TridentTuple tuple, TridentCollector collector) {

        double tempReading = tuple.getDouble(1);
        String createDate = tuple.getString(2);
        String deviceId = tuple.getString(3);

        if (tempReading > maxAlertTemp )
        {
            collector.emit(new Values (
                    "reading above bounds",
                    tempReading,
                    createDate,
                    deviceId
            ));
            System.out.println("Emitting above bounds: " + tempReading);
        } else if (tempReading < minAlertTemp)
        {
```

```
            collector.emit(new Values (
                    "reading below bounds",
                    tempReading,
                    createDate,
                    deviceId
            ));
            System.out.println("Emitting below bounds: " + tempReading);
        }
    }
}
```

Returning to `AlertTopology` one last time, the last call we chain to the topology is
`parallelismHint`. The effect of this call is the same as was demonstrated for the bolts
in the classic Storm topology. It will ensure there is one instance of the spout, the
dynamically generated bolt hosting the `ParseTelemetry` function, and the instance of
the bolt hosting the `EmitAlert` function for each partition in Event Hubs.

```
topology.newStream("stream-" + spoutConfig.getTopologyName(), spout)
    .each(new Fields("message"), new ParseTelemetry(), new Fields("temp",
    "createDate", "deviceId"))
    .each(new Fields("message", "temp", "createDate", "deviceId"),
    new EmitAlert(65, 68), new Fields("reason"))
    .parallelismHint(spoutConfig.getPartitionCount());

return topology.build();
```

The final line returns the `StormTopology` instance that we execute and run in exactly
the same way as the classic Storm version. It is worth noting that the calls to `each`
make it appear like we are processing the stream in a tuple-at-a-time fashion, but
under the covers the `OpaqueEventHubSpout` is emitting a batch of tuples at a time
(usually with several hundred tuples to a batch), and it is these batches that flow
down the stream.

Batch Operations

Trident contains various operations, such as aggregates, that can perform their work
on the batch (selecting the minimum value from the batch, counting the number of
tuples in a batch, etc).

For a more complete exploration of these operations in the Trident API, see the docu‐
mentation (*https://storm.apache.org/releases/0.10.0/Trident-API-Overview.html*).

Storm with tick tuples

Another approach to implementing micro-batch processing with Storm centers on
the use of a "tick" tuple to define the batch. The idea is that the topology will, on a
periodic basis you configure, emit a special kind of tuple called a *tick tuple*. In your

bolt code, you can identify this tuple as being different from the other tuples because it comes from a different stream. This enables you to build bolts that buffer up tuples, only to release them or an aggregation tuple calculated from them, when the tick tuple arrives. In other words, you can create a micro-batch that is defined by the window of time between tick tuples. Prior to Storm 1.0.0, this was a common basic pattern that was implemented in order to perform time-window-based calculations (such as counting the number of alert tuples over the last 15 minutes).

To examine how we might extend the AlertTopology (the classic Storm topology), take a look at the TickTuples sample from *http://bit.ly/2bzcV7q*.

In the sample, we want to count how many alert tuples were emitted by each bolt within a 10-second window. Using a tick tuple amounts to two steps. First, you need to set the topology configuration so that it emits a tick tuple on the interval you configure. Second, you build your bolts to check if the input tuple comes from the special tick stream, and if so perform your micro-batch calculation (if not, your bolt processes the tuple as it normally would).

Let's begin with the configuration. This can be seen in AlertTopology, where the only change needed is within the submitTopology method, where we add a configuration setting for the Config.TOPOLOGY_TICK_TUPLE_FREQ_SEQS and provide a value of 10. When submitted with our topology, this will cause a tick tuple to be emitted every 10 seconds.

```
protected void submitTopology(String[] args, StormTopology topology)
throws Exception {
    Config config = new Config();
    config.setDebug(false);

    config.put(Config.TOPOLOGY_TICK_TUPLE_FREQ_SECS, 10);

    if (args != null && args.length > 0) {
        StormSubmitter.submitTopology(args[0], config, topology);
    } else {
        config.setMaxTaskParallelism(2);

        LocalCluster localCluster = new LocalCluster();
        localCluster.submitTopology("test", config, topology);
        Thread.sleep(600000);
        localCluster.shutdown();
    }
}
```

Then we need to alter our bolts to be aware of this tick tuple. In the case of ParseTelemetry we just want to log that a tick tuple was received:

```
public void execute(Tuple input, BasicOutputCollector collector) {

    if (input.getSourceComponent()
```

```
        .equals(Constants.SYSTEM_COMPONENT_ID) //Handle Tick Tuple
            && input.getSourceStreamId().equals(Constants.SYSTEM_TICK_STREAM_ID)) {
        System.out.println("ParseTelemetry Tick tuple received.");
    }
    else { //Handle data tuple

        String value = input.getString(0);

        ObjectMapper mapper = new ObjectMapper();
        try {
            JsonNode telemetryObj = mapper.readTree(value);

            if (telemetryObj.has("temp")) //assume must be a temperature reading
            {
                Values values = new Values(
                        telemetryObj.get("temp").asDouble(),
                        telemetryObj.get("createDate").asText(),
                        telemetryObj.get("deviceId").asText()
                );

                collector.emit(values);
            }
        } catch (IOException e) {
            System.out.println(e.getMessage());
        }
    }
}
```

In the implementation of execute, observe that we check that the source component
is a system component and the ID of the source stream is the system tick stream. If
both are true, then we know the tuple is a tick tuple.

Next, let's look at how we perform the counting of alert tuples within the implementation of the EmitAlerts bolt:

```
protected int alertCounter;

public void execute(Tuple input, BasicOutputCollector collector) {

    if (input.getSourceComponent()
    .equals(Constants.SYSTEM_COMPONENT_ID) //Handle Tick Tuple
            && input.getSourceStreamId().equals(Constants.SYSTEM_TICK_STREAM_ID)) {
        System.out.println("=== EmitAlert: " + alertCounter
        + " alerts emitted in tick window. +++");
        alertCounter = 0;
    }
    else { //Handle data tuple
        double tempReading = input.getDouble(0);
        String createDate = input.getString(1);
        String deviceId = input.getString(2);

        if (tempReading > maxAlertTemp) {
```

```
        collector.emit(new Values(
                "reading above bounds",
                tempReading,
                createDate,
                deviceId
        ));
        System.out.println("Emitting above bounds: " + tempReading);
        alertCounter++;
    } else if (tempReading < minAlertTemp) {
        collector.emit(new Values(
                "reading below bounds",
                tempReading,
                createDate,
                deviceId
        ));
        System.out.println("Emitting below bounds: " + tempReading);
        alertCounter++;
    }
  }
}
```

We create a protected member field, `alertCounter`, in the class to store the count that is incremented within the tick window. Each time we emit an alert tuple, we increment `alertCounter`. Each time we receive a tick tuple, we print out the current value of `alertCounter` and then reset the counter back to zero.

Azure Stream Analytics

Azure Stream Analytics is a fully managed, real-time event processing engine. This makes it very different from Storm and Spark on HDInsight from the perspective that there are no clusters you have to provision or manage—you provision a Stream Analytics job and start it. The micro-batch processing performed by a Stream Analytics job is described through a combination of configuration (by specifying the input source of the streaming data and the output sink for the results of your job) and any data transformation is expressed using declarative SQL. All of these steps are performed within the Azure Portal. Beyond a browser, there is no code and no IDE or specialized authorizing environment required.

Without having any infrastructure, Stream Analytics is capable of handling high event throughput from 1 MB/s on the low end up to 1 GB/s on the high end. The extreme levels of throughput in this range are achieved by a combination of using the partitions provided by Event Hubs, the manner in which data is partitioned in the SQL queries, and the way in which data is partitioned on output. The service is built following a pay-as-you-go model based on streaming unit (SU) usage and the amount of data processed by the system; as you need more capacity you can add extra SUs, which each provide 1 MB/s of additional capacity.

Stream Analytics is primarily aimed at processing input streams of data from Event Hubs, and thus its inputs connect directly to Event Hubs and IoT Hubs for stream ingestion. Stream Analytics can also connect directly to Azure Blob Storage to ingest historical data. The inputs support data formatted in Avro, UTF-8-encoded CSV (alternate field delimiters supported are semicolon, space, tab, or pipe), or UTF-8-encoded JSON.

CSV Handling

CSVs ingested from Blob Storage must have a row header, where each header label is unique. Additionally, files read from Blob Storage are processed only once, so any updates to a previously processed blob will not be processed by a Stream Analytics job.

In addition to streaming input data, Stream Analytics jobs can pull slowly changing reference data from Azure Blob Storage. This reference data can be used to enrich the streaming input data—for example, to look up device metadata from device IDs—and is treated like any other event stream within the data transformations. Reference data supports the same data formats as the streaming inputs.

Results can be written from Stream Analytics to Azure Blob Storage or Table Storage, SQL Database, Data Lake Store, DocumentDB, Event Hubs, Service Bus Topics/Queues, and Power BI.

The data transformations are expressed in a query language that is largely a subset of T-SQL with added language extensions for expressing temporal semantics using windowing.

Examples of Stream Analytics SQL

For examples of typical query patterns, see the Microsoft Azure documentation (*http://bit.ly/2mR06cB*).

A query definition can consist of a single step (e.g., `SELECT * FROM eventhub`), or it can contain multiple steps (either as multiple independent queries or as a sequence of queries and subqueries defined using the `WITH` keyword). The latter approach yields two benefits.

On the one hand, multiple independent queries can be used to describe multiple independent transformations within the same Stream Analytics job. For example, you could have one query step that reads all data from an Event Hub and writes it out to Blob Storage to support cold path analytics, and within the same job have another query step that reads the same data from the Event Hub but perhaps filters it for alert conditions and writes it out to a SQL database. You can have up to 60 inputs and up to 60 outputs per job.

On the other hand, multiple related queries and subqueries are written in a single job, with data partitioning in mind, to maximize the parallel processing that occurs on the data stream.

Partitioning Streaming Data

Detailed coverage of partitioning streaming data is beyond the scope of this book, but the approach is summarized nicely in the Microsoft Azure documentation (*http://bit.ly/2o5oTe7*).

When a job input, query, and output have all been specified, you can start the Stream Analytics job. When starting a job, you can specify a Start Output value that dictates the point in time at which the job begins to process data from the source. The default setting for a new job is Job Start Time, which means any data received after the job's start time will immediately be processed. As Event Hubs and Blob Storage may contain data that predates the Job Start Time, you can also specify a Custom Time in the past to process this historical data, or a time in the future to delay the processing until some point in the future. Jobs can be stopped and restarted. When a previously stopped job is restarted, the Last Stopped Time becomes an option that resumes the job from where the processing left off when it was stopped.

Comparison of Stream Analytics Versus Storm on HDInsight

Given that you've now read about both Stream Analytics and Storm, you can cement your understanding of the differences between the two in the Microsoft Azure documentation (*http://bit.ly/2nJYy9v*).

With this background in mind, let's take a look at what it takes to provide the same alert processing we have shown for Spark and Storm using Stream Analytics.

Provisioning a Stream Analytics job

Before you can configure your job inputs, outputs, and query definition, you need to provision a new Stream Analytics job. Follow these steps:

1. From the Azure Portal, select New.

2. Select Intelligence + Analytics in the blade that appears.

3. Select "Stream Analytics job" (Figure 5-15).

Figure 5-15. Selecting a Stream Analytics job in the Azure Portal

4. In the blade that appears, provide a name for the job, then choose the subscription in which to deploy it, the resource group, and the location (it should be in the same region as your input Event Hub), as shown in Figure 5-16.

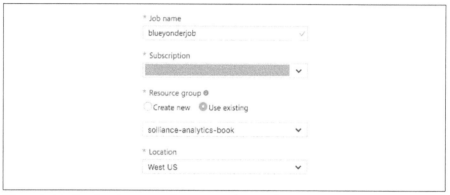

Figure 5-16. Configuring a new Stream Analytics job.

5. Click Create to provision the job.

6. Once the job is created, open it in the Azure Portal.

7. On the blade for the Stream Analytics job, underneath Job Topology, click Inputs (Figure 5-17).

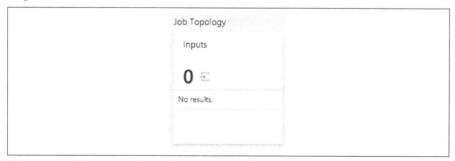

Figure 5-17. The inputs tile on the Stream Analytics Job blade.

8. In the blade that appears, click Add.

9. On the "New input" blade, provide a name for your new input (e.g., eventhub). This is the label you will need to use in your SQL query in the context of the FROM clause.

10. Set the Source Type to "Data stream" and the Source to "Event hub."

11. Use the "Subscription," "Service bus namespace," "Event hub name," and "Event hub policy name" to select the Event Hub you have created for the sample solution, so it can receive data from the SimpleSensorConsole device simulator application.

12. For the telemetry created by the simulator, you should leave the "Event serialization format" as JSON and the "Encoding" as UTF-8 (since the simulator sends the telemetry payload as UTF-8-encoded JSON). See Figure 5-18.

Figure 5-18. Configuring an Event Hub source for a Stream Analytics job.

13. Select Create to add the input.

14. Back on the blade for the Stream Analytics job, under Job Topology, select Outputs (Figure 5-19).

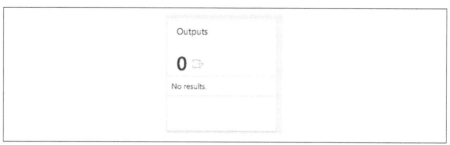

Outputs

0

No results.

Figure 5-19. The outputs tile on the Stream Analytics Job blade in the Azure Portal.

15. On the Outputs blade, select Add.

16. In this case, we will output alert telemetry to Azure Blob Storage. To do so provide an alias (e.g., blobs).

17. Change the Sink drop-down to "Blob storage."

18. Use the "Subscription" and "Storage account" drop-downs to select the storage account to which you want to write the output files.

19. For the container, select an existing container.

20. For the Path pattern, specify a subfolder path that will be used beneath the container. For our purposes, it should read simply {date}.

21. Using the "Date format" drop-down that is enabled, select "YYYY/MM/DD." This will effectively write the blob data under the path *<containerName>/ YYYY/MM/DD/<filename>*.

22. Leave "Event serialization" as JSON, "Encoding" as UTF-8, and "Format" as "Line separated" (so that each line contains a complete JSON document). See Figure 5-20.

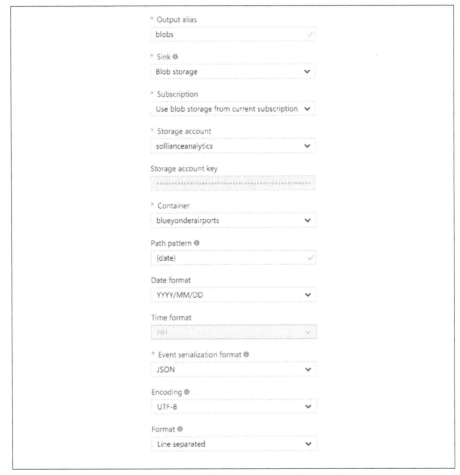

Figure 5-20. Configuring a blob sink for a Stream Analytics job.

23. Select Create to add the output.

24. Back on the blade for the Stream Analytics job, under Job Topology, select Query.

25. On the query blade, within the query text area, add the following query:

```
SELECT *
INTO blobs
FROM eventhub
WHERE temp < 65.0 OR temp > 68.0
```

26. Select Save.

27. Close the query blade.

28. Back on the blade for the Stream Analytics job, select Start.

29. Leave the "Job output start time set" to Now, and select Start (Figure 5-21).

Figure 5-21. Setting the Job output start time for a Stream Analytics job.

30. Run the `SimpleSensorConsole` (provided with this book's sample files) and select the Event Hub option to prime the Event Hub with some telemetry.

31. The job will take a few minutes to start, after which you should check the container in Blob Storage you configured as the output for new files (which you can do via the portal by selecting the Storage account and selecting Blobs). See Figure 5-22.

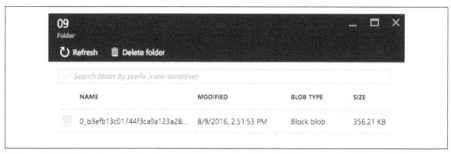

Figure 5-22. Viewing the listing of blobs emitted by the Stream Analytics job.

As you can see from the preceding steps, the only coding you perform to implement the logic for the stream processing is the simple SQL query; the rest is configuration.

Summary

In this chapter we dug deeper into how consumers from Event Hubs can be implemented to process events in a micro-batch fashion, using our alerting example as a reference across multiple options. We looked at implementing processing applications in Apache Spark using Spark Streaming coded in the Scala language. We introduced using Storm with Trident and with tick tuples to perform event processing, implementing the solution in Java. We also covered using Azure Stream Analytics jobs to implement stream processing by using a variant of SQL.

In the next chapter, we will increase our latency tolerance from seconds, as required by stream processing, to minutes and even hours as we look at the options for building batch processing applications.

CHAPTER 6

Batch Processing in Azure

In this chapter we explore the options for performing batch processing in Azure (Figure 6-1). Just as we did for real-time processing (which aimed for subsecond processing), we will use a latency definition of batch processing. Think of batch processing as those queries or programs that take tens of minutes, hours, or even days to complete.

Batch processing is used in a variety of scenarios, from the initial data munging efforts to a more complete ETL (extract-transform-load) pipeline, to preparing data for ultimate consumption over very large data sets or where the computation takes significant time. In other words, batch processing is a step in your lambda architecture processing pipeline—one that either leads to further interactive exploration (downstream analytics), provides the modeling-ready data for machine learning, or lands the data in a data store optimized for analytics and visualization.

A concrete example of batch processing is transforming a large set of flat, unstructured CSV files into a schematized (and structured format) that is ready for further querying. Along with this, typically the format is converted from the raw formats used for ingest (such as CSV) to binary formats that are more performant for querying because they store data in a columnar format, and often provide indexes and inline statistics about the data contained.

An important concept you will see in action throughout the technologies highlighted in this chapter is that of *schema on read*. The idea is that instead of having to already have the data in a format where the schema is applied, you can apply the schema while loading the data from disk. This enables scenarios like the CSV one just described, because you can take the data in whatever format it arrives and overlay a schema so that you can then work with that data.

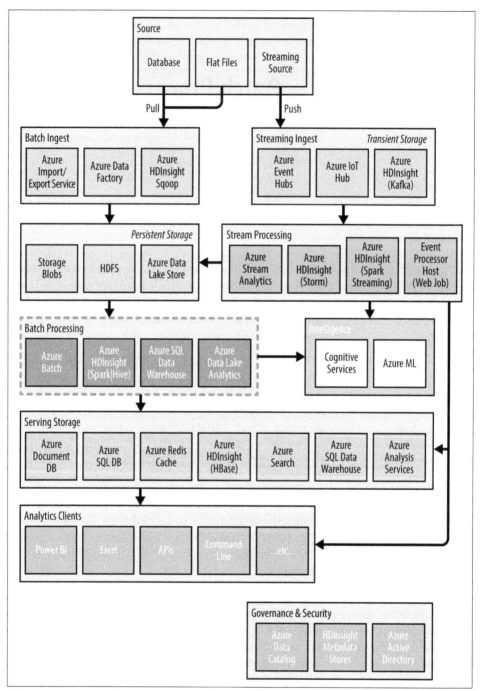

Figure 6-1. In this chapter we focus on the components used for batch processing.

Another important concept that is leveraged by almost all batch processing systems is the notion of *external* and *managed* (or *internal*) tables. Here the idea centers on the authority provided to the batch processing solution over the data. A managed table provides schema on read over data that the processing solution "owns"—that is to say, it controls the lifecycle of the data and it is the only system expected to be interacting with the data. This is in contrast to external tables, whereby the underlying data is expected to be shared between the batch processing solution and other systems, so the former would not have any expectations of control over the lifecycle of the under-lying data.

To illustrate batch processing in action in this chapter, we will return to the Blue Yon-der Airlines scenario. For the purposes of this chapter, we'll examine a input data set consisting of CSV files representing flight (and flight delay) information for multiple years' worth of data. We will examine how we can apply schema to this data and for-mat it for subsequent querying, such as interactive analytics (which we cover in the next chapter). The process we use for Blue Yonder could extend to include additional processing and transformation of the data, but with the basics of internal and external tables and schema on read under your belt you will be well equipped to approach batch processing challenges in general.

Batch Processing with MapReduce on HDInsight

The MapReduce programming model is designed for creating applications to batch process big data sets in parallel. At its core it splits large data sets and converts them into collections of key/value pairs for processing. The first step of MapReduce, the map, applies some function that takes data rows of keys and values as input and returns a list of new key/value pairs as output. In other words, for an input key/value pair, the output key can differ from the input key. Additionally, the output can have multiple key/value pairs with the same key (hence the output is really viewed as a list of key/value pairs).

```
map(key1,value) -> list<key2,value2>
```

The second and final step takes as input the list of key/value pairs produced from the map step, processing for each key the list of associated values to generate a new list of values.

```
reduce(key2, list<value2>) -> list<value3>
```

By ensuring that each MapReduce operation is independent of all other ongoing MapReduce operations, you have a solution that enables the operations to be run in parallel on different keys and lists of data. This parallel processing is one of the important benefits of the MapReduce model that makes it useful for processing big data sets.

Apache Hadoop MapReduce

Apache Hadoop MapReduce is an implementation of the MapReduce programming model that provides an embarrassingly parallel map phase where the data is split into subsets to be processed, followed by a reduce phase where the output of the map phase is aggregated to yield the desired result. The term *embarrassingly parallel* is used to indicate a pattern whereby each task performing the processing does so in isolation from and with no communication with any of the other tasks processing the data (the opposite pattern is one where each task communicates directly with every other task as a part of its processing, such as is done in Message Passing Interface, or MPI, based solutions).

A tenet of the MapReduce implementation is that given a cluster of nodes (e.g., servers), you can improve processing times by limiting the amount of time spent moving data between compute nodes across the network. This process of moving the data to the compute is called a *shuffle*. MapReduce takes the alternate approach of moving the computation to the data whenever possible (i.e., running the code on the same node that is storing the data), thereby eliminating the time-consuming shuffle. The storage underpinning the compute is assumed to be a distributed filesystem, which in most cases is HDFS.

You can think of Hadoop MapReduce as encompassing three components:

MapReduce API
    The end-user API for programming the application.

MapReduce framework
    The runtime implementation of map, sort, shuffle, merge, and reduce.

MapReduce system
    The backend infrastructure running the user's MapReduce application, managing cluster resources, and scheduling the concurrent jobs.

The Apache Hadoop MapReduce system has two major components, each of which runs as a process on a node: a master JobTracker and multiple per-node slave Task-Tracker (see Figure 6-2). The JobTracker does two things:

Resource management
    Manage the TaskTrackers; track resource consumption and availability

Job lifecycle management
    Schedule individual job tasks with the TaskTrackers, tracking their progress and providing fault tolerance for transient failures

The TaskTracker follows the instructions given to it by the JobTracker, which are either to launch tasks or kill tasks. It also provides periodic task status back to the JobTracker.

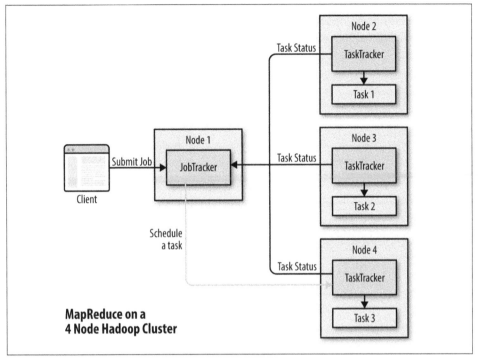

Figure 6-2. The relationship between the client that submits a MapReduce job, the compute nodes that run the Tracker processes (the JobTracker and subordinate TaskTrackers), and the tasks that are ultimately executed.

In Hadoop 1, clusters would run MapReduce with the responsibilities defined previously and would rely on the HDFS for storage of source data, intermediate results (i.e., the results of a map step), and the final output (i.e., the results of a reduce step).

Hadoop 2 introduced some very dramatic changes that addressed the particular limitations of MapReduce. These limitations centered on the poor performance that resulted from always having to write intermediate results to disk, low cluster utilization that surfaced as a result of the rigid number of map and reduce "slots" that were available in the cluster, the inability to describe a processing pipeline that was anything other than a map followed by a reduce, and in a broader sense, the lack of flexibility to leverage the cluster to do any other form of distributed processing that was not a MapReduce workload.

The response to these limitations in Hadoop 2 is Apache YARN (Yet Another Resource Manager), which provides both resource management and a distributed application framework. YARN changes its perspective on the resources it manages from managing MapReduce jobs (as was done in Hadoop 1) on the cluster to managing more generic applications, where applications can be instances of MapReduce or even newer workloads like Spark. YARN takes the approach of splitting up the two responsibilities of the JobTracker. The resource management responsibilities become the duties of a global ResourceManager, and the job lifecycle management responsibilities become the duties of a per-application ApplicationMaster (Figure 6-3).

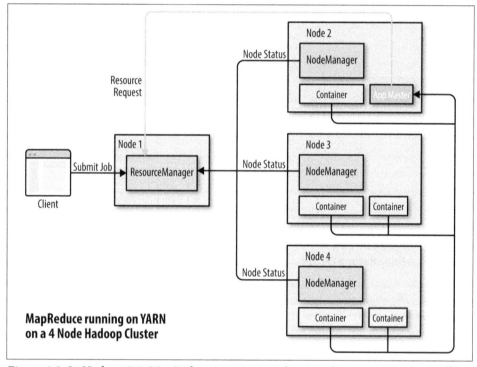

Figure 6-3. In Hadoop 2.0, MapReduce is just an application that runs atop the YARN managed cluster.

The ResourceManager manages the allocation of resources among all the applications in the system. The Scheduler component of the ResourceManager doles out resources in packages of defined CPU, memory, disk, and network capacities called *resource containers*.

Each node runs a slave process called the NodeManager, which is responsible for launching containers, monitoring container resource usage, and reporting resource usage to the ResourceManager. Containers within each node support two forms of processing: an ApplicationMaster or execution of the tasks required by the application. One ApplicationMaster is created per application instance. It has the responsibility of negotiating the resource containers from the Scheduler of the

ResourceManager, and then tracking the status and monitoring the progress of the allocated resource containers executing across the cluster.

The final major modification introduced in the move to YARN is that MapReduce becomes simply a type of application (that implements just the MapReduce algorithm) that runs on the YARN-managed cluster.

In Azure, whenever you provision any type of HDInsight cluster, you are provisioning YARN, and it is YARN the provides the underlying resource management for Apache Hive, Pig, Spark, and Storm applications, to name a few.

Authoring MapReduce Programs

We will not cover directly authoring MapReduce programs in this book. Instead, we will focus on applications like Hive whose output is a MapReduce program, or non-MapReduce applications like Spark, each of which run on the YARN cluster provided by HDInsight. If you are curious about directly programming and running Java-based MapReduce jobs on HDInsight, see the Microsoft Azure documentation (*http://bit.ly/2mQENbc*).

Batch Processing with Hive on HDInsight

Apache Hive is a data warehouse system for Hadoop that enables data summarization, querying, and analysis by using HiveQL (a query language similar to SQL). Hive can be used to interactively explore your data or to create reusable batch processing jobs. Hive provides support for familiar objects like databases, tables, views, user-defined functions, and indexes that are typically found in relational databases. Hive supports most of the data types you would expect (`bigint`, `binary`, `boolean`, `char`, `decimal`, `double`, `float`, `int`, `smallint`, `string`, `timestamp`, and `tinyint`), but also has specialized support for arrays, maps, and structs. The primary benefits of Hive are that it allows you to project a structure on unstructured (or semi-structured) data, providing you an interface to query data residing in HDFS without having to write programs using MapReduce.

It is worth emphasizing the Hive is not database—it simply provides a mechanism to project database structure on data you store in HDFS and then lets you query that data using HiveQL. Unlike a typical database, Hive has no control over the structure of the underlying storage; it can only apply schema to the data stored in response to queries. In other words, it provides schema on read. If the underlying data does not match the expected schema, Hive will try to work around errors so that the query can execute. For example, if the schema expects numbers, but the stored fields are non-numeric strings, then Hive will return `null` for those fields.

When you query Hive with HiveQL, your queries are implicitly converted into Map-Reduce or Tez (which we cover in greater detail in the next chapter), or Spark jobs.

Hive-on-Spark

The option of executing HiveQL queries via Spark jobs is called Hive-on-Spark. Hive-on-Spark is in its early days and not yet available in HDInsight. It is a part of Hive 2.x, so it will become an option for HDInsight when HDInsight adds support for Hive 2.x. As HDInsight is based on HortonWorks HDP, watch for Horton-Works to release HDP 2.5, which should include Hive 2.x, and a release of HDI with HDP 2.5 should follow shortly thereafter.

Hive can be used to query against data stored as text files (e.g., CSV) as well as some of the more specialized binary formats that have emerged over the years, including sequence files (the original key/value format used by MapReduce) and the columnar formats ORC, RCFile, and Parquet.

Internal and External Tables

As previously mentioned, Hive supports the concept of internal and external tables. Hive uses internal (aka managed) and external tables to capture intent—that is, the intended ownership of a table and its data. Internal tables imply Hive is expected to have full ownership, whereas external tables imply Hive is sharing access to the data with other applications that have access to the same instance of HDFS.

Internal tables have their data physically located in a location managed by Hive itself. External tables are effectively references to data located at some path external to Hive. The major difference between the two occurs when tables are created and when they are dropped. An internal table, when created, copies the data files into Hive's managed location, and when the table is dropped Hive also deletes the data from disk. An external table, when created, leaves the data at its source location and when the table is dropped, Hive does not delete the underlying data, only the structure metadata.

Partitioning Tables

Tables, both internal and external, can be horizontally partitioned (i.e., the table is split into sets of rows).

Partitioning tables changes how Hive structures the data storage. Hive will now create subdirectories reflecting the partitioning structure, where the folder name takes the format: *<fieldName>=<value>*. In this approach, the fields used for partitioning can be removed from the data files themselves and expressed only once in the path leading up to the data files, which saves space.

Table Reference

For a detailed guide on all the options for creating a partitioned table, see the Apache Hive wiki (*http://bit.ly/2nK0UVS*).

Views

A view allows a query to be saved and treated like a table. It is a logical construct, as it does not store data like a table. In other words, materialized views are not currently supported by Hive.

View Reference

For a good reference on the syntax used for creating a view, see the Apache Hive wiki (*http://bit.ly/2mV4t7q*).

Indexes

Hive has some limited indexing capabilities. There are no keys in the usual relational database sense, and since Hive is generally in the business of overlaying structure without modifying the storage format, applying the equivalent of primary (or clustered) indexes that change sort order of the data on disk is not an approach Hive supports. That said, you can build a secondary index on columns to speed up some operations. The index data for a table is stored in another table.

When you declare an index, you specify an index handler that implements the desired indexing strategy. The two most common ones are BITMAP (which is optimized for columns that have few distinct values, such as gender) and COMPACT (which is optimized for queries performing point lookups). Indexing of external tables and views is supported in addition to indexing internal tables.

It is important to note that indexes have to be manually rebuilt when the underlying table data changes.

Indexes are supported only when MapReduce is used as the engine for Hive. When Tez is used, index builds will fail. You should instead use ORC storage (which includes inlined indexes) and partitions.

Index Management HiveQL Syntax

For documentation on creating and managing indexes, see the Apache Hive wiki (*http://bit.ly/2nCJLgd*).

Databases

In Hive a database is basically a logical grouping of tables; think of it as a table catalog or namespace. Hive has one out-of-the-box database called default, which is used when no other database is explicitly specified.

Each database gets its own subfolder below Hive's warehouse directory by default. You can specify an alternate location for a database external to the warehouse directory if desired. The exception to this is the default database, which effectively is the root of the warehouse folder, which means any internal tables you create within it are folders that are peers to other databases.

Database HiveQL Syntax Reference

For details on the HiveQL syntax for managing databases, see the Apache Hive wiki (*http://bit.ly/2nShak9*).

Using Hive on HDInsight

Now let's explore these concepts concretely on an HDInsight cluster. Before we begin, make sure you provision a new HDInsight cluster. Strictly speaking, you can use any of the cluster types, since they all include Hive, but if Hive is the main technology you're after you should deploy with a cluster type of Hadoop. This leaves the choice of operating system open, so you can use either Linux- or Windows-based clusters. We recommend deploying Linux clusters since this provides more robust functionality than Windows (specifically in that it includes Apache Ambari, which has more polished interfaces for Hive). Thus, we will assume a Linux deployment of HDInsight in this section. Just for reference, here are click-by-click steps:

1. Log in to the Azure Portal.
2. Select New→Data + Analytics→HDInsight.
3. On the New HDInsight blade, provide a unique name for your cluster.
4. Choose your Azure subscription.
5. Click Select Cluster Type.
6. On the "Cluster type configuration" blade, set the cluster type to Hadoop, operating system to Linux, version to Hadoop 2.7.1, and cluster tier to Standard. Click Select.
7. Click "credentials."
8. Set the admin login username and password, then the SSH username and password, and click Select.
9. Click Data Source.

10. For a Hadoop cluster (and by extension for Hive), you are required to associate an Azure Storage account and optionally Azure Data Lake Store with your cluster. Select an existing Azure Storage account or create a new one as desired. This Storage account will provide the default storage for your cluster.

11. Modify the container name as desired. This container name will act as the root folder for your HDInsight cluster.

12. Choose the location nearest you.

13. Optionally, if you want to use Azure Data Lake Store, select "Cluster AAD identity" and either create a new AAD Service Principal or select an existing one. In order to configure an AAD Service Principal, you must be logged into the Azure Portal as the subscription owner (co-admin users will not be able to successfully perform this step). After your cluster is done provisioning, be sure to go to your Data Lake Store instance, and give the service principal you created in this step access to your Data Lake Store (Figure 6-4).

Figure 6-4. Configuring Data Lake Store access for the new cluster.

14. Click Select.

15. Click Pricing.

16. Set the number of worker nodes to 4 (you do not need more to run the sample), and adjust the worker node size and head node size as desired (any of the smaller available options will work).

17. Click Select on the Pricing blade.

18. Click Resource Group and select an existing one or create a new Resource Group as desired. You should now have all the settings specified.

19. Click Create to begin creating the HDInsight cluster. It will take about 25 minutes to complete. When it's ready, continue with the next section to begin your Hive exploration.

Storage on HDInsight

When you provision an HDInsight cluster, you are required to provision a new Azure Storage account or associate an existing one with your cluster. Also, you must specify a blob container within that associated Storage account that HDInsight will treat as the root of the HDFS.

With regards to internal tables, the default Azure Storage container associated with the cluster is used, and internal tables are stored under the path */hive/warehouse*.

External tables may be created over data that lives in a different location under the root container, but could also be created over data existing in different containers or even different Azure Storage accounts that have been associated with the cluster.

In addition to providing a default Azure Storage account, you can also associate Azure Data Lake Store with your HDInsight cluster (Figure 6-5). When you do so, this enables you to use Azure Data Lake Store for the storage of your external table data. Internal tables will continue to store their data on the HDInsight cluster's configured container within the default Azure Storage account.

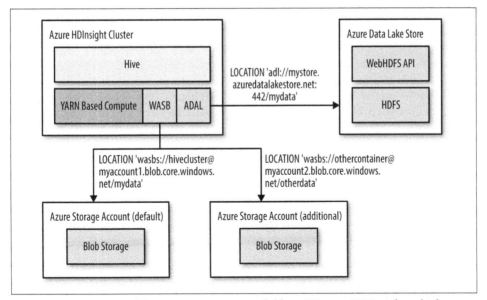

Figure 6-5. Overview of the storage options available to Hive on HDInsight, which allows for associating a mix of Azure Storage accounts and Azure Data Lake Stores.

Batch Processing Blue Yonder Airports Data

Now that you have your HDInsight cluster provisioned, make sure that you have uploaded the flight delay data (see Chapter 2) to the Azure Storage account or the Azure Data Lake Store that you have associated with your cluster and from which you will be querying. In our steps that follow, we uploaded the data to the path */flightdata* in both data stores.

There are two primary modes of executing HiveQL queries. You can SSH into the head node of the cluster and run your queries using the Hive shell, or you can use a browser to access Ambari and use the Hive View GUI for querying. We show examples of both.

The flight delay data set has a few real-world challenges that we will show you how to address as well. Here is the gist of the challenges and how we will address them.

Challenges with the data set:

1. Each CSV file has a header row, which needs to be skipped over.
2. The OriginCityName and DestCityName fields themselves have a comma in their value (e.g., "city, state"), which causes the fields after them to not align to the headers.

3. The source data is in CSV, but we'd prefer to use a more performant format for later analytic querying.

Solution to the challenges:

1. You can tell Hive to skip the first row of each file, to treat it as a header, by providing the `skip.header.line.count` table property when you define your external table.

2. When defining the schema for the load, create two columns for OriginCityName, and two columns for DestCityName. Then, in your transformation script, you can merge these values back together as desired, but keep the correct field count and header to value alignment.

3. For Hive, we can migrate the data into ORC for improved compression and query performance.

Creating an External Table

In this section, we will begin the process of preparing the flight delay data for analytics by overlaying a schema. We will accomplish this by using the Ambari Hive View to execute our HiveQL scripts.

1. Open a browser and navigate to
   https://<YOURCLUSTERNAME>.azurehdinsight.net/#/main/views.

2. When prompted, log in with the admin credentials you created when provisioning the cluster.

3. In the list of views that appears, select Hive View (Figure 6-6).

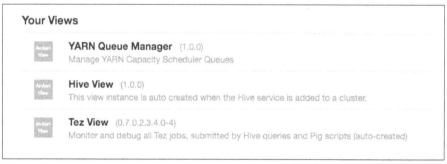

Figure 6-6. The list of views available from the Ambari Hive View.

4. In the Database Explorer area, under the Databases tab, click the default hyperlink to view the tables that your default Hive database currently contains (it should only have hivesampletable). See Figure 6-7.

Figure 6-7. Listing showing the created Hive table

5. Next, in the Query Editor area, under the Worksheet tab, paste the following query into the text area:

```
CREATE EXTERNAL TABLE FlightData
(
Year INT,
Quarter INT,
Month INT,
DayofMonth INT,
DayOfWeek STRING,
FlightDate STRING,
UniqueCarrier STRING,
AirlineID STRING,
Carrier STRING,
TailNum STRING,
FlightNum STRING,
OriginAirportID STRING,
OriginAirportSeqID STRING,
OriginCityMarketID STRING,
Origin STRING,
OriginCityName1 STRING,
OriginCityName2 STRING,
OriginState STRING,
OriginStateFips STRING,
OriginStateName STRING,
OriginWac STRING,
DestAirportID STRING,
DestAirportSeqID STRING,
DestCityMarketID STRING,
Dest STRING,
DestCityName1 STRING,
DestCityName2 STRING,
DestState STRING,
DestStateFips STRING,
DestStateName STRING,
DestWac STRING,
CRSDepTime INT,
DepTime INT,
DepDelay INT,
DepDelayMinutes INT,
DepDel15 BOOLEAN,
DepartureDelayGroups INT,
```

```
DepTimeBlk STRING,
TaxiOut INT,
WheelsOff INT,
WheelsOn INT,
TaxiIn INT,
CRSArrTime INT,
ArrTime INT,
ArrDelay INT,
ArrDelayMinutes INT,
ArrDel15 BOOLEAN,
ArrivalDelayGroups INT,
ArrTimeBlk STRING,
Cancelled BOOLEAN,
CancellationCode STRING,
Diverted BOOLEAN,
CRSElapsedTime INT,
ActualElapsedTime INT,
AirTime INT,
Flights INT,
Distance INT,
DistanceGroup INT,
CarrierDelay INT,
WeatherDelay INT,
NASDelay INT,
SecurityDelay INT,
LateAircraftDelay INT,
FirstDepTime INT,
TotalAddGTime INT,
LongestAddGTime INT,
DivAirportLandings BOOLEAN,
DivReachedDest BOOLEAN,
DivActualElapsedTime INT
)
ROW FORMAT DELIMITED FIELDS TERMINATED BY ','
STORED AS TEXTFILE
LOCATION 'adl://solliance.azuredatalakestore.net:443/flightdata'
TBLPROPERTIES ("skip.header.line.count"="1");
```

Let's explore the syntax a bit, before you run the script.

In the first line we provide the name of the table, and of course, we indicate that we want an external table by using the keyword EXTERNAL:

```
CREATE EXTERNAL TABLE FlightData
```

Then we provide an open parenthesis and list all of the columns in the table and a close parenthesis. Each column provides the name (as you will use in your queries) and the data type. It's important to list these columns in the same order as they appear in each of the CSV files:

```
(
Year INT,
Quarter INT,
Month INT,
...
DivReachedDest BOOLEAN,
DivActualElapsedTime INT
)
```

Following the columns, we indicate how Hive should parse this CSV file—namely by specifying that the fields (columns) are delimited by commas, that rows are line-delimited, and that we are dealing with a TEXTFILE (as opposed to ORC, SEQUENCE FILE, RCFILE, etc.):

```
ROW FORMAT DELIMITED FIELDS TERMINATED BY ','
STORED AS TEXTFILE
```

Then we get to the line that tells Hive where the files actually live, via the LOCATION keyword:

```
LOCATION 'adl://solliance.azuredatalakestore.net:443/flightdata'
```

We are telling Hive that our files live in Azure Data Lake Store. This is indicated by the adl:// prefix. The name of the Azure Data Lake Store is indicated as the subdomain (solliance, in this case). Finally, the folder in which the files exist is the path component of the URL (flightdata, in this case). If you have multiple levels of subfolders, you can express those in the path as you would expect (e.g., /flightdata/ 2016). The syntax for this URL to Azure Data Lake Store is summarized as follows:

```
LOCATION 'adl://[STORENAME].azuredatalakestore.net:443/[FOLDER]'
```

It is important to note that LOCATION requires you to provide a path to a folder and not to an individual file.

If we wanted to use Azure Blob Storage instead as the source for our CSV files, all we would change is the URL used in the LOCATION. For example:

```
LOCATION
'wasbs://myhive@solexpanalytics1.blob.core.windows.net/flightdata'
```

For Azure Storage, the URL prefix needs to be wasbs:// (short for Windows Azure Storage Blobs SSL), and then you need to provide the Storage account name, container name, and subfolder path below the container as follows:

```
LOCATION
'wasbs://[container]@[account].blob.core.windows.net/[subfolder]'
```

The last line in our script tells Hive to skip over the first line in each CSV file, since this line contains the column names and not any actual data:

```
TBLPROPERTIES ("skip.header.line.count"="1");
```

Returning to the Ambari Hive View you should have open in the browser:

1. Before you run the script, make sure you modify the LOCATION URL to point to where you have the flight delay data stored.

2. Click the Execute button (Figure 6-8).

Figure 6-8. The Execute button.

3. When you see Query Process Results (Status: Succeeded), as shown in Figure 6-9, your external table metadata has been created.

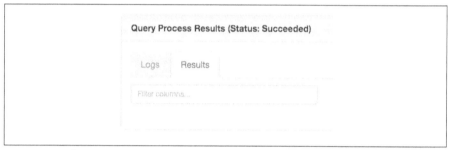

Figure 6-9. The query process results dialog showing success.

4. In Database Explorer, click the Refresh button (Figure 6-10).

Figure 6-10. The Refresh button.

5. Click on your default database and you should see your new table in the list (Figure 6-11).

Figure 6-11. Viewing the new table in the Hive tables underneath the default database.

Congratulations, you've created your first Hive external table!

Next, issue a query against this table:

1. Click the New Worksheet button to open a new query tab (Figure 6-12).

Figure 6-12. The New Worksheet button.

2. Paste the following query into the worksheet and click Execute:

```
SELECT * FROM flightdata LIMIT 100;
```

This query will return just the first 100 rows from the external table. You should see results similar to Figure 6-13.

flightdata.year	flightdata.quarter	flightdata.month	flightdata.dayofmonth	flightdata.dayofweek	flightdata.fligh
2014	1	1	1	3	2014-01-01
2014	1	1	2	4	2014-01-02
2014	1	1	3	5	2014-01-03
2014	1	1	4	6	2014-01-04
2014	1	1	5	7	2014-01-05
2014	1	1	6	1	2014-01-06

Figure 6-13. The results of querying the first 100 rows from the flightdata external table.

Creating an Internal Table

Now let's look at creating an internal table from the data contained in our flightdata external table. Because an internal table will represent a copy of the data contained in the external table, a typical reason you create one is to change the storage format from the raw format used at ingest to one that is more performant for analytic queries. For Hive, there are a few options, but ORC is one of the preferred formats.

More About ORC

If you're curious about the ORC file format, you can find a comprehensive description in the Apache Hive wiki (*http://bit.ly/ 2nK72NV*).

In the steps that follow, we will use a different approach to run our HQL queries. We will use SSH and the Hive shell. If you prefer to keep using the Ambari Hive View, you absolutely can.

1. SSH into your HDInsight cluster (recall this means running something akin to `"ssh [username]@[clustername]-ssh.azurehdinsight.net"`).

2. When prompted, enter the password for your user.

3. At the shell, type **hive** to launch the Hive shell.

4. Copy the following script to create the schema for an internal table stored using the ORC format. Be sure to modify the URL in the location so it points to the default Azure Storage account.

5. Paste your modified script into the Hive shell and press Enter to execute it.

```
CREATE EXTERNAL TABLE flightdataorc
(
Year INT,
Quarter INT,
Month INT,
DayofMonth INT,
DayOfWeek STRING,
FlightDate STRING,
UniqueCarrier STRING,
AirlineID STRING,
Carrier STRING,
TailNum STRING,
FlightNum STRING,
OriginAirportID STRING,
OriginAirportSeqID STRING,
OriginCityMarketID STRING,
Origin STRING,
OriginCityName1 STRING,
OriginCityName2 STRING,
OriginState STRING,
OriginStateFips STRING,
OriginStateName STRING,
OriginWac STRING,
DestAirportID STRING,
DestAirportSeqID STRING,
DestCityMarketID STRING,
Dest STRING,
DestCityName1 STRING,
DestCityName2 STRING,
DestState STRING,
DestStateFips STRING,
DestStateName STRING,
DestWac STRING,
CRSDepTime INT,
```

```
        DepTime INT,
        DepDelay INT,
        DepDelayMinutes INT,
        DepDel15 BOOLEAN,
        DepartureDelayGroups INT,
        DepTimeBlk STRING,
        TaxiOut INT,
        WheelsOff INT,
        WheelsOn INT,
        TaxiIn INT,
        CRSArrTime INT,
        ArrTime INT,
        ArrDelay INT,
        ArrDelayMinutes INT,
        ArrDel15 BOOLEAN,
        ArrivalDelayGroups INT,
        ArrTimeBlk STRING,
        Cancelled BOOLEAN,
        CancellationCode STRING,
        Diverted BOOLEAN,
        CRSElapsedTime INT,
        ActualElapsedTime INT,
        AirTime INT,
        Flights INT,
        Distance INT,
        DistanceGroup INT,
        CarrierDelay INT,
        WeatherDelay INT,
        NASDelay INT,
        SecurityDelay INT,
        LateAircraftDelay INT,
        FirstDepTime INT,
        TotalAddGTime INT,
        LongestAddGTime INT,
        DivAirportLandings BOOLEAN,
        DivReachedDest BOOLEAN,
        DivActualElapsedTime INT
        )
        ROW FORMAT DELIMITED
        FIELDS TERMINATED BY ','
        STORED AS ORC
        LOCATION 'wasbs://solspark1612@sollianceanalytics2.blob.core.windows.net
        /flightdata_orc';
```

You should see output similar to the following after your script runs:

```
OK
Time taken: 2.944 seconds
```

Let's recap what we accomplished in this script. In the STORED AS line we specified ORC so that the data is stored using ORC instead of plain text. Also, you modified the LOCATION to point to your default Azure Storage account blob container and sub-folder path.

```
STORED AS ORC
LOCATION
'wasbs://solspark1612@sollianceanalytics2.blob.core.windows.net/flightdata_orc';
```

This script only created the metadata describing the table. Now we need to actually copy the data from the external table into this internal table.

To accomplish the copy, run the following script in your Hive session:

```
INSERT OVERWRITE TABLE flightdataorc SELECT * FROM flightdata;
```

After a few minutes, your internal table should contain a copy of all the data from the raw CSV files represented by the external table, except stored in the binary columnar format ORC.

Did You Know?

Microsoft engaged with the community to design the Optimized Row Columnar (ORC) format.

After the insert query completes, you now have a table ready for some initial analytics querying, which we will cover in the next chapter.

Batch Processing with Pig on HDInsight

Apache Pig is a platform for producing data processing programs using a scripting language known as Pig Latin. It provides a simpler alternative to programming complex MapReduce applications in Java.

We will not cover Pig in detail in this book, except to say that if you have become familiar from the previous section with how to set up Hadoop on HDInsight and are comfortable connecting to the head node using SSH to run Hive, then running Pig should be familiar territory for you: you basically run the Pig command at the SSH terminal instead of Hive.

Want More Pig?

For a comprehensive overview of running Pig on HDInsight, see the Microsoft Azure documentation (*http://bit.ly/2n81E3N*).

Batch Processing with Spark on HDInsight

Apache Spark running on HDInsight provides a few options one could use for batch processing. At the lowest level lies Spark Core and the RDD API, which lets you perform parallel operations on Spark's distributed data. Atop this sits the Spark SQL module, which provides the DataFrame API and DataSet API as well as support for issuing SQL queries directly against the DataFrame API.

These higher-level abstractions prove useful in batch processing both because they simplify the development effort (as they are more expressive) and because they often perform better than the raw RDD APIs (because they include extra information used in optimizing queries before they execute). In this book, we'll focus on Spark SQL and its constituent DataFrame API. We will introduce batch processing with DataFrame in this chapter and explore its support for SQL querying in the next.

So what is a `DataFrame`? Simply put, it is a distributed collection of data organized into named columns (notice we said named columns only, not named and typed columns).

A `DataFrame` is created from one of a variety of sources. Parquet files are the default data source, but the complete list of built-in sources includes:

- Parquet
- JSON
- ORC
- Text files
- Hive tables
- JDBC sources

Spark Packages

There are many more sources available than just those that are built in. See the Spark Packages website (*https://spark-packages.org/*) for libraries you can use to interact with other data sources.

For an HDInsight cluster, you are likely reading flat files either from the Azure Storage account associated with your cluster, an attached Azure Storage account, or an Azure Data Lake Store (see Figure 6-14).

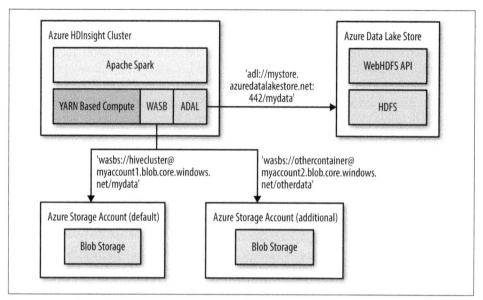

Figure 6-14. Examples of accessing files stored in Azure from Spark on HDInsight.

You may recall from Chapter 5 that when we want to interact with Spark in a program, we always start with the `SparkContext`.

To use Spark SQL and the DataFrame API, we use one of two other contexts that wraps the `SparkContext`: the `SQLContext` or the `HiveContext`. They both provide the same functionality, but the `HiveContext` provides extra support for working with data stored in Apache Hive.

In most situations where you run a Spark program, an instance of `SQLContext/Hive Context` has already been created for you in addition to the base `SparkCon text`. When reading from sources you use an instance of `DataFrameReader`, which is accessed from the `SQLContext` via the `read` method (`sqlContext.read`). This part gets a little confusing because there are multiple ways to get at the same `DataReader` for a particular source, so let's list them both so it's easy to compare. Each of the built-in sources has a helper method that simplifies the syntax:

```
sqlContext.read.parquet("path/to/files")
sqlContext.read.json(path/to/files")
sqlContext.read.orc("path/to/files")
sqlContext.read.jdbc(url, tableName, properties)
sqlContext.read.text("path/to/files")
sqlContext.read.table("hiveTableNameOrtempTableName")
```

Alternately, you can specify the data source format by using the `format` method, which can take the full type name or its short name such as:

```
sqlContext.read.format("org.apache.spark.sql.parquet").load("path")
sqlContext.read.format("parquet").load("path") //short format
```

The return value of any of these calls is a DataFrame instance. With a DataFrame in hand, you can use Spark SQL's language integrated query format (if you're familiar with LINQ in .NET, this should be very familiar), or issue SQL against it. We'll show the latter in the next chapter, and explore the former here. You can use your LINQ-based script to transform the data as you see fit, and then write the results back out.

DataFrame Operations

For a complete example of the types of operations you apply against a DataFrame, see the Spark documentation (*http://bit.ly/2mQAbSy*).

The object used to write your results back somewhere is a DataFrameWriter. When you're writing to sources your format options are similar to reading, except you are using a DataWriter instance acquired off of a DataFrame instance you wish to persist. The examples of this approach using the helper methods are as follows:

```
dataFrame.write.parquet("path/to/files")
dataFrame.write.json("path/to/files")
dataFramet.write.orc("path/to/files")
dataFrame.write.jdbc(url, tableName, properties)
dataFrame.write.text("path/to/files")
```

Spark SQL also has a notion of external and internal tables. External tables are effectively created as per-session temporary tables, using dataFrame.registerTempTable("tableName") from a DataFrame instance sourced from either a SQLContext or a HiveContext. The schema describing the table is all that Spark really maintains, and when the table is deleted or expires with the session, the underlying data remains untouched, albeit the schema is lost.

Spark SQL's notion of internal tables has everything to do with creating managed tables in Hive. You can create permanent, managed tables in Hive (that other Hive clients can query without using Spark) using saveAsTable from a DataFrame instance. Only when you are working with a HiveContext can DataFrames be saved as persistent tables; DataFrame sources from a SQLContext cannot be saved as Hive tables. Here is an example of DataFrame created from an existing RDD; note that the DataFrame was created using the HiveContext:

```
val flightsDF = hiveContext.createDataFrame(resultRDD)
flightsDF.write.saveAsTable("FlightDelaysSummaryRDD")
```

DataSet API

The DataSet API aims to unify the benefits of the RDD APIs with the benefits of the DataFrame API. As of Spark 1.6.1, the DataSet API is experimental and separate from DataSet. There is a long-term goal of unifying them in the early releases of Spark 2.0. One way to quickly understand the difference between the two is to describe a DataFrame as consisting of a collection of Row objects, where each field in the Row is accessed via generic dictionary-like access, and the type is applied on access. A DataSet, however, aims to provide strong typing to the collection of objects at compile time, such that each item in the collection is an instance of a class with typed properties that match the schema of the underlying data. Put another way, in the future a DataFrame will simply be an extension of DataSet where each collection element is of type Row, but you will tend to work with DataSets of Person or DataSets of Flights, for example.

With these basic concepts in mind, let's look at applying the DataFrame API to batch processing the flight delay data. We will not cover how to deploy HDInsight with Spark in this section. If you need a refresher, see Chapter 5 where we went step by step to deploy Spark on HDInsight.

Batch Processing Blue Yonder Airports Data

Now that you have your HDInsight cluster provisioned, make sure that you have uploaded the flight delay data (see Chapter 2) to the Azure Storage account or the Azure Data Lake Store that you have associated with your cluster and from which you will be querying. In our steps that follow, we uploaded the data to the path */flightdata* in both data stores.

There are two primary modes of executing Spark SQL queries. You can SSH into the head node of the cluster and run your queries using the Spark shell, or you can use a browser to access a Jupyter notebook for querying. In this section, we will show examples using the former.

The flight delay data set has a few real-world challenges that we will show you how to address as well. Here is the gist of the challenges and how we will address them:

Challenges with the data set:

1. Each CSV file has a header row, which needs to be used to drive the schema.

2. The OriginCityName and DestCityName fields themselves have a comma in their value (e.g., "city, state"), which causes the fields after them to not align to the headers.

3. After processing the data set, we have an extra phantom column with a name of "" (empty string). We need to remove this column.

4. The source data is in CSV, but we'd prefer to use a more performant format.

Solution to the challenges:

1. Using spark-csv, you can infer the schema from the files (which uses the header rows for the column names and then makes passes over the data to infer the column data type).

2. The spark-csv parser recognizes the nested comma correctly, so it's not a problem in this case.

3. Create a new data frame from the original that drops the column with the name "".

4. For Spark, we can migrate the data into ORC for improved compression and query performance.

Creating an External Table

In order to use the Spark SQL API in Scala, we will SSH into the head node of our HDInsight cluster. Recall this means running a command similar to the following:

```
ssh <user>@<clusterName>-ssh.azurehdinsight.net
```

You will be prompted for your password and then you should be ready to run the following commands.

To run Scala code, we can use the `spark-shell` command. Note that because we want to use the spark-csv package to help us process the flight delay data CSV files, we need to launch it using the package option. In your SSH session, run the following:

```
$SPARK_HOME/bin/spark-shell
  --packages com.databricks:spark-csv_2.11:1.4.0
```

This will ensure that our Spark session has access to the spark-csv package (and takes care of automatically downloading it from the Spark Packages repository).

Once Spark Shell has started up, run the following code (be sure to modify the string provided to the `load` method to match your environment):

```
val flightData = sqlContext.read.format("com.databricks.spark.csv").
option("header","true").
option("inferSchema","true").
load("adl://[datalakestore].azuredatalakestore.net:443/flightdata")
```

This creates a `DataFrame` over the flight data, using the spark-csv library to parse the data, ignoring header rows, and inferring the schema from the header rows and by sampling the data to infer the data types. In our case we loaded it from Azure Data Lake Store, but you can change the parameter string passed into the `load` method to use Azure Storage instead:

```
val flightData = sqlContext.read.format("com.databricks.spark.csv").
option("header","true").
option("inferSchema","true").
load("wasbs://[container]@[acct].blob.core.windows.net/flightdata")
```

Next, spot-check that your data loaded OK by taking a preview look at it:

```
flightData.select("FlightDate","Carrier","OriginCityName",
"DestCityName").show()
```

The results of this should appear similar to the following:

```
+----------+-------+---------------+---------------+
|FlightDate|Carrier|OriginCityName|   DestCityName|
+----------+-------+---------------+---------------+
|2014-01-01|     AA|   New York, NY|Los Angeles, CA|
|2014-01-02|     AA|   New York, NY|Los Angeles, CA|
|2014-01-03|     AA|   New York, NY|Los Angeles, CA|
|2014-01-04|     AA|   New York, NY|Los Angeles, CA|
|2014-01-05|     AA|   New York, NY|Los Angeles, CA|
|2014-01-06|     AA|   New York, NY|Los Angeles, CA|
|2014-01-07|     AA|   New York, NY|Los Angeles, CA|
|2014-01-08|     AA|   New York, NY|Los Angeles, CA|
|2014-01-09|     AA|   New York, NY|Los Angeles, CA|
|2014-01-10|     AA|   New York, NY|Los Angeles, CA|
|2014-01-11|     AA|   New York, NY|Los Angeles, CA|
|2014-01-12|     AA|   New York, NY|Los Angeles, CA|
|2014-01-13|     AA|   New York, NY|Los Angeles, CA|
|2014-01-14|     AA|   New York, NY|Los Angeles, CA|
|2014-01-15|     AA|   New York, NY|Los Angeles, CA|
|2014-01-16|     AA|   New York, NY|Los Angeles, CA|
|2014-01-17|     AA|   New York, NY|Los Angeles, CA|
|2014-01-18|     AA|   New York, NY|Los Angeles, CA|
|2014-01-19|     AA|   New York, NY|Los Angeles, CA|
|2014-01-20|     AA|   New York, NY|Los Angeles, CA|
+----------+-------+---------------+---------------+
only showing top 20 rows
```

Next, take a look at the schema that was inferred by running the following:

```
flightData.printSchema
```

The output of this should appear as follows:

```
root
 |-- Year: integer (nullable = true)
 |-- Quarter: integer (nullable = true)
 |-- Month: integer (nullable = true)
 |-- DayofMonth: integer (nullable = true)
 |-- DayOfWeek: integer (nullable = true)
```

```
|-- FlightDate: string (nullable = true)
|-- UniqueCarrier: string (nullable = true)
|-- AirlineID: integer (nullable = true)
|-- Carrier: string (nullable = true)
|-- TailNum: string (nullable = true)
|-- FlightNum: integer (nullable = true)
|-- OriginAirportID: integer (nullable = true)
|-- OriginAirportSeqID: integer (nullable = true)
|-- OriginCityMarketID: integer (nullable = true)
|-- Origin: string (nullable = true)
|-- OriginCityName: string (nullable = true)
|-- OriginState: string (nullable = true)
|-- OriginStateFips: integer (nullable = true)
|-- OriginStateName: string (nullable = true)
|-- OriginWac: integer (nullable = true)
|-- DestAirportID: integer (nullable = true)
|-- DestAirportSeqID: integer (nullable = true)
|-- DestCityMarketID: integer (nullable = true)
|-- Dest: string (nullable = true)
|-- DestCityName: string (nullable = true)
|-- DestState: string (nullable = true)
|-- DestStateFips: integer (nullable = true)
|-- DestStateName: string (nullable = true)
|-- DestWac: integer (nullable = true)
|-- CRSDepTime: integer (nullable = true)
|-- DepTime: integer (nullable = true)
|-- DepDelay: double (nullable = true)
|-- DepDelayMinutes: double (nullable = true)
|-- DepDel15: double (nullable = true)
|-- DepartureDelayGroups: integer (nullable = true)
|-- DepTimeBlk: string (nullable = true)
|-- TaxiOut: double (nullable = true)
|-- WheelsOff: integer (nullable = true)
|-- WheelsOn: integer (nullable = true)
|-- TaxiIn: double (nullable = true)
|-- CRSArrTime: integer (nullable = true)
|-- ArrTime: integer (nullable = true)
|-- ArrDelay: double (nullable = true)
|-- ArrDelayMinutes: double (nullable = true)
|-- ArrDel15: double (nullable = true)
|-- ArrivalDelayGroups: integer (nullable = true)
|-- ArrTimeBlk: string (nullable = true)
|-- Cancelled: double (nullable = true)
|-- CancellationCode: string (nullable = true)
|-- Diverted: double (nullable = true)
|-- CRSElapsedTime: double (nullable = true)
|-- ActualElapsedTime: double (nullable = true)
|-- AirTime: double (nullable = true)
|-- Flights: double (nullable = true)
|-- Distance: double (nullable = true)
|-- DistanceGroup: integer (nullable = true)
|-- CarrierDelay: double (nullable = true)
```

```
|-- WeatherDelay: double (nullable = true)
|-- NASDelay: double (nullable = true)
|-- SecurityDelay: double (nullable = true)
|-- LateAircraftDelay: double (nullable = true)
|-- FirstDepTime: integer (nullable = true)
|-- TotalAddGTime: double (nullable = true)
|-- LongestAddGTime: double (nullable = true)
|-- DivAirportLandings: integer (nullable = true)
|-- DivReachedDest: double (nullable = true)
|-- DivActualElapsedTime: double (nullable = true)
|-- DivArrDelay: double (nullable = true)
|-- DivDistance: double (nullable = true)
|-- Div1Airport: string (nullable = true)
|-- Div1AirportID: integer (nullable = true)
|-- Div1AirportSeqID: integer (nullable = true)
|-- Div1WheelsOn: integer (nullable = true)
|-- Div1TotalGTime: double (nullable = true)
|-- Div1LongestGTime: double (nullable = true)
|-- Div1WheelsOff: integer (nullable = true)
|-- Div1TailNum: string (nullable = true)
|-- Div2Airport: string (nullable = true)
|-- Div2AirportID: integer (nullable = true)
|-- Div2AirportSeqID: integer (nullable = true)
|-- Div2WheelsOn: integer (nullable = true)
|-- Div2TotalGTime: double (nullable = true)
|-- Div2LongestGTime: double (nullable = true)
|-- Div2WheelsOff: integer (nullable = true)
|-- Div2TailNum: string (nullable = true)
|-- Div3Airport: string (nullable = true)
|-- Div3AirportID: integer (nullable = true)
|-- Div3AirportSeqID: integer (nullable = true)
|-- Div3WheelsOn: integer (nullable = true)
|-- Div3TotalGTime: double (nullable = true)
|-- Div3LongestGTime: double (nullable = true)
|-- Div3WheelsOff: string (nullable = true)
|-- Div3TailNum: string (nullable = true)
|-- Div4Airport: string (nullable = true)
|-- Div4AirportID: string (nullable = true)
|-- Div4AirportSeqID: string (nullable = true)
|-- Div4WheelsOn: string (nullable = true)
|-- Div4TotalGTime: string (nullable = true)
|-- Div4LongestGTime: string (nullable = true)
|-- Div4WheelsOff: string (nullable = true)
|-- Div4TailNum: string (nullable = true)
|-- Div5Airport: string (nullable = true)
|-- Div5AirportID: string (nullable = true)
|-- Div5AirportSeqID: string (nullable = true)
|-- Div5WheelsOn: string (nullable = true)
|-- Div5TotalGTime: string (nullable = true)
|-- Div5LongestGTime: string (nullable = true)
|-- Div5WheelsOff: string (nullable = true)
```

```
|-- Div5TailNum: string (nullable = true)
|-- : string (nullable = true)
```

The astute reader should notice the last column that was inferred does not really exist in the source data—it is simply an artifact resulting from how each line in the flight delay data ends in a comma. So drop this extra column (which is named empty string, "") by running:

```
val flightDataCleaned = flightData.drop("")
```

Now, `flightDataCleaned` represents a well-cleaned external table. Let's save this as a managed table in a format that is more performant than text and that will also save the schema. Run the following to save a copy of the data in the ORC format (be sure to modify the string passed to `save` so it accurately targets your Data Lake Store or Azure Storage account):

```
flightDataCleaned.write.format("orc").
save("adl://[lake].azuredatalakestore.net:443/flightdataorcspark")
```

Congratulations! You've successfully batch processed your first set of CSV data using Spark SQL! You are now ready to perform further processing on the data or perform analytic querying as we will demonstrate in the next chapter.

Batch Processing with SQL Data Warehouse

Azure SQL Data Warehouse is a massively parallel processing (MPP) distributed database system, based on the SQL Server relational database engine. In fact, it uses specialized instances of Azure SQL Database as the compute nodes in the underlying cluster. SQL Data Warehouse spreads your data across many shared-nothing storage and processing units. SQL Data Warehouse provides its functionality as a Platform-as-a-Service (PaaS) function, where your need to manage any of the nodes that make up the cluster is completely removed (in fact, you have no way of accessing these nodes directly). To query SQL Data Warehouse, you use T-SQL.

From a high level, Azure SQL Data Warehouse consists of four main elements (Figure 6-15):

Control node

> The control node manages and optimizes queries. It is the frontend that interacts with all applications and connections (i.e., it is ultimately what you connect to when querying SQL Data Warehouse). The control node is powered by SQL Database. When you submit a T-SQL query to SQL Data Warehouse, the control node transforms it into separate queries that run on each compute node in parallel.

Compute nodes

The compute nodes are SQL databases that store your data and process your query in parallel. After processing, the compute nodes pass the results back to the control node. To finish the query execution, the control node aggregates the results and returns the final result to client application.

Storage

Just like for Hive, SQL Data Warehouse has a notion of external and internal table storage. Its internal storage relies on Azure Premium Disk Storage, where each disk (e.g., a page file in Premium Storage) is directly attached to a single compute node, and that data is locally redundant. Unlike Hive, however, SQL Data WareHouse is a database and the internal data is completely managed by the database engine and stored in SQL Server's own format for data files. Owing to a feature called PolyBase, SQL Data Warehouse can also attach standard Azure Storage blobs directly and project a schema on read over files in Blob Storage. You access this functionality by creating external tables.

Data Movement Service

Data Movement Service (DMS) is a Windows service that runs alongside SQL Database on all the nodes and is responsible for moving (e.g., shuffling) data between the nodes. DMS gives the compute nodes access to data they need for joins and aggregations.

In addition to enabling access to Azure Storage from SQL Data Warehouse queries, PolyBase is the recommended tool for loading and extracting large volumes of data, as it is designed to leverage the massively parallel processing architecture of SQL Data Warehouse. PolyBase supports many of the common flat file formats, including delimited text (UTF-8 only), ORC, RCFILE, and Parquet.

What makes SQL Data Warehouse unique among the batch processing options in Azure is that you can pause, and also easily resume, the compute. When you do so, the compute control and compute nodes are effectively deallocated, but your data remains in storage. If you are using internal table storage, you need to resume the SQL Data Warehouse instance to query the data. However, if you are using external table storage, then you can use the tool of your choice to query and interact with the data stored in Azure Blob Storage. When your SQL Data Warehouse instance is paused, you only pay for the storage used and not the compute (which can create significant savings for bursty batch processing workloads).

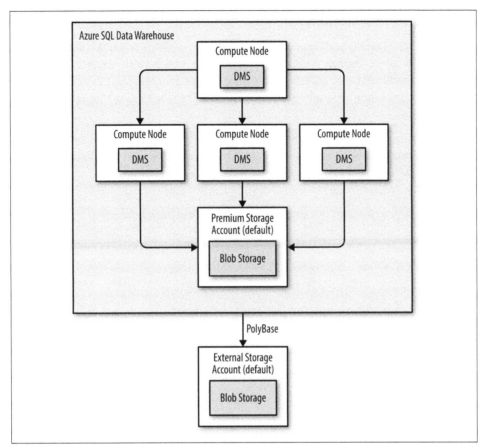

Figure 6-15. Overview of the main elements in SQL Data Warehouse.

The capacity of the SQL Data Warehouse instance is measured in Data Warehouse units (which is a blended measure of CPU, network, memory, and I/O capacity). While your cluster is running, you can adjust the resources available to it by adding or removing Data Warehouse units.

In addition to external and internal tables, SQL Data Warehouse supports many of the features you would expect from its SQL Server heritage, including indexes on tables (both clustered and nonclustered b-tree indexes as well as clustered columnar indexes), temporary tables, partitioned tables, stored procedures, user-defined functions (returning a scalar value only), nonmaterialized views, database schemas, and databases.

Using SQL Data Warehouse

Given that SQL Data Warehouse provides PolyBase, which lets you load flat file data ingested into Blob Storage, SQL Data Warehouse shines with Extract, Load, and Transform workloads that take the data from Azure Storage, load it into SQL Data Warehouse's premium storage, and perform the transformations after the fact as desired.

In this section, we will explore how to provision and than use an instance of SQL Data Warehouse to create an external table from which we load the flight delay data into a SQL Data Warehouse internal table, preparing it for subsequent transformation or analytics.

To begin, let's provision an instance of Azure SQL Data Warehouse:

1. Log in to the Azure Portal (*https://portal.azure.com*).
2. Select New→Data + Storage→SQL Data Warehouse.
3. Provide a name for the SQL Data Warehouse database.
4. Set your subscription and resource group as desired.
5. Leave the select source set to "Blank database."
6. Select Server.
7. Create a new server or use an existing server as desired.
8. Set the performance to 100 DWU. (You will not need any more for this example.)
9. Select Create.

Your Azure SQL Data Warehouse should be ready within a few minutes.

Batch Processing Blue Yonder Airports Data

For the following steps that issue queries against SQL Data Warehouse, you can use either Visual Studio 2015 or SQL Server Management Studio. The latter is a free download from Microsoft (*http://go.microsoft.com/fwlink/?LinkID=824938*) and at the moment offers better support for SQL Data Warehouse, so we will use it in the steps that follow. You will need a Windows-based machine for these steps (albeit you are very likely to replicate these steps using the tool of your choice on any operating system that can make connections to SQL Database).

In the context of SQL Data Warehouse, the flight delay data set has a few real-world challenges that we will show you how to address as well. Here is the gist of the challenges and how we will address them:

Challenges with the data set:

---

1. Each CSV file has a header row, which needs to be skipped over.

2. The OriginCityName and DestCityName fields themselves have a comma in their value (e.g., "city, state"), which causes the fields after them to not align to the headers.

3. The source data is in CSV, but we'd prefer to use a more performant format.

Solution to the challenges:

1. You can tell SQL Data Warehouse to skip the first row of each file by defining a `filter` clause in the query (i.e., that ignores rows having a value present in the column header) that loads the data from the external table into the internal table.

2. You need to specify the `string_delimiter` to be a double quote when defining the external file format used by the external table.

3. We can load the data into an internal table (stored on Azure Premium Storage) for improved compression and query performance.

Storing the Credentials to Azure Storage

In this section, we will begin the process of preparing the flight delay data by creating a data source for the Azure Storage account that contains the flight delay CSV files.

1. Launch SQL Server Management Studio, and in the "Connect to Server" dialog, enter the name of the server hosting your SQL Data Warehouse in Azure.

2. Set the authentication to SQL Server Authentication and provide the username and password you entered when provisioning the server.

3. Select Connect (see Figure 6-16).

Figure 6-16. Connecting to SQL Data Warehouse.

4. From the File menu, select New→New Query with Current Connection.

5. In the query document that appears, paste the following script.

```
CREATE MASTER KEY;

CREATE DATABASE SCOPED CREDENTIAL AzureStorageCreds
WITH IDENTITY = '[identityName]'
,    Secret = '[azureStorageAccountKey]'
;

CREATE EXTERNAL DATA SOURCE azure_storage
WITH
(
    TYPE = HADOOP
,   LOCATION =
'wasbs://[containername]@[accountname].blob.core.windows.net/[path]'
,   CREDENTIAL = AzureStorageCreds
);
```

You will need to modify and replace the variables within this script to suit your environment:

[identityName]

Replace this with any label you want to use for the credential storing the key to your Azure Storage account.

[azureStorageAccountKey]

Replace this with the key of your Azure Storage account.

[containername]

Replace this with the name of the container in Blob Storage that contains your flight data files.

[accountname]

Replace this with the name of your Azure Storage account.

[path]

Replace this with the subfolder path to the folder where your flight data files are located.

With this portion of the script in place, you have effectively stored the connection string to your Azure Storage account within SQL Data Warehouse. Next, you will define the structure of the data it contains.

Below the SQL you already added, add the following lines:

```
CREATE EXTERNAL FILE FORMAT text_file_format
WITH
(
```

```
        FORMAT_TYPE = DELIMITEDTEXT
,   FORMAT_OPTIONS  (
                        FIELD_TERMINATOR =',',
            STRING_DELIMITER = '"',
                        USE_TYPE_DEFAULT = TRUE
                )
);
```

This script defines the format of the files that will be read. Think of it as simply configuration telling the parser used by SQL Data Warehouse how to interpret the flight data CSV files. The FORMAT_TYPE is set to DELIMITEDTEXT to indicate it is a delimited text file. The FIELD_TERMINATOR is set to a comma to indicate that the values in a line of text are separated by commas. Setting STRING_DELIMITER to a double quote (") helps with the situation when string values in a line of text have commas within them. For example, in a row the OriginCityName may appear like:

"abc", "San Diego, CA", "def"

Without the STRING_TERMINATOR being properly set to a double quote, the comma between San Diego and CA would accidentally be treated as a field terminator, so the single string value "San Diego, CA" would be interpreted as two strings—"San Diego" and "CA"—which is obviously not desired.

Finally the USE_TYPE_DEFAULT is set to TRUE to indicate the default value for the data type should be used when a value is missing (e.g., a numeric type would default to 0, a string column would default to the empty string "").

CREATE EXTERNAL FILE FORMAT

For more details on all the options supported by this statement, see *https://msdn.microsoft.com/library/dn935026.aspx*.

Now you are ready to define the schema for the external table. Below the SQL script for the file format, add the following:

```
CREATE EXTERNAL TABLE FlightDelays
(
[Year] varchar(255),
[Quarter] varchar(255),
[Month] varchar(255),
[DayofMonth] varchar(255),
[DayOfWeek] varchar(255),
FlightDate varchar(255),
UniqueCarrier varchar(255),
AirlineID varchar(255),
Carrier varchar(255),
TailNum varchar(255),
```

```
FlightNum varchar(255),
OriginAirportID varchar(255),
OriginAirportSeqID varchar(255),
OriginCityMarketID varchar(255),
Origin varchar(255),
OriginCityName varchar(255),
OriginState varchar(255),
OriginStateFips varchar(255),
OriginStateName varchar(255),
OriginWac varchar(255),
DestAirportID varchar(255),
DestAirportSeqID varchar(255),
DestCityMarketID varchar(255),
Dest varchar(255),
DestCityName varchar(255),
DestState varchar(255),
DestStateFips varchar(255),
DestStateName varchar(255),
DestWac varchar(255),
CRSDepTime varchar(128),
DepTime varchar(128),
DepDelay varchar(128),
DepDelayMinutes varchar(128),
DepDel15 varchar(255),
DepartureDelayGroups varchar(255),
DepTimeBlk varchar(255),
TaxiOut varchar(255),
WheelsOff varchar(255),
WheelsOn varchar(255),
TaxiIn varchar(255),
CRSArrTime varchar(128),
ArrTime varchar(128),
ArrDelay varchar(255),
ArrDelayMinutes varchar(255),
ArrDel15 varchar(255),
ArrivalDelayGroups varchar(255),
ArrTimeBlk varchar(255),
Cancelled varchar(255),
CancellationCode varchar(255),
Diverted varchar(255),
CRSElapsedTime varchar(255),
ActualElapsedTime varchar(255),
AirTime varchar(255),
Flights varchar(255),
Distance varchar(255),
DistanceGroup varchar(255),
CarrierDelay varchar(255),
WeatherDelay varchar(255),
NASDelay varchar(255),
SecurityDelay varchar(255),
LateAircraftDelay varchar(255),
FirstDepTime varchar(255),
```

```
TotalAddGTime varchar(255),
LongestAddGTime varchar(255),
DivAirportLandings varchar(255),
DivReachedDest varchar(255),
DivActualElapsedTime varchar(255),
DivArrDelay varchar(255),
DivDistance varchar(255),
Div1Airport varchar(255),
Div1AirportID varchar(255),
Div1AirportSeqID varchar(255),
Div1WheelsOn varchar(255),
Div1TotalGTime varchar(255),
Div1LongestGTime varchar(255),
Div1WheelsOff varchar(255),
Div1TailNum varchar(255),
Div2Airport varchar(255),
Div2AirportID varchar(255),
Div2AirportSeqID varchar(255),
Div2WheelsOn varchar(255),
Div2TotalGTime varchar(255),
Div2LongestGTime varchar(255),
Div2WheelsOff varchar(255),
Div2TailNum varchar(255),
Div3Airport varchar(255),
Div3AirportID varchar(255),
Div3AirportSeqID varchar(255),
Div3WheelsOn varchar(255),
Div3TotalGTime varchar(255),
Div3LongestGTime varchar(255),
Div3WheelsOff varchar(255),
Div3TailNum varchar(255),
Div4Airport varchar(255),
Div4AirportID varchar(255),
Div4AirportSeqID varchar(255),
Div4WheelsOn varchar(255),
Div4TotalGTime varchar(255),
Div4LongestGTime varchar(255),
Div4WheelsOff varchar(255),
Div4TailNum varchar(255),
Div5Airport varchar(255),
Div5AirportID varchar(255),
Div5AirportSeqID varchar(255),
Div5WheelsOn varchar(255),
Div5TotalGTime varchar(255),
Div5LongestGTime varchar(255),
Div5WheelsOff varchar(255),
Div5TailNum varchar(255)
)
WITH
(
LOCATION = '/',
DATA_SOURCE = azure_storage,
```

```
FILE_FORMAT = text_file_format,
REJECT_TYPE = value,
REJECT_VALUE = 100000
);
```

The CREATE EXTERNAL TABLE syntax should look familiar all the way up to the WITH clause. Let's examine each of the parameters in the WITH clause. LOCATION provides a path beneath the container and subfolder path that you specified in the external data source configuration. DATA_SOURCE is how you tell SQL Data Warehouse to use the data source you configured previously. FILE_FORMAT is how you apply the file format you defined previously. REJECT_TYPE and REJECT_VALUE collectively define when SQL Data Warehouse aborts processing because the data is not sufficiently aligned with the schema. REJECT_TYPE can have the values of either value or percentage. When specifying a REJECT_TYPE of value, you need to provide a number to REJECT_VALUE that represents the fixed numeric threshold above which the query processing will be aborted. When specifying a REJECT_TYPE of percentage, you must provide a value between 0 and 100, to indicate the percentage of rows that must fail before the query is aborted. If you specify a REJECT_TYPE of percentage you also need to specify REJECT_SAMPLE_VALUE with an integer that indicates the number of rows SQL Data Warehouse needs to have considered before it starts to calculate the percentage.

CREATE EXTERNAL TABLE

For the complete documentation on the CREATE EXTERNAL TABLE syntax in SQL Data Warehouse, see the Microsoft documentation (*https://msdn.microsoft.com/en-us/library/dn935021.aspx*).

Now, press the Execute button in SQL Server Management Studio to run this query.

When it completes, your external table is ready. Try the following query to see a sample of the data:

```
SELECT Top 100 * FROM FlightDelays;
```

Now you are ready to use this external table as a source from which to load an internal table. In the same query script (or a new one), copy and paste the following SQL:

```
CREATE TABLE FlightDelaysStaging
WITH (DISTRIBUTION = ROUND_ROBIN)
AS
SELECT * FROM FlightDelays
WHERE [Year] <> 'Year';
```

In this script, we are creating a new internal table (notice this is indicated by the absence of the EXTERNAL keyword). We are also setting the DISTRIBUTION to ROUND_ROBIN, which will basically mean that rows will be distributed among all the underlying storage distributions in a round-robin fashion. The AS keyword lets us specify a query, and in this case we select all the data in the FlightDelays external table except those whose Year column has a value of the string `'Year'`. This is how we can make sure that the header rows of each CSV are not copied over into our internal table.

CREATE TABLE

For the complete documentation on the CREATE TABLE syntax in SQL Data Warehouse, see *http://bit.ly/2nnE2KH*.

Run the SQL script you just added. To verify that you do not have any header values in the row data, run the following script:

```
SELECT [Year], Count(*) FROM FlightDelaysStaging Group By [Year];
```

The results should only show year values in the Year column of the results, similar to Figure 6-17 (the query may take a few moments to complete).

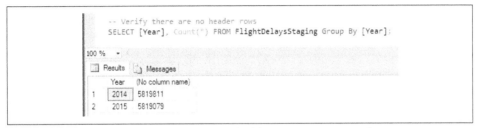

Figure 6-17. Results of querying an internal table in SQL Data Warehouse.

Congratulations! You've just performed your first ELT operation using PolyBase to load an internal table from data stored in Azure Storage. Your data in the internal table is now ready for further processing or analytic querying, as we will demonstrate in the next chapter.

Batch Processing with Data Lake Analytics

Azure Data Lake Analytics provides a Platform-as-a-Service approach to performing analytics on big data. In fact, of all of the batch processing options presented in this chapter, it is the one service that is most fully a PaaS solution because your interface with Data Lake Analytics focuses on writing job scripts, running jobs, and managing jobs. You are never exposed to the operational aspects of the distributed architecture running under the covers.

When you run a job with Data Lake Analytics, you control the scale of the compute applied and pay only for the resources you allocated for that particular job. In other words, you are not paying for a cluster that is sitting around waiting for a job to arrive; you pay only when you have a job actually executing.

Data Lake Analytics has its origins in Cosmos, a solution Microsoft uses internally for analytics in Bing, Office 365, Skype, Windows, and Xbox Live, handling queries of tens of thousands of users daily and driving hundreds of petabytes daily across exabytes of data. As a data platform service it provides many of the features you would expect from a data store, including databases, database schemas, views, internal and external tables, indexes, user-defined functions, and stored procedures. It also supports invoking code source from user-provided code modules in the form of .NET assemblies.

It also has some differences from the other processing solutions we have seen so far. For starters, the language used to author jobs is neither largely functional (e.g., Scala in Spark) nor largely declarative (e.g., SQL in SQL Data Warehouse)—it is a hybrid of both. In Azure Data Lake Analytics, you author scripts using a new language called U-SQL, and the idea is that you get the best of both T-SQL and C# worlds. Historically speaking, U-SQL emerged from Scope, a SQL-like language for scale-out data processing that is based on Dryad and used within Microsoft for formulating queries within Cosmos.

We will dive into an example of U-SQL shortly, but before we do, keep in mind it does have some differences from both SQL and C#:

- All keywords such as SELECT have to be in UPPERCASE.
- The type system and expression language inside clauses like SELECT and predicates like WHERE are in C#.
- The data types are the C# types (int, string, double?, etc.)
- The data types use C# NULL semantics, and the comparison operations inside a predicate follow C# syntax (e.g., a == "foo" instead of a = 'foo').
- This also means that the values are full .NET objects, allowing you to easily use any method to operate on the object (e.g., "a,b,c".Split(',')).

Another difference from the other processing solutions is how Azure Data Lake Analytics defines the notion of external tables and managed (aka internal) tables. At the time of this writing, external tables are used for querying data stored in Azure SQL Database, Azure SQL Data Warehouse, and SQL Server running within an Azure virtual machine.

You can use U-SQL to query files stored in Azure Blob Storage and Azure Data Lake Store, but these are defined as queries that are encapsulated in U-SQL views or U-SQL table-valued functions—they do not get the traditional external table representation we have seen with the other options.

Data Lake Analytics refers to internal tables as managed tables. Here, just as for SQL Data Warehouse, managed tables "own" their data. Both the table definition (the metadata) as well as the table data are being managed via the metadata system. The data for managed tables is stored in the default instance of Azure Data Lake Store that is associated with the Azure Data Lake Analytics instance at the time of provisioning. See Figure 6-18.

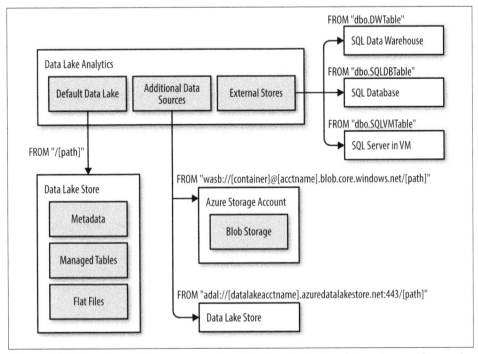

Figure 6-18. Overview of the storage options for Data Lake Analytics along with samples of the FROM clause used to target those sources in U-SQL scripts.

Using Data Lake Analytics

In this section, we will explore how to provision a Data Lake Analytics account, associating it with a Data Lake Store, and show how to schematize and load CSV data from the Data Lake Store, wrap the query in a view, and then query against that view to create a new managed table with a copy of the data.

To begin, let's provision an instance of Azure Data Lake Analytics:

1. Log in to the Azure Portal (*https://portal.azure.com*).
2. Select New→Data + Analytics→Data Lake Analytics.
3. Provide a name for your Data Lake Analytics account.

4. Choose the subscription and resource group as desired.

5. Choose a location (it should be the same as where you provisioned your Azure Data Lake Store or Azure Storage accounts).

6. Select Data Lake Store, and select your existing Data Lake Store or create a new one.

7. Select Create.

Your Azure Data Lake Analytics account should be ready within a few minutes.

Batch Processing Blue Yonder Airports Data

In the context of Azure Data Lake Analytics, the flight delay data set has a few real-world challenges that we will show you how to address as well. Here is the gist of the challenges and how we will address them:

Challenges with the data set:

1. Each CSV file has a header row, which needs to be skipped over.

2. The OriginCityName and DestCityName fields themselves have a comma in their value (e.g., "city, state"), which causes the fields after them to not align to the headers.

3. The source data has a trailing comma after each row.

4. The source data is in CSV, but we'd prefer to use a more performant format.

Solution to the challenges:

1. You can tell Azure Data Lake Analytics to skip the header row in each file by using the text extractor and provide the value of 1 for the skipFirstNRows parameter in the constructor.

2. You need to use the text extractor and provide the value of true for the quoting parameter in the constructor.

3. You need to add an extra field to your schema to capture this phantom column, which you can discard in a subsequent query.

4. We can load the data into a managed table that has a clustered index.

Processing with U-SQL

Let's begin by authoring a U-SQL query that creates a view by applying schema on read over the flight delay data that has been uploaded to the Data Lake Store.

For the following steps that create U-SQL scripts for executing within Data Lake Analytics, you can use either Visual Studio 2015 or the Azure Portal, as we will essentially only be working with a text-based script. We will highlight the steps using the Azure Portal.

Authoring U-SQL with Visual Studio 2015

For instructions on how to use Visual Studio to author and execute a U-SQL script, see the Microsoft Azure documentation (*http://bit.ly/2mQPURv*).

Within the Azure Portal, navigate to your Data Lake Analytics accounts and follow these steps:

1. Select New Job in the command bar.

2. In the New U-SQL Job blade, provide a name for the job. Optionally, set the priority (lower numbers give a job a higher priority to resources over a job with higher priorities in your Data Lake Analytics account) and set the parallelism (note this affects your cost, and for the purposes of this demo even a parallelism of 1 will suffice).

3. Within the text area, paste the following script:

```
DROP VIEW IF EXISTS FlightDelaysView;

CREATE VIEW FlightDelaysView
AS
    EXTRACT Year int,
            Quarter int,
            Month int,
            DayofMonth int,
            [DayOfWeek] int,
            FlightDate string,
            UniqueCarrier string,
            AirlineID int,
            Carrier string,
            TailNum string,
            FlightNum string,
            OriginAirportID int,
            OriginAirportSeqID int,
            OriginCityMarketID int,
            Origin string,
            OriginCityName string,
            OriginState string,
            OriginStateFips string,
            OriginStateName string,
            OriginWac int,
            DestAirportID int,
```

```
DestAirportSeqID int,
DestCityMarketID int,
Dest string,
DestCityName string,
DestState string,
DestStateFips string,
DestStateName string,
DestWac int,
CRSDepTime string,
DepTime string,
DepDelay double?,
DepDelayMinutes double?,
DepDel15 double?,
DepartureDelayGroups string,
DepTimeBlk string,
TaxiOut double?,
WheelsOff string,
WheelsOn string,
TaxiIn double?,
CRSArrTime string,
ArrTime string,
ArrDelay double?,
ArrDelayMinutes double?,
ArrDel15 double?,
ArrivalDelayGroups string,
ArrTimeBlk string,
Cancelled double?,
CancellationCode string,
Diverted double?,
CRSElapsedTime double?,
ActualElapsedTime double?,
AirTime double?,
Flights double?,
Distance double?,
DistanceGroup double?,
CarrierDelay double?,
WeatherDelay double?,
NASDelay double?,
SecurityDelay double?,
LateAircraftDelay double?,
FirstDepTime string,
TotalAddGTime string,
LongestAddGTime string,
DivAirportLandings string,
DivReachedDest string,
DivActualElapsedTime string,
DivArrDelay string,
DivDistance string,
Div1Airport string,
Div1AirportID string,
```

```
                    Div1AirportSeqID string,
                    Div1WheelsOn string,
                    Div1TotalGTime string,
                    Div1LongestGTime string,
                    Div1WheelsOff string,
                    Div1TailNum string,
                    Div2Airport string,
                    Div2AirportID string,
                    Div2AirportSeqID string,
                    Div2WheelsOn string,
                    Div2TotalGTime string,
                    Div2LongestGTime string,
                    Div2WheelsOff string,
                    Div2TailNum string,
                    Div3Airport string,
                    Div3AirportID string,
                    Div3AirportSeqID string,
                    Div3WheelsOn string,
                    Div3TotalGTime string,
                    Div3LongestGTime string,
                    Div3WheelsOff string,
                    Div3TailNum string,
                    Div4Airport string,
                    Div4AirportID string,
                    Div4AirportSeqID string,
                    Div4WheelsOn string,
                    Div4TotalGTime string,
                    Div4LongestGTime string,
                    Div4WheelsOff string,
                    Div4TailNum string,
                    Div5Airport string,
                    Div5AirportID string,
                    Div5AirportSeqID string,
                    Div5WheelsOn string,
                    Div5TotalGTime string,
                    Div5LongestGTime string,
                    Div5WheelsOff string,
                    Div5TailNum string,
                    Garbage1 string
        FROM "/flightdata/On_Time_On_Time_Performance_2014_1.csv"
        USING Extractors.Text(',', null, null, null,
                    System.Text.Encoding.UTF8, true, false, 1);
```

This script should seem reasonably familiar if you have worked with SQL. However, let's take a look at a few of the details that are easy to overlook in the familiar-looking syntax.

In the first line, we drop the view definition if it already exists.

After that, we begin the CREATE VIEW syntax and provide a name for the view (Flight DelaysView, in this case). Following that line, we encounter the AS keyword where the query definition for the view usually begins. Here, we encounter the EXTRACT keyword. The EXTRACT keyword is how we tell U-SQL to define a schema on demand (i.e., the parameters list following the EXTRACT keyword) and apply over data read at the location specified in the FROM clause—in our case, reading the CSV file found in the *flightdata* directory underneath the root of our Data Lake Store. Here we are referring to a single CSV file of the flight delay data, but we could also provide the path to a folder that contains many CSV files.

How Azure Data Lake Analytics parses the files at the FROM location is controlled by the use of an extractor, which is defined following the USING keyword:

```
USING Extractors.Text(',', null, null, null,
                System.Text.Encoding.UTF8, true, false, 1);
```

Notice from the Extractors object we use the Text factory method to create an instance of the text extractor. Observe also that we are passing in parameters to configure the extractor so it properly reads the flight data CSV.

The parameters for the Text factory method are defined as follows:

```
Text(
  System.Char delimiter, //the delimiter character between fields
  System.String rowDelimiter, //the string separating rows
  System.Nullable<System.Char> escapeCharacter, //used to
  //escape delimiter chars
  System.String nullEscape, //the string to put in place of null
  System.Text.Encoding encoding, //the text encoding of the files
  System.Boolean quoting, //ignore delimiters appearing within
  //quoted strings
  System.Boolean silent, //ignore rows that don't match schema
  System.Int32 skipFirstNRows // the number of header rows to skip over
);
```

So now you should understand that we have configured our text extractor to use a comma as the field delimiter, expect the text to be UTF-8 encoded, properly handle string values (like "Los Angeles, CA") by ignoring the comma within quoted strings, and skip over the first row of data (which has only the column headers).

U-SQL currently supports three different extractors that all work on text files. There is the text extractor as was just shown and also Csv and Tsv, which are simply specialized variants of text preconfigured for comma-separated value files and tab-separated value files, respectively. You can also develop custom extractors and use them here.

Extractors

For detailed documentation on all the extractors and their parameters, see the Microsoft Azure documentation (*http://bit.ly/2n7XPvi*).

Returning to our query, take a look back at the parameters list. Did you notice anything unusual? Did you happen to notice that the data type of `DepDelay` is a "double?" and `Carrier` is a "string"? These are C# types. The ? in `double?` means that the field is nullable.

Now run the script by selecting Submit Job in the command bar at the top of the New U-SQL Job blade. It will take about 30 seconds to run, after which you will have your view defined and ready for querying (see Figure 6-19).

Figure 6-19. Successfully creating a view from U-SQL in the Azure Portal.

Once the job is complete, close the blade displaying Job Summary and you should be back at the New Job blade where you can author another U-SQL script. Now, replace the script that's there with the following script, which we will use to query the data. And, by using an outputter (the opposite of an extractor), we can save the results of the query to another CSV file in Azure Data Lake Store.

```
@results =
    SELECT *
    FROM FlightDelaysView;
```

```
OUTPUT @results
TO "/flightdataout/Output/On_Time_On_Time_Performance_2014_copy.csv"
USING
Outputters.Text(',', null, null, null, System.Text.Encoding.UTF8,
true, null);
```

Run the query, which should take about 90 seconds with 1 unit of parallelism. While you are waiting for the query to complete, take a look at the syntax of the previous query. We assigned the `SELECT * FROM FlightDelaysView` to something that looks like a variable in T-SQL. The `@results` object is called a rowset variable. Each query expression that produces a rowset can be assigned to a variable. Note that the assigment does not force the execution, it merely names the query expression. It is the `OUTPUT` keyword that causes the `@results` expression to be evaluated and its results ultimately written to a CSV file (Figure 6-20).

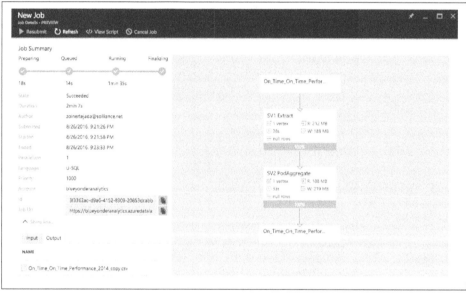

Figure 6-20. Results of creating a CSV output from querying the view. Notice the directed acyclic graph visualization of the script execution.

When your query completes its execution in the Azure Portal, observe the summary and the view of the directed acyclic graph (recall Azure Data Lake Analytics runs on YARN, so this should seem familiar by now). If desired, you can navigate to the path in your Azure Data Lake Store and see your output file.

Now, let's look at copying the view data into a managed table. To do this, close the summary blade, and in the New U-SQL Job blade paste the following query:

```
DROP TABLE IF EXISTS FlightDelays;

CREATE TABLE FlightDelays(
    INDEX idx_year CLUSTERED (Year)
    PARTITIONED BY RANGE (Year)
) AS
SELECT *
FROM FlightDelaysView;
```

Submit the job. While it runs, let's review the query. We create a managed table with CREATE TABLE. Inside of that, we must specify both which column to create the clustered index on and the columns to use to partition the data.

Creating Managed Tables

For the full documentation on the syntax for creating managed tables, see the Microsoft documentation (*https://msdn.micro soft.com/library/azure/mt718728.aspx*).

Following the AS keyword, we query the data from our view. Notice that the schema for the new FlightDelays table is automatically inferred from the underlying query, as we did not have to specify any of the columns involved in the view (Figure 6-21).

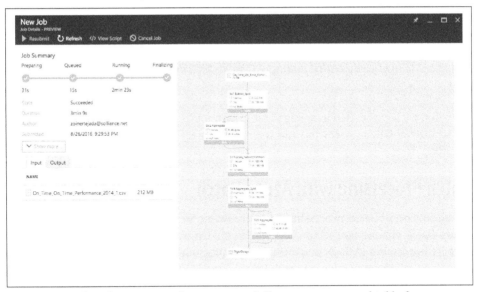

Figure 6-21. The job summary after we successfully create a managed table from a query against the view.

The query should take about 3 minutes to complete with 1 unit of parallelism. When it is finished, in the Azure Portal go back to your Data Lake Analytics account, and select Data Explorer. If you expand Catalog, your Data Lake Store, master, and then Tables, you should see your new managed table (Figure 6-22).

Figure 6-22. The newly created managed table in the Data Lake Analytics Data Explorer view.

Now that we have created a managed table from our CSV data, we are better prepared for additional batch processing and interactive querying, as we will show in the next chapter.

Batch Processing with Azure Batch

No discussion of batch processing in Azure would be complete without Azure Batch. Azure Batch enables you to run high-performance computing (HPC), embarassingly parallel processing (MPP), and message passing interface (MPI)–based workloads, where as a platform service it schedules the work to run on a managed collection of virtual machines that can scale automatically to meet the demands of your job.

Azure Batch is very powerful, but it is also quite different from the data-oriented solutions we've covered thus far because it is designed to be much more generic. For example, what if the unstructured data you wanted to batch process was not CSV data, but rather photographic images, and what if instead of querying data your processing consisted of performing image-processing tasks (such as edge detection)?

While you might be able to engineer a solution that uses Spark on HDInsight for this, this workload is clearly not the type of big data batch processing Hive, SQL Data Warehouse, or Data Lake Analytics is designed for. Thus, Azure Batch may form a part of a larger data pipeline, where the outputs of the Azure Batch processing may well be data that is more easily manipulated by the technologies we've covered in this chapter.

Given these differences, we will not cover Azure Batch in any greater detail except to ensure the reader is aware of it should the right workload arise.

Want More Azure Batch?

Azure Batch is a rich and powerful platform service. If you are curious to learn more about it, see the Microsoft Azure documentation (*http://bit.ly/2nJOjln*).

Orchestrating Batch Processing Pipelines with Azure Data Factory

We introduced Azure Data Factory in Chapter 2, showing how to build a simple pipeline that orchestrates the copying of data from an on-premises network share to either an Azure Storage account or to Azure Data Lake Store. This pipeline was built with a Copy activity.

In the context of this chapter on batch processing, it is worth mentioning that Azure Data Factory has the following data transformation activities that you can use to kick off your batch processing as part of a larger pipeline that is orchestrated by Azure Data Factory:

Hive activity
    Run a HiveQL script from a file stored in Blob Storage.

Pig activity
    Run a Pig Latin script from a file stored in Blob Storage.

MapReduce
    Run a MapReduce program from a JAR file stored in Blob Storage.

Stored procedure activity
    Execute a stored procedure in Azure SQL Data Warehouse

Data Lake Analytics U-SQL
    Execute a U-SQL job.

Want More Azure Data Factory?

For more details on using Azure Data Factory to orchestrate your batch processing, including sample pipelines, see the Microsoft Azure documentation (*http://bit.ly/2nCBSHN*).

Summary

In this chapter we took a broad perspective on the batch processing options available in Azure, where we used a latency definition of batch processing as those queries or programs that take tens of minutes, hours, or even days to complete. We covered multiple batch processing options that run on Azure HDInsight (Hive, Pig, Spark, MapReduce), as well as SQL Data Warehouse and Azure Data Lake Analytics. We also touched on Azure Batch and put it in context relative to all of the other options we covered.

In the next chapter, we will dial back and reduce our latency tolerance from tens of minutes, as is typical of batch processing, to the hopefully shorter latencies we expect as we explore the data interactively and apply more advanced analytics on our prepared data.

CHAPTER 7

Interactive Querying in Azure

In this chapter, we look at various techniques that are useful to achieving interactive query performance (Figure 7-1). For our purposes in this chapter, this means querying batch data at "human" and "humane" (pun intended) interactive speeds, which with the current generation of technologies means results are ready in time frames measured in seconds to minutes.

The fundamental concept introduced in this chapter that is universal to all the data stores we cover is understanding how to prune large data sets during query processing to achieve faster query execution. The concept seems fairly obvious—if you reduce the amount of data that the query engine has to read through, then your queries will be faster. Exactly how you reduce the data set size is where you get into the various techniques these data stores utilize, including:

Indexes

Creating indexes over the data can help the query engine identify the data files to include and which to skip over by consulting a separate set of data that represents the index, which is presumably significantly smaller than the source data set. In some cases, such as for data stored using ORC, indexes are automatically created and stored with the data files to aid in identifying complete files to exclude from processing as well as large segments of a file that can be ignored because they do not contain the values of interest.

Partitions

All of the data stores in this chapter have a notion of a table that acts to group data into rows that share a similar schema. Partitions are used to split very "tall" tables with lots of rows into separate files, whereby each file on disk contains only the data for a partition.

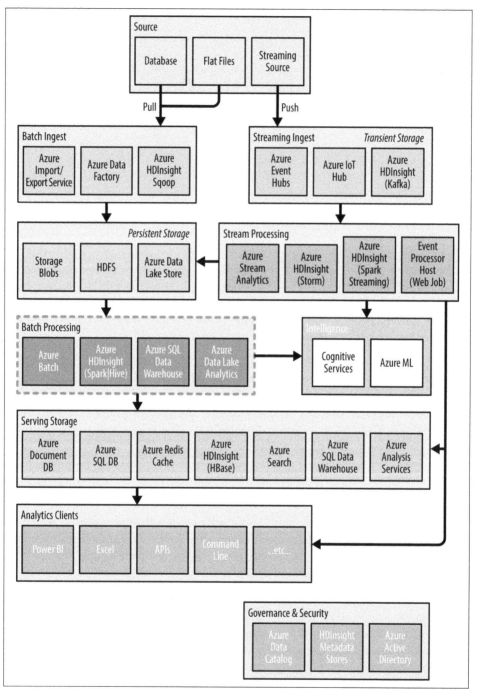

Figure 7-1. This chapter focuses on achieving "interactive" query latencies with batch processing components.

Predicate pushdown

When the filter (or WHERE clause) of a query is applied in deciding what data files to load or which to ignore, you are in effect pushing the filter (aka predicate) down toward the storage layer instead of waiting to apply it after you have read all of the data from disk.

To apply these concepts, we will continue with the data prepared in the previous chapter for Blue Yonder Airports. This time, Blue Yonder Airports is interested in exploring the data to understand, for any given airport, which three months of the year seem to incur flight delays longer than five minutes. They want to focus their initial expenditures for these three months on at-gate amenities to improve the guest experience.

Interactive Querying with Azure SQL Data Warehouse

Azure SQL Data Warehouse provides a handful of features that help reduce query latency and improve the interactive querying experience and center on distributions and indexes.

Partitions and Distributions

SQL Data Warehouse supports two separate concepts for spreading table data among all nodes that make up its cluster. When you create a table in SQL Data Warehouse, your table's data is automatically divided across 60 databases. Each of these individual databases is referred to as a *distribution*. The act of assigning a row to given distributions takes place when data is loaded into each table. During table creation, we configure the algorithm the SQL Data Warehouse follows in deciding how to allocate a given row by setting the distribution method.

SQL Data Warehouse supports the following distribution methods:

ROUND_ROBIN

Randomly distributes data evenly across distributions. As your data is loaded, each row is sent to the next distribution in the circular list of distributions.

HASH

Distributes data based on hashing values from a single column that you select. The hashing algorithm and resulting distribution is deterministic, so for a given input value you will always hash to the same value and by extension the same distribution.

All tables in SQL Data Warehouse must specify a distribution method. If you do not explicitly declare one when creating a table, it will default to ROUND_ROBIN. Here is an example of creating a table with an explicit ROUND_ROBIN distribution method:

```
CREATE TABLE flights
(
 flightNum int NOT NULL,
 airlineName varchar(20),
 ...,
 DepDelay REAL
)
WITH
(
 DISTRIBUTION = DISTRIBUTION = ROUND_ROBIN
)
```

Here is an example of creating the same table with using the HASH method (notice that in this case we need to provide the name of single column used as an input to the hash):

```
CREATE TABLE flights
(
 flightNum int NOT NULL,
 airlineName varchar(20),
 ...,
 DepDelay REAL
)
WITH
(
 DISTRIBUTION = HASH (flightNum)
)
```

Partitioning is also supported on all SQL Data Warehouse tables, irrespective of their distribution method. As you would expect, partitions can be used to improve query performance by scanning only the qualifying partitions needed to satisfy a query, and ideally avoiding a full table scan.

As with most other data stores we cover in this book, creating a table with too many partitions can hurt performance. The general rule of thumb is to create partitions in the tens to hundreds of partitions and not in the thousands. That said, be aware of the interaction between distributions and partitions. Since any table of the gate will be distributed into 60 distributions, your data will automatically be split there and you initially may not need any partitions. For example, if you create a table with 100 partitions (a reasonable count by our rule of thumb), you would actually be partitioning your data into 6,000 partitions (because 60 distributions × 100 partitions = 6,000 partitions), which is far too many partitions.

Creating a partition in SQL Data Warehouse is a little different from the process you may be familiar with from SQL Server. Instead of defining the partitioning function (which describes the value boundaries) and scheme (which describes the mapping between a partition and its underlying file group) that are used during table creation to partition the data, in SQL Data Warehouse you must explicitly define the partition boundaries inline with the CREATE TABLE statement. For example:

```
CREATE TABLE flights
(
 flightNum int NOT NULL,
 airlineName varchar(20),
 ...,
 DepDelay REAL
)
WITH
(
 PARTITION (flightNum RANGE LEFT FOR VALUES (100, 200, 300, 400))
)
```

The previous query would create a table with five partitions based on the boundary value provided, and a row would be inserted into the appropriate partition based on the value of its flightNum field.

Indexes

SQL Data Warehouse provides three different index options (clustered columnstore indexes, clustered indexes, and nonclustered indexes) and one no-index option for table data. Let's briefly examine each of these index options.

Clustered columnstore index

The clustered columnstore index stores data in a columnar format, and provides the actual storage for the entire table. The structure of a columnstore table index slices the table into groups of rows, creatively referred to as rowgroups. The columnstore format organizes the data first into column segments. A column segment is a column of data from within a rowgroup, where each rowgroup contains one column segment for every column in the table. This approach enables each column segment to be compressed and stored together on disk. Clustered columnstore indexes perform best when each row group has between 100,000 and 1M rows.

You can create a clustered columnstore index using the following syntax within the WITH clause:

```
CREATE TABLE flights
(
 flightNum int NOT NULL,
 airlineName varchar(20),
 ...,
 DepDelay REAL
)
WITH
(
 DISTRIBUTION = DISTRIBUTION = ROUND_ROBIN,
 CLUSTERED COLUMNSTORE INDEX
)
```

If you create a table without specifying any index options, a clustered columnstore index will be the default.

Clustered index

A clustered index provides a primary index created on a rowstore (i.e., row-oriented storage) table. It is responsible for the physical sort order of the data on disk. These are akin to primary indexes in other relational databases. Clustered indexes may outperform clustered columnstore indexes when a single row needs to be quickly retrieved.

Nonclustered index

A nonclustered index provides a secondary index on a rowstore table. It is secondary in the sense that the table usually already has a primary clustered index that defines the physical sort order on disk, and the nonclustered index contains a copy of part or all of the rows and columns in the underlying table.

Heap table

A heap table is a table without any index at all, and by extension no sorting is applied to the physical layout of the data on disk. A heap table is often the most performant way to load data into SQL Data Warehouse, since it does not have to sort the data prior to writing it out. Also, for small tables (i.e., less than 100M rows), heap tables might be an option.

> **Clustered and Nonclustered Index Syntax**
>
> We won't cover the syntax for creating clustered and nonclustered rowstore indexes in this book, as the columnar format is typically the preferred structure for a data warehouse. If you are interested in the syntax, see *http://bit.ly/2nnCi44*. (*http://bit.ly/2nnCi44*)

Interactive Exploration of the Blue Yonder Airports Data

In this section, we will pick up where we left off in the previous chapter, so make sure you have your SQL Data Warehouse instance running with the managed table FlightDelaysStaging.

You can execute the following queries using any tool that can connect to SQL Server, but we will demonstrate the results using SQL Server Management Studio connected to our instance of SQL Server Data Warehouse.

Let's begin by partitioning this data so it better suits the needs of Blue Yonder Airports. Since each airport is an entity, they want to focus queries at the airport first. For example, to understand which three months experience the most delays, they would start by narrowing the data by origin airport, say San Diego International (airport code SAN) and then performing analytics from there.

As a first query, let's examine how many distinct origin airports the data set contains:

```
SELECT count(distinct origin)
FROM FlightDelaysStaging
WHERE year = 2015
```

Note that we have 322 distinct origin airports (Figure 7-2).

Figure 7-2. Results displayed in SQL Server Management Studio showing the number of distinct origin airports in the data set for the year 2015.

Next, let's identify the top 30 busiest airports by departures:

```
SELECT Top(30) origin, count(*) counted
FROM FlightDelaysStaging
WHERE year = 2015
GROUP BY origin
ORDER BY count(*) DESC
```

The results appear as shown in Figure 7-3.

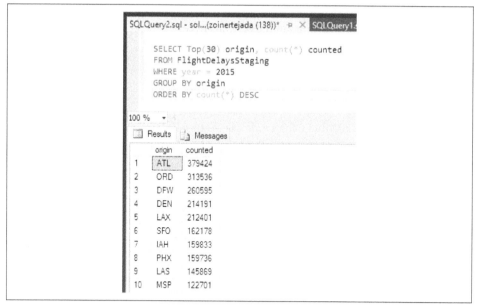

Figure 7-3. Sample of top 30 busiest airports by departures in 2015.

This gives us a sense of how many rows each airport would typically have to deal with to understand its operations, each in the few hundred thousands at most. In other words, pretty small.

Given the requirement that all queries will take the perspective of an origin airport, we could consider partitioning the data by origin airport. However, there really is no need to partition, because the automatic partitioning into 60 distributions is more than sufficient (and already results in very small distributions). However, to support future growth, it would be wise to distribute data so that rows describing a given airport are located in the same distribution. We can accomplish this by creating a new table using a HASH distribution on the Origin column as follows:

```
CREATE TABLE DepartureFlightData
WITH (DISTRIBUTION = HASH(Origin) )
AS
SELECT * FROM FlightDelaysStaging
```

Now we are ready to perform our analytics query for the busiest months:

```
SELECT Month, Count(*)
FROM DepartureFlightData
WHERE origin='SAN' AND Cast(DepDelay as REAL) > 15
GROUP BY Month
```

The results of this query appear similar to Figure 7-4.

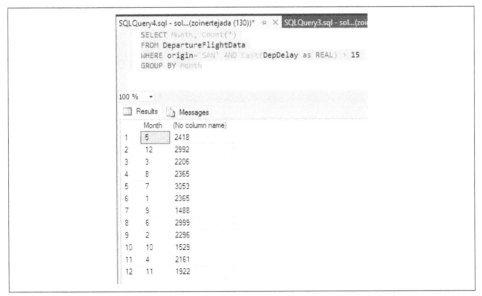

Figure 7-4. Results showing the month ordinals and number of flights having greater than 15-minute delays for the airport with code SAN.

So, from this we can conclude that for the San Diego International Airport, Blue Yonder Airports should really focus on the customer experience during the months of July, August, and December.

Interactive Querying with Hive and Tez

In 2009, Hive started out as a data warehouse solution intended for batch analytics (read: long waits until results ready). Hortonworks launched an initiative in 2013 called Stinger to make Hive more suitable for interactive SQL queries common in the enterprise, thereby reducing the query latency. The Stinger initiative, delivered in 2014, is included with and enabled by default in HDInsight, and evolves Hive's traditional architecture by providing the following core enhancements:

ORC file format
    The ORC (Optimized Row Columnar) file format provides compressed column-oriented storage. When it comes to data pruning, the Hive engine avoids having to read data for columns it is not querying. It also provides lightweight, inline indexes that support predicate push-down efforts to reduce the reading of unnecessary data. The ORC file format divides the data into files, and within a file into stripes consisting of 200 megabytes' worth of data. Within each stripe, the data is stored in column order (a set of data for column 1 appears, then a set of data for column 2, etc.). Each file has a footer that provides statistics (in the form of an index) about the data contained at the file level and the stripe level. Additionally,

each stripe has its own index that helps to summarize the data contained within the stripe. This index includes the minimum and maximum values contained for each column within a group of 10,000 rows within the stripe. In short, engines that understand how to read ORC files use the indexes that the ORC files contain to prune unnecessary I/O.

Vectorized SQL engine

Instead of processing a single row's worth of data at a time, the gist of vectorized execution is to process 1,024 rows' worth of data at a time. The idea here is to leverage data locality principles—the data for one row is probably surrounded by other rows that are going to be queried, so it makes sense to load and process them in the same effort.

Apache Tez

Tez is an application framework completely separated from MapReduce that is used for general data processing tasks that execute on YARN. Think of it this way: instead of generating a MapReduce program to execute on the cluster, Tez generalizes map and reduce tasks into a *directed acyclic graph* (DAG) that describes the program to execute as a graph where the vertices represent tasks (map or reduce) and the edges represent the data connection between tasks. The design of this framework directly addresses the performance shortcomings of MapReduce, such as always having to have a reduce step follow a map step, or always having to write intermediate results to disk between steps. In Hive, the Tez framework is referred to as an *engine*, where it is the alternative to the Map-Reduce engine.

In short, to leverage the benefits of Stinger you need to make sure to store your data in the ORC file format, and configure Hive to use vectorized SQL execution as well as the Tez engine. These are enabled by default in HDInsight, so you do not have to do any special configuration to leverage Stinger.

Stinger.next

The enhancements to Hive from the Stinger initiative will continue in Stinger.next, which aims to bring subsecond query performance to Hive. The key enhancements here include long-running daemon processes in the cheekily named Live Long and Process (LLAP). LLAP provides a host of functionality that enables subsecond performance and in-memory caching, leveraging HBase for the metadata catalog to speed metadata operations, and support for Spark as an alternative engine to Tez and MapReduce (called Hive on Spark).

Indexes

When it comes to indexes, Hive has limited indexing capabilities, and these generally only come into use when you have overridden Hive on HDInsight's default configuration to use the MapReduce engine instead.

 Hive Indexes and You

For details on the indexes supported by Hive, see the Apache Hive wiki (*http://bit.ly/2n7XOri*).

Instead of defining explicit table indexes, you should be leveraging the inline indexes automatically provided by the ORC file format along with partitioning your tables.

Partitions

Partitioning directly controls how Hive constructs the folder hierarchy leading up to the data files that make up a table. Hive creates subdirectories reflecting the partitioning structure, where the folder name takes the format: *<fieldName>=<value>*. The `fieldName` represents the name of the column in the source data, and `value` represents that actual value for that partition. One way to understand this is to visualize the filesystem as a tree:

```
flightdata
- airport=LAX
---- year=2015
-------- 000000_0.orc
-------- 000001_0.orc
- airport=SAN
---- year=2015
-------- 000000_0.orc
```

In the previous listing, the flightdata table is partitioned by airport code at the top level, and then by year. As you can see, this is expressed in the names of the folders leading up to the ORC files that have the data for the particular partition. You can think of this approach as indexing the data by way of the folder path leading up to it. The insight is that if you partition correctly, the query engine gets to ignore entire directories' worth of data files during query processing (as would be the case if we were after only data for the SAN airport—we could ignore the data under the LAX folder). This is just another example of how to prune large data sets.

Interactive Exploration of the Blue Yonder Airports Data

In this section, we will pick up where we left off in the previous chapter, so make sure you have your HDInsight cluster ready with the ORC-based internal table flightdataorc.

You can execute the following queries using either the Ambari Hive View or an SSH session running the Hive shell.

Running Hive Queries from Visual Studio

When you have the HDInsight Tools for Visual Studio installed (which are installed with Azure SDK 2.5.1 or later), you can also use Visual Studio's Server Explorer to view your tables and run Hive queries. If you are curious, try the queries in this chapter using the steps described here (*http://bit.ly/2n7VwbF*).

Let's begin by partitioning this data so it better suits the needs of Blue Yonder Airports. Since each airport is an entity, they want to focus queries at the airport first. For example, to understand which three months experience the most delays, they would start by narrowing the data by origin airport, say San Diego International (airport code SAN), and then performing analytics from there.

One approach is to partition all of the flight delay data in the flightdataorc table by the value of the origin field (which indicates a flight that is departing from that airport). With Hive, an important consideration is to keep the number of partitions to a reasonable number—a few hundred to at most a thousand. If you grow beyond that, you run the risk of creating too many small partitions, and that can get you in trouble because the result is too many small files, which can overload your HDFS nodes.

So let's begin by understanding how many partitions we would have if we partitioned by origin airport:

```
SELECT count(distinct origin)
FROM flightdataorc
WHERE year = 2015;
```

If you run the preceding query, you would find that in 2015 there were 322 distinct origin airport values. Since the number of airports is not likely to change dramatically over time, this seems like a reasonable way to partition the data. It would be tempting, for example, to further partition by year (i.e., airport code and then year), but consider with only three years' worth of data you would be hitting close to a thousand partitions (3 years × 322 airports = 966 partitions), and worse, the number of partitions grows significantly (by over 300) each year.

To get some additional context, run the following query so we get a sense of just how many rows would be in each partition if we partitioned only by origin airport:

```
SELECT origin, count(*) FROM flightdataorc
WHERE year = 2015
GROUP BY origin;
```

Running this query would provide insights like:

1. ATL, or Hartsfield-Jackson Atlanta International Airport, has the most flights in 2015 with 379,424.

2. LAX, or Los Angeles International Airport, has 212,401 flights.

3. SAN, or San Diego International Airport, has 76,416 flights.

Why do we care about flight counts departing from each airport? Because the number of flights represents the number of rows we will have in each partition, assuming we partition by origin airport. These are not huge numbers of rows—10 years' worth of data might have 4M rows in the ATL partition, and it strikes a good balance between having partitions whose row count is too high and having too many partitions.

Confident we have a good partitioning strategy, let's look at how we actually create a partitioned internal table by running the following:

```
CREATE TABLE departureflightdata
(
Year INT,
Quarter INT,
Month INT,
DayofMonth INT,
DayOfWeek STRING,
FlightDate STRING,
UniqueCarrier STRING,
AirlineID STRING,
Carrier STRING,
TailNum STRING,
FlightNum STRING,
OriginAirportID STRING,
OriginAirportSeqID STRING,
OriginCityMarketID STRING,
--Origin STRING,
OriginCityName1 STRING,
OriginCityName2 STRING,
OriginState STRING,
OriginStateFips STRING,
OriginStateName STRING,
OriginWac STRING,
DestAirportID STRING,
DestAirportSeqID STRING,
DestCityMarketID STRING,
Dest STRING,
DestCityName1 STRING,
DestCityName2 STRING,
DestState STRING,
DestStateFips STRING,
DestStateName STRING,
DestWac STRING,
CRSDepTime INT,
DepTime INT,
```

```
    DepDelay INT,
    DepDelayMinutes INT,
    DepDel15 BOOLEAN,
    DepartureDelayGroups INT,
    DepTimeBlk STRING,
    TaxiOut INT,
    WheelsOff INT,
    WheelsOn INT,
    TaxiIn INT,
    CRSArrTime INT,
    ArrTime INT,
    ArrDelay INT,
    ArrDelayMinutes INT,
    ArrDel15 BOOLEAN,
    ArrivalDelayGroups INT,
    ArrTimeBlk STRING,
    Cancelled BOOLEAN,
    CancellationCode STRING,
    Diverted BOOLEAN,
    CRSElapsedTime INT,
    ActualElapsedTime INT,
    AirTime INT,
    Flights INT,
    Distance INT,
    DistanceGroup INT,
    CarrierDelay INT,
    WeatherDelay INT,
    NASDelay INT,
    SecurityDelay INT,
    LateAircraftDelay INT,
    FirstDepTime INT,
    TotalAddGTime INT,
    LongestAddGTime INT,
    DivAirportLandings BOOLEAN,
    DivReachedDest BOOLEAN,
    DivActualElapsedTime INT
    )
    PARTITIONED BY (Origin STRING)
    STORED AS ORC;
```

In the previous data definition language query, we declare a managed table just as we did previously, with two notable differences. The second to last has a PARTITIONED BY clause that lists the column name and type of the column to partition by; here we identify that we want to partition by the Origin column, which has a type of STRING. Because we identified the partitioning column in the PARTITIONED BY clause, we should not redefine it in the columns listing that defines the schema of the table—note that Origin is commented out to highlight this fact.

Now we have an empty table and are ready to load data into it. But how do we load data into the right partitions of a table, given that each partition is basically just a folder (or folder hierarchy)? Because we want to insert into a partitioned table, Hive

---

does not allow us to use the CREATE TABLE AS syntax, but we can still use a plain INSERT statement augmented with a clause that identifies the partition column to use from the source query by running the following:

```
INSERT OVERWRITE TABLE departureflightdata
PARTITION (Origin)

    SELECT
    Year ,
    Quarter ,
    Month ,
    DayofMonth ,
    DayOfWeek ,
    FlightDate ,
    UniqueCarrier ,
    AirlineID ,
    Carrier ,
    TailNum ,
    FlightNum ,
    OriginAirportID ,
    OriginAirportSeqID ,
    OriginCityMarketID ,
    --Origin ,
    OriginCityName1 ,
    OriginCityName2 ,
    OriginState ,
    OriginStateFips ,
    OriginStateName ,
    OriginWac ,
    DestAirportID ,
    DestAirportSeqID ,
    DestCityMarketID ,
    Dest ,
    DestCityName1 ,
    DestCityName2 ,
    DestState ,
    DestStateFips ,
    DestStateName ,
    DestWac ,
    CRSDepTime ,
    DepTime ,
    DepDelay ,
    DepDelayMinutes ,
    DepDel15 ,
    DepartureDelayGroups ,
    DepTimeBlk ,
    TaxiOut ,
    WheelsOff ,
    WheelsOn ,
    TaxiIn ,
    CRSArrTime ,
    ArrTime ,
```

```
            ArrDelay ,
            ArrDelayMinutes ,
            ArrDel15 ,
            ArrivalDelayGroups ,
            ArrTimeBlk ,
            Cancelled ,
            CancellationCode ,
            Diverted ,
            CRSElapsedTime ,
            ActualElapsedTime ,
            AirTime ,
            Flights ,
            Distance ,
            DistanceGroup ,
            CarrierDelay ,
            WeatherDelay ,
            NASDelay ,
            SecurityDelay ,
            LateAircraftDelay ,
            FirstDepTime ,
            TotalAddGTime ,
            LongestAddGTime ,
            DivAirportLandings ,
            DivReachedDest ,
            DivActualElapsedTime ,
            Origin
            FROM flightdataorc;
```

In the previous query, notice that the PARTITION clause identifies the column Origin
as the column containing the value used to partition each row. Reading further down,
observe that we commented out Origin from its original position and made it the
very last column we select. Hive follows a convention that the columns referenced in
order in the PARTITION clause are listed in the same order as the last columns in the
query. In this case we only used one column, Origin. If we had three (say Origin,
Year, and Quarter) columns in the PARTITION clause, then the last three columns
before the FROM clause would need to be Origin, Year, and Quarter. With this syntax,
we are able to dynamically insert data into the right partitions—this is what Hive calls
dynamic partitioning.

If you take a look at the departureflightdata on disk (in Azure Storage or Azure Data
Lake Store according to your cluster), you will see the partitioning structure clearly,
as shown in Figure 7-5.

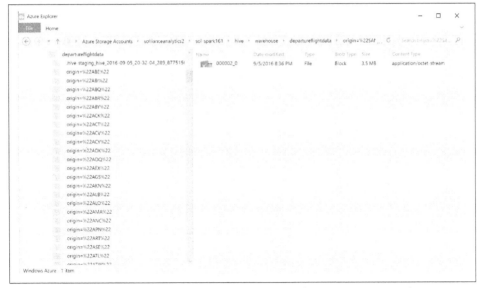

Figure 7-5. Folder structure resulting from partitioning by origin airport code.

With our data set now nicely partitioned by origin airport, let's take the perspective of a single airport (say SAN) and find the count of delays that are greater than 15 minutes. Run the following query against your instance of Hive:

```
SELECT Month, Count(*)
FROM departureflightdata
WHERE origin='SAN' AND DepDelay > 15
GROUP BY Month;
```

You should see a result set that looks like the following:

month	_c1
5	2418
9	1488
11	1922
1	2365
2	2296
7	3053
10	1529
12	2992
3	2206
4	2161
6	2999
8	2365

A quick scan of this (or if you are so bold, another query) reveals that the top three months with the most delays are:

- 7: July
- 6: June
- 12: December

So it would seem Blue Yonder Airports should focus their efforts on customer experience in the earlier summer months and the December holiday season.

Where's the Tez?

One thing you may not have noticed while you ran these queries was the framework being run under the covers. Unless you changed your default settings, your queries were executing using Tez on HDInsight. This is a fact you can confirm if you look closely at the console output when the query is running (you will see mention of "starting Tez session" or "DAG finished in XX.YY seconds").

Interactive Querying with Spark SQL

Spark SQL and the DataFrame API enable interactive querying of data sets in a few different ways. First, Spark SQL's support for performant columnar formats like Parquet and ORC enable pruning of large data sets at query processing time by virtue of predicate pushdown and table partitions. Second, once a data set has been loaded in-memory across the cluster, iterative querying (which is common when you are exploring data during interactive querying) benefits, as the data is served directly from memory instead of from disk.

Indexes

Currently, Spark SQL has no support for indexes. Table indexes (compact, bitmap, and bloom) from Hive are also not supported yet—meaning that if you have created a table in Hive that has these indexes and try to query it via a HiveContext in Spark, the indexes will not be used in the query processing. Just as for Hive, you can get some index help by saving your data to ORC files, so when the data is being loaded the inline indexes within the ORC file can help to prune the data that has to actually be read.

Partitions

Spark SQL uses the same approach to expressing partitions on disk as does Hive (see "Interactive Querying with Hive and Tez" on page 269), whereby the partitions are subfolders whose names are key/value pairs, where the key is the partition column name and the value is the particular value for the data represented in that partition. You can partition a DataFrame at save time by using the `partitionBy` method prior to invoking the `save` method:

```
mydataframe.write.format("orc").partitionBy("name").save("mydata")
```

The `partitionBy` method takes a list of string names representing the columns in order by which to partition the DataFrame's data.

Interactive Exploration of the Blue Yonder Airports Data

In this section, we will pick up where we left off in the previous chapter, so make sure you have your Spark HDInsight cluster ready with the ORC-based data set available as flightdataorcspark, as was shown there.

The following scripts can be run using either the Jupyter notebook or the Spark shell within an SSH session. For our purposes here, we'll use the Jupyter notebook so we can also leverage some of its chart visualization features. Recall you can open Jupyter from the blade for your HDInsight cluster, selecting Cluster Dashboards, selecting Jupyter, and then logging in with your admin credentials.

Once you have the Jupyter website open, select New and then Spark to create a new notebook for running Scala-based Spark programs.

The first thing you will need to is to create a DataFrame loaded with the ORC data you created in the previous chapter. If you were using Azure Data Lake Store, this would appear as follows:

```
val flightData = sqlContext.read.format("orc")
.load("adl://[lake].azuredatalakestore.net:443/flightdataorcspark")
```

Similarly, you would load from Azure Storage by using the *wasbs:* scheme and path:

```
val flightData = sqlContext.read.format("orc")
.load(
"wasbs://[container]@[acct].blob.core.windows.net/flightdataorcspark"
)
```

Now that we have this data in a DataFrame, we can query it using the Language Integrated Query approach as we showed in the previous chapter, or we can explore it using SQL. To be able to issue queries using SQL, we first need to register a temporary table that represents the DataFrame:

```
flightData.registerTempTable("flightdatatemp")
```

Make sure you run these cells in your Jupyter notebook before proceeding.

Next, let's explore the number of distinct origin airports. Within a Jupyter notebook, you can use what's called "magics" to issue specialized commands, such as SQL statements. In a new cell in the notebook, enter the following and run it:

```
%%sql
SELECT count(distinct origin)
FROM flightdatatemp
WHERE year = 2015
```

Note that the magic that is responsible for interpreting the cell's script as SQL instead of Scala is %%sql. Once the query returns, you should see output similar to Figure 7-6.

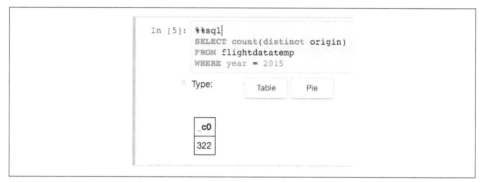

Figure 7-6. The results table indicates there are 322 distinct origins in the data represented by the flightdatatemp temporary table.

This gives us a sense for how many partitions we will create when we partition the data by origin. Next, let's take a look at about how much data will appear in the largest partitions:

```
%%sql
SELECT * FROM
(SELECT origin, count(*) counted FROM flightdatatemp
WHERE year = 2015
GROUP BY origin) departures
ORDER BY counted DESC
LIMIT 30
```

The results showing the top 30 busiest airports in 2015 should appear as shown in Figure 7-7.

Given that we are happy that we have a reasonable number of partitions and a reasonable size for partitions, let's save the DataFrame in a partitioned format back to storage by running the following:

```
flightData.write.format("orc").partitionBy("origin").save(
"adl://[lake].azuredatalakestore.net:443/departureflightdata")
```

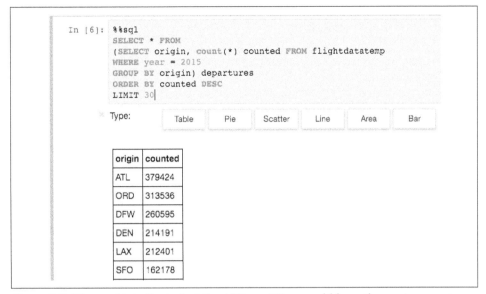

```
In [6]:  %%sql
         SELECT * FROM
         (SELECT origin, count(*) counted FROM flightdatatemp
         WHERE year = 2015
         GROUP BY origin) departures
         ORDER BY counted DESC
         LIMIT 30
```

Type:

| Table | Pie | Scatter | Line | Area | Bar |

origin	counted
ATL	379424
ORD	313536
DFW	260595
DEN	214191
LAX	212401
SFO	162178

Figure 7-7. The results indicate that the ATL partition would have the most rows, at 379,424 rows.

Substitute the WASB string as the input to the `save` method if you were using Azure Storage instead. Note that all we needed to do was invoke the `partitionBy` method and tell it the name of the column to partition by (in our case, the origin column).

If we open up our favorite tool for exploring storage, we can observe the partitioned folder structure, with ORC files at the leaf nodes of each directory tree (Figure 7-8).

solliance
Data Lake Store - PREVIEW

▼ Filter ☐ New Folder ⬆ Upload ▣ Access ✏ Rename Folder ≔ Folder Properti... 🗑 Delete Folder ⟳ Refresh

solliance ▸ departureflightdata ▸ Origin=SAN

NAME	SIZE	LAST MODIFIED
part-r-00000-44773b04-36ea-4065-8bfe-bfca2c045233.orc	189 KB	9/6/2016, 6:03:16 AM	...
part-r-00001-44773b04-36ea-4065-8bfe-bfca2c045233.orc	189 KB	9/6/2016, 6:03:15 AM	...
part-r-00002-44773b04-36ea-4065-8bfe-bfca2c045233.orc	186 KB	9/6/2016, 6:03:18 AM	...

Figure 7-8. Viewing the partitioned folder structure for the origin=SAN partition of the departureflightdata table in Azure Data Lake Store.

Now, before we can query against this partitioned version, we need to load it into a DataFrame. Run the following in your notebook:

```
val departureFlightData = sqlContext.read.format("orc").load(
"adl://[lake].azuredatalakestore.net:443/departureflightdata")
departureFlightData.registerTempTable("departureflightdatatemp")
```

Now we are ready to write our analytic query against this table. Run the following in a new cell in your notebook:

```
%%sql
SELECT Month, Count(*)
FROM departureflightdatatemp
WHERE origin='SAN' AND DepDelay > 15
GROUP BY Month
```

When the results appear, select the Bar button to visualize the results as a bar chart. Notice that June, July, and December have the most delays over 15 minutes in duration—these are the months Blue Yonder Airports should focus on for the San Diego airport (Figure 7-9).

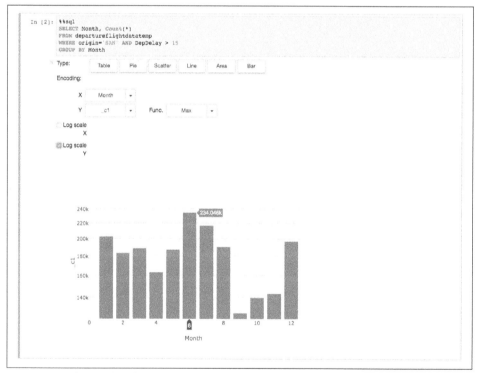

Figure 7-9. The results of the SQL query against the partitioned data, showing the results as a bar chart in a Jupyter notebook.

Interactive Querying with USQL

Azure Data Lake Analytics is primarily aimed at batch analytics, but there are a few features it supports that can help bring down the query processing time into the realm of interactive querying.

Like SQL Data Warehouse, Azure Data Lake Analytics supports indexes, partitions, and distributions, with some limitations.

Tables in Azure Data Lake Analytics currently must have a clustered index (e.g., columnar indexes and heap tables are not supported). Tables can be split into partitions or directly into distributions. Furthermore, partitions can be split into distributions. In addition to defining a clustered index, every table must define a distribution scheme that determines how rows are assigned to the distributions that make up a table or partition of a table.

Azure Data Lake Analytics supports the following four distribution schemes:

RANGE
Distributes rows based on an ordered list of columns where the system will automatically determine the bounds for the distribution. In effect, each distribution will contain a range of rows in sorted order between a minimum value inclusive and maximum value exclusive for the columns in the range.

HASH
Distributes rows according to the hash of a list of columns.

DIRECT_HASH
Distributes rows according to the hashed value of a single, integer column.

ROUND_ROBIN
Assigns rows to distributions in a round-robin fashion irrespective of any column values.

Interactive Exploration of the Blue Yonder Airports Data

In this section, we will pick up where we left off in the previous chapter, so make sure you have your Azure Data Lakes Analytics instance ready with the managed table available as FlightDelays, as was shown there.

We will execute the U-SQL jobs using the Azure Portal (as was shown in the previous chapter), but of course you are free to try alternatives such as Visual Studio.

Let's begin by getting the count of the distinct airports in the data set in 2014:

```
@results =
    SELECT COUNT(DISTINCT Origin) AS Counted
    FROM FlightDelays
    WHERE Year == 2014;

OUTPUT @results
TO "/flightdataout/Output/counts.csv"
USING Outputters.Csv();
```

If you open the output file (*counts.csv*), you should confirm the count is 301 distinct origins for the year 2014.

You can view the top 30 busiest airports by departures by executing the following query:

```
@results =
    SELECT Origin, COUNT(*) AS Counted
    FROM FlightDelays
    WHERE Year == 2014
    GROUP BY Origin
    ORDER BY Counted DESC
    FETCH 30 ROWS;

OUTPUT @results
TO "/flightdataout/Output/counts.csv"
USING Outputters.Csv();
```

You should find that in 2014, the busiest airport was ATL.

Next, let's examine how we might partition the table by using a HASH distribution, to help with the requirement that most queries will center on a single airport:

```
CREATE TABLE DepartureFlightData(
    INDEX idx_year_month_day_flightnum CLUSTERED (Year, Month, DayofMonth,
    FlightNum)
    PARTITIONED BY HASH (Origin)
) AS
SELECT *
FROM FlightDelays;
```

Note in the previous query that we were required to provide a definition for the clustered index (for which we defined the composite Year, Month, DayofMonth, and FlightNum), and defined the HASH distribution on the Origin column within the PARTITIONED BY clause.

With our table partitioned, now we can query for the busiest months:

```
@results =
SELECT Month, COUNT(*) AS Counted
FROM DepartureFlightData
WHERE Origin == "SAN" AND DepDelay  > 15
GROUP BY Month;
```

```
OUTPUT @results
TO "/flightdataout/Output/counts.csv"
USING Outputters.Csv();
```

Summary

In this chapter we explored various techniques within Hive, Spark, SQL Data Warehouse, and Azure Data Lake Analytics to further prepare the flight data for exploratory analytics, and then we issued some analytic queries to help Blue Yonder Airports better understand their "busy" seasons during which flights are most delayed.

In the next chapter, we will look at layering in intelligence to our data pipeline by exploring the options for creating and operationalizing machine learning models.

CHAPTER 8

Hot and Cold Path Serving Layer in Azure

In this chapter we focus on the end goal of the lambda architecture—enabling the querying of the results of all the processing performed. To this end, we will examine the Azure services that support querying of both hot path data and cold path data by client applications and BI tools, which we will collectively refer to as the *serving layer* (see Figure 8-1).

The serving layer collectively deals with data from both the hot path and the cold path. It is further subdivided into a speed serving layer, which represents the subset of incrementallyprocessed hot path data that has not yet been processed by the batch techniques of the cold path, and the batch serving layer that contains the batch-processed output of the cold path.

The main idea behind the speed serving layer is that it supports a high degree of query flexibility—that is to say, it provides a query model enabling the client applications to ask the questions they need, be it direct lookups or more complex analytic queries. In other words, the serving layer has strong support for random reads. The serving layer also has low latency; these queries should return results in subseconds to seconds.

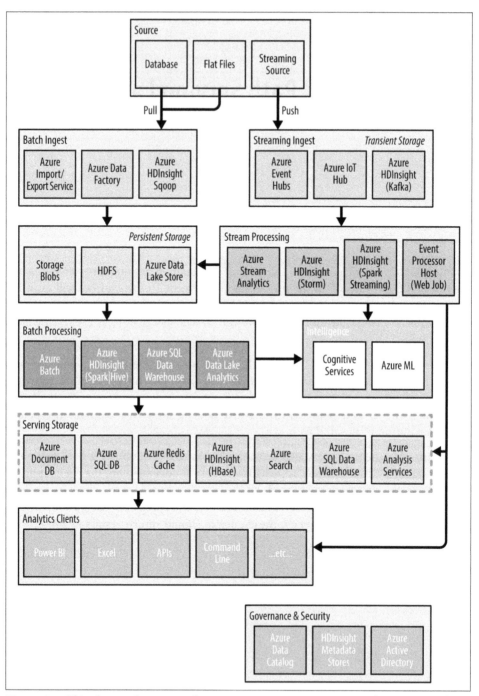

Figure 8-1. This chapter focuses on the serving storage components in the Azure analytics pipeline.

For the speed serving layer, because of the subsetting of the data, the actual volumes of data that it needs to store and process are usually measured in tens or hundreds of gigabytes to at most a few terabytes, as opposed to the much higher scale we need to handle in the cold path. This data volume reduction opens the door to using a wide variety of data stores in the speed serving layer. The key aspects of the speed serving layer are:

Random reads

> Support for quickly locating data during random read style queries. Usually support for random reads is enabled via indexes.

Random writes

> The data store needs to support random writes inserting data from the streaming sources with very low latency (e.g., measured in milliseconds), since any preparation work needed to create a batch and batch load data into the data store would typically introduce undesired delays in making the hot data available to clients.

Data expiration

> The data stores can provide a mechanism to automatically purge the data in the speed serving layer once it has landed in the batch serving layer. Some data stores offer a time to live (TTL) on each record managed by the data store, whereby those records exceeding the TTL are automatically purged from the data store. In some scenarios this is sufficient, because there is enough of a time overlap between the TTL and the time it takes for the batch serving layer to get the same data that it is never the case that data is purged from the speed serving layer but has not arrived in batch serving layer. In other cases, the application coordinating the data processing pipeline has to orchestrate this purging of data from the speed serving layer after it has successfully written the data to the batch serving layer.

Approximation

> Some data stores can minimize their read and write latency by reducing the amount of data actually stored. Oftentimes the data is approximated or stored using specialized algorithms that summarize the data within a tolerable margin of error.

The batch serving layer has a different set of characteristics. The key aspects of the batch serving layer are:

Random reads

> For the batch serving layer, indexes play an equally important role to support both point lookup and analytic style queries that may span large swaths of the data they manage.

Batch writes

The batch serving layer need not support random writes; since the requirement of the batch serving layer is to enable querying over the latest set of batch-processed data, loading data in batches consisting of the processed views is all that is required. Random writes add complexity and overhead (such as having to deal with compaction of unused space resulting from deleted or updated data and enforcing synchronization to present the correct value for read after write scenarios). Swapping in bulk sets of data representing the latest run of batch-processed, cold path data and swapping out the old data are techniques often leveraged by data stores in the batch serving layer.

Azure Redis Cache

Azure Redis Cache provides the open source Redis cache in the form of a managed service. At its core Redis provides a distributed, in-memory cache that, when deployed in Azure, can support production workloads using either a replicated primary/secondary configuration or a scaled-out cluster involving many nodes and providing as much as 530 GB of cache storage.

The fact that all data is stored in memory should suggest that Redis is particularly good at handling random reads and random writes—and it is. Redis is a key/value store where the key is always a string, but the value can be one of the many supported types. Under the covers, values that use primitive types like strings and numbers are always represented as string values. However, Redis provides commands that can atomically parse and manipulate numeric values (such as to increment or decrement the number). Redis also supports structures as values including lists, sets, sorted sets, hashes, and bit arrays. Redis also provides a unique structure, the HyperLogLog, which can be very useful for counting unique inputs at scale using a slight approximation (with an error of less than 1%) while using very little memory. Finally, Redis also supports setting an expiration on keys so that once the TTL has elapsed the key (and its value) are automatically removed from the data store.

Redis Reference

To get a better idea of the capabilities of Redis, see the complete list of commands for Redis by visiting *http://redis.io/commands*. Follow that up with this excellent summary of Redis data types: *http:// redis.io/topics/data-types-intro*.

Given that Redis operates in-memory, the I/O latency for performing random read/ write operations is minimized versus the same performed on disk. In Azure Redis Cache, the latency you experience is a combination of the latency of performing the operation within Redis plus the network latency of the round-trip between your client application and Redis Cache. You minimize network latency simply by deploying your Redis cache in the same location as the service or client applications that use it. Additionally, you can control throughput of your Redis instance by the selection of the pricing tier—this will determine the available network bandwidth and the peak requests per second. While Redis is accessed over the network (like any other data store), for most applications you will see latencies predominantly in the low double-digit millisecond range (e.g., 3–20 ms), which is pretty low latency indeed.

Benchmarking Azure Redis Cache

Your application latency may vary. If you are curious, you can run your own benchmarks on your Azure Redis Cache instance to see if you have it configured and sized correctly. This involves setting up a Windows VM in the same region as your Azure Redis Cache instance and running a command-line executable against it.

You can download the Redis benchmark for Windows from *https://github.com/MSOpenTech/redis/releases*.

Once you have done that, see this page (*http://bit.ly/2o55Alg*) for samples of the benchmark commands.

Given the support for random reads/writes, data expiration, and approximation, Azure Redis Cache fits well in the speed serving layer to enable client applications to query the hot path data.

Because Redis maintains all data in memory, its maximum size will always have significantly lower limits than disk-based data stores. The current limit of 530 GB is likely plenty to support a window of hot path data for a few hours, but certainly not likely to support all of the data produced from batch processing. Hence, it is not a good candidate for the batch serving layer.

Redis in the Speed Serving Layer

Let's turn our attention to applying Redis to support the speed serving layer for Blue Yonder Airports.

First, we need to deploy an instance of Azure Redis Cache. We can easily accomplish this using the Azure Portal:

1. Log in to the Azure Portal (*https://portal.azure.com*) and select New→Data + Storage→Redis Cache.

2. Provide a DNS name for your Redis Cache instance, then choose a subscription, resource group, and location.

3. For the pricing tier, you can use any tier for this example. For production, you are likely to use Premium so that you can leverage the total memory made available by the cluster.

4. If you selected a Premium tier, on the Redis Cluster setting, you should enable clustering and indicate how many nodes are in the cluster (and also the total amount of cluster memory) by adjusting the shard count slider. Also, note that if you selected Premium tier, you can enable Redis Database (RDB) backup, which will take snapshots on an interval. With Premium, you can also opt to provision the cluster within an Azure virtual network (meaning that your Azure hosted applications can access Redis without having to go through a public endpoint).

5. Select Create to provision your Redis Cache.

With your Redis Cache instance in hand, clone the sample project from *http://bit.ly/ 2bJDLOi*.

This Visual Studio solution contains a project called CachingEventProcessorHost-WebJob, which shows an event processor host consuming events from an Event Hubs instance (which can also be IoT Hub), and storing the results of later querying. For simplicity, it periodically queries the cache to the log output to show the approach to querying Redis. This project uses the Redis C# StackExchange libraries.

Open the solution in Visual Studio, expand the CachingEventProcessorHostWebJob, and then open *app.config* to set the following settings:

`redisConnectionString`
From the Azure Portal, navigate to your Redis Cache instance, and select Settings and then Access Keys. On the Access Keys blade, copy the value under the label "Primary conneciton string (StackExchange.Redis)" and paste it into the value of this app setting in *app.config*.

`eventHubConnectionString`
The connection string to your Event Hub endpoint that has read permissions.

`eventHubName`
The name of your Event Hub.

`eventHubConsumerGroup`
The name of the consumer group for the event processor to use if you created one; otherwise, leave this as $Default.

`storageAccountName`
The Azure Storage account name where the event processor will checkpoint its progress.

storageAccountKey

The key to the aforementioned Storage account.

This project follows the same structure as was covered in Chapter 4, in "EventProcessorHost" on page 170. This project provides a different implementation for the event processor that writes to the Redis Cache and periodically queries it. Let's explore how it uses Redis.

Open *CachingProcessor.cs* and scroll down to the ProcessEvents method, which looks as follows:

```
private void ProcessEvents(IEnumerable<EventData> events)
{
    IDatabase cache = Connection.GetDatabase();

    foreach (var eventData in events)
    {
        try
        {
            var eventBytes = eventData.GetBytes();
            var jsonMessage = Encoding.UTF8.GetString(eventBytes);
            var evt = JObject.Parse(jsonMessage);

            JToken temp;
            TempDataPoint datapoint;

            if (evt.TryGetValue("temp", out temp))
            {
            datapoint = JsonConvert.DeserializeObject<TempDataPoint>(
                    jsonMessage);
            cache.StringSet("device:temp:latest:" +
                        datapoint.deviceId, jsonMessage);
            cache.KeyExpire("device:temp:latest:"+
                        datapoint.deviceId,
                        TimeSpan.FromMinutes(120));
            cache.HyperLogLogAdd("device:temp:reportcounts:" +
                        datapoint.deviceId, jsonMessage);
            }
        }
        catch (Exception ex)
        {
            LogError(ex.Message);
        }
    }
}
```

In the first line, we get a connection to the Redis instance, and then the default database. The Connection property is lazily initialized with the redisConnectionString value you updated in *app.config*. Then we loop over each event received from the Event Hub, and extract and parse the JSON to examine if it contains a temperature value. If it does, we want to cache it. This brings us to the first use of Redis, to cache a value:

```
cache.StringSet("device:temp:latest:" +
            datapoint.deviceId, jsonMessage);
```

The way primitive values are cached is by providing a string key name and a value that is serialized as a string. Notice the way we structure the string that makes up the key (`"device:temp:latest:123"`)—it looks like a namespace prefixed in front of the device ID, and that's exactly how its used. With Redis you only have a single database (on a clustered deployment), and you don't have any notion of tables. However, if you use prefixes for your keys, then you can query for the keys that match a substring of the namespace and thereby query for all keys in that "table"—for example, to retrieve the latest temperature reading for all devices. We'll show how we query that in a moment. For now, take a look at the second parameter we provide to `StringSet`: the JSON-formatted string representing the event payload.

In the next line, we set time to live on the newly added key by using the `KeyExpire` method:

```
cache.KeyExpire("device:temp:latest:"+ datapoint.deviceId,
            TimeSpan.FromMinutes(120));
```

In this line, we are instructing Redis that this key and its value should be deleted after 120 minutes, assuming that's more than enough time for our cold path processing to include this data. If we run into a situation where it is not long enough (e.g., the cold path processing is down for maintenance), we can always extend the TTL by making another call to `KeyExpire`.

Following that, we show an example of using `HyperLogLog`, which takes a set-based approach to counting, whereby the count of items in the set (the cardinality of the set) is the number of unique items in the set:

```
cache.HyperLogLogAdd("device:temp:reportcounts:" + datapoint.deviceId,
            jsonMessage);
```

The way to think about `HyperLogLog` in this case is that we are using it to count the number of unique JSON message temperature payloads sent by the device. Alternately, if the device sent the same temperature reading with the same timestamp multiple times, these would yield the same JSON string and `HyperLogLog` would count it as having happened only once. This should elucidate a core value of the `HyperLogLog` approach in the speed serving layer: it can be used to easily deduplicate counts coming from hot path data.

Reading values from Redis using C# is fairly straightforword as well. In *CachingProcessor.cs*, we have the method `PrintSnapshotStatus`, which is called periodically by the event processor:

```
private void PrintStatusSnapshot()
{

    try
    {
        var redisClient = new StackExchangeRedisCacheClient(
                        Connection, new NewtonsoftSerializer());
        var keys = redisClient.SearchKeys(
                "device:temp:latest:" + "*");
        var dict = redisClient.GetAll<TempDataPoint>(keys);

        Console.WriteLine("========================");
        Console.WriteLine("Latest Temp Readings: ");
        foreach (var key in dict.Keys)
        {
            Console.WriteLine($"\t{key}:\t{dict[key].temp}");
        }

        IDatabase cache = Connection.GetDatabase();
        var countKeys = redisClient.SearchKeys("device:temp:reportcounts:" + "*");

        Console.WriteLine("========================");
        Console.WriteLine("Latest Report Counts: ");
        foreach (var key in countKeys)
        {
            Console.WriteLine($"\t{key}:\t{cache.HyperLogLogLength(key)}");
        }
    }
    catch (Exception ex)
    {
        LogError("PrintStatusSnapshot: " + ex.Message);
    }

}
```

Note that in this case, we wrap the connection in an instance of StackExchangeRedis
CacheClient. This provides some extra functionality, including the ability to scan all
keys that match a pattern and return them as a list, which we can then use to get all
the values for those keys:

```
var redisClient = new StackExchangeRedisCacheClient(
                Connection, new NewtonsoftSerializer());
var keys = redisClient.SearchKeys(
            "device:temp:latest:" + "*");
var dict = redisClient.GetAll<TempDataPoint>(keys);
```

The important piece in the call to SearchKeys is the use of the asterisk (*) to enable
the matching of any key that starts with device:temp:latest. The call to GetAll gets
us back a dictionary of key/value pairs that we can iterate over to see the latest cached
temperature readings by device:

```
    foreach (var key in dict.Keys)
    {
        Console.WriteLine($"\t{key}:\t{dict[key].temp}");
    }
```

Following that loop in `PrintStatusSnapshot`, we query the `HyperLogLog` counts for each key:

```
    IDatabase cache = Connection.GetDatabase();
    var countKeys = redisClient.SearchKeys("device:temp:reportcounts:" + "*");

    Console.WriteLine("========================");
    Console.WriteLine("Latest Report Counts: ");
    foreach (var key in countKeys)
    {
        Console.WriteLine($"\t{key}:\t{cache.HyperLogLogLength(key)}");
    }
```

Notice that in this case we use `SearchKeys` to get the list of keys to use in retrieving values, but we need to make each lookup individually by using `HyperLogLogLength`. This call returns the count of distinct temperature reports for each device.

If you run the project, the output should be similar to the following (depending on how much data you have in your Event Hub):

```
========================
Latest Temp Readings:
        device:temp:latest:1:    65
========================
Latest Report Counts:
        device:temp:reportcounts:1:      29705
Checkpoint partition 1 progress.
Checkpoint partition 3 progress.
Checkpoint partition 2 progress.
Checkpoint partition 0 progress.
```

You can also deploy this project as a Web Job in Azure as desired (which will greatly improve the processing speed by eliminating the network latency).

Document DB

Azure DocumentDB is a PaaS offering that enables the scalable storage and querying of schemaless JSON documents with response times in the order of milliseconds, and it enables you to scale the service along the axis required by your applications—be it storage capacity (e.g., total storage in GBs), query throughput (e.g., queries per second), or both. DocumentDB can be queried using SDKs for .NET, Node.js, Java, or Python, or via its REST endpoints. In addition, there is the DocumentDB Hadoop Connector, which enables you to interact with DocumentDB from Hive, Pig, and MapReduce. Users can also write queries in a SQL syntax or leverage the SDK's language-specific constructs to generate and issue the necessary SQL on their behalf.

DocumentDB Hadoop Connector

The DocumentDB Hadoop Connector is something you install into your HDInsight cluster during provisioning time. For step-by-step instructions on how to install the connector, see the Microsoft Azure documentation (*http://bit.ly/2nCL2DR*).

For the GitHub repository containing the connector source code and documentation, see *http://bit.ly/2o5epeK*.

The structure of DocumentDB is as follows. At the very lowest level you have complete, individual JSON documents. These documents are stored in collections, which are logical containers for storing document data. Collections can store a mix of documents having differing schemas—essentially, a schema is never explicitly defined at write time, and is used in schema-on-read fashion. Collections can consist of either a single partition or be created to support multiple partitions. Each partition has a fixed 10 GB of SSD-backed storage and a configurable throughput with a maximum of 10K request units (RUs) per second. RUs are a logical metric of provisioned throughput that quantify the reserved amount of resources (CPU, memory, and IOPS) available for read and write operations. In addition to storing documents, collections can also manage triggers (pre-action and post-action), stored procedures, and user-defined functions, all of which are programmed in JavaScript and run server-side.

Estimating RUs

To help you estimate the RU requirements for your workload, Microsoft has provided a web-based calculator that enables you to upload a sample of your JSON documents and provides an estimate of RU needs based upon read, write, update, and delete operations per second that you specify. See *https://www.documentdb.com/capacityplanner*.

Collections are grouped into a database, which acts as the security boundary at which you define users and permissions. Databases are themselves organized into a database account that controls aspects such as georeplication, default consistency settings, and the master access keys.

Given this hierarchy, it should come as no surprise that we scale DocumentDB by scaling collections, which we achieve in a scale-out fashion by adding partitions.

When you provision a collection, you specify its partitioning mode, which can either be Single Partition or Partitioned. If you select Single Partition, then your collection will have a maximum capacity of 10 GB and 10K RUs. If you select Partitioned, then you eliminate those hard limits. In the case of a partitioned collection, the number of partitions is automatically determined by DocumentDB based on the storage size and the provisioned throughput of the collection. In fact, partition management is fully managed by Azure DocumentDB—you do not have to write any code or manage your partitions to deal with tasks like adding, removing, and rebalancing partitions. For your part, during collection provisioning you need to provide a partition key (the path to the value in the JSON document whose hashed value will determine partition assignment for that document). After that, DocumentDB will take care of ensuring that documents with the same partition key land in the same partition.

With regards to indexing, by default all document properties of all documents are indexed, but you can alter the indexing policy to specify which document paths to include or exclude from the index to improve write performance and lower index storage costs. Additionally, collections can be configured to index lazily (i.e., asynchronously to the `write` operation), which also improves write performance.

All DocumentDB partitions are replicated to multiple replicas for high availability. DocumentDB offers a unique mechanism for improving write performance—tunable consistency levels (between replicas) that are scoped to a single user request. Document DB provides four consistency levels; from strongest (heaviest write impact, but greatest consistency across replicas) to weakest (lowest write impact, but lowest consistency across replicas), they are:

Strong
> Reads are globally (across any and all replicas) guaranteed to return the most recent version of a document. A write is visible only after it is synchronously committed by the majority quorum of replicas. A client can never see an uncommitted or partial write and is always guaranteed to read the latest acknowledged write.

Bounded Staleness
> Globally guarantees that the reads may lag behind writes by at most K versions of a document or by a specified time interval.

Session
> Enables local guarantees for a client to "read your own writes"—in other words, ensuring a client sees changes consistent within its session.

Eventual
> Provides the weakest of guarantees, essentially saying that DocumentDB is not enforcing a quorum of replicas to have acknowledged the change before acknowledging the write to a client—replicas will asynchronously become consistent at some undetermined point in time after the write. The client, for its part, sees the write as a "fire and forget," knowing that only the primary replica acknowledged the change.

You can specify the default consistency level for all collections by configuring it on the database account. However, each read or query request can specify its desired consistency level.

Document DB in the Speed Serving Layer

Given that DocumentDB serves data off of SSD storage and its measured propensity to service random reads 99% of the time in under 10 ms and random writes 99% of the time under 15 ms, it makes a great candidate for landing hot path data and enabling querying against it using a SQL syntax. Features like eventual consistency and lazy indexing enable you to trade some degree of read-time accuracy in favor of improved write performance to better meet the demands of your workload. Partitioned collections, and the automatic partition management provided by DocumentDB, help ensure that as your hot path gets "hotter" you can scale by adding more partitions with more RUs.

DocumentDB supports specifying a time to live on documents within collections, which is also beneficial to managing the size of your hot path data stores. With the TTL behavior, documents can be automatically purged from the database after a period of time. The default TTL can be set at the collection level, and overridden on a per-document basis. The TTL value is set in seconds and is calculated from the delta between the _ts property (that captures the time when the document was last modified) and the current time. While the documents are physically deleted by the system in the background, the documents are marked as unavailable as soon as the document has expired. This means no operations will be allowed on these documents after this time, and they will be excluded from the results of any queries performed.

Figure 8-2. Example of enabling time to live on a collection in the Azure Portal and setting the default expiration to 10 minutes (600 seconds).

In addition to the SDKs, DocumentDB provides click-to-configure integration with Stream Analytics, making it an easy destination for data ingested from Event Hubs and processed by Stream Analytics.

Let's examine this flow to store the Blue Yonder Airports telemetry data from Event Hubs using a Stream Analytics job. In the Azure Portal, create a new DocumentDB account, by selecting New→Databases→DocumentDB. To create a DocumentDB account you only need to provide an ID for the account, select the NoSQL API (which for our purposes you can leave at DocumentDB), and choose a subscription, resource group, and location (Figure 8-3).

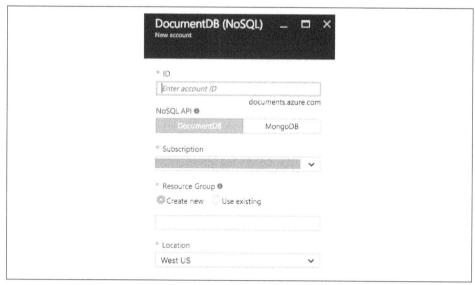

Figure 8-3. Creating a new DocumentDB account in the Azure Portal.

With your DocumentDB account ready, select Add Database in the DocumentDB Account blade. This only requires an ID for the database. With your database in place, from its blade in the Portal, select Add Collection. Here you will need to provide an ID for the collection, choose the pricing tier (Standard is sufficient for our purposes), and set the partitioning mode to Partitioned. You should also set the RUs as desired (the minimum is 10,100 RUs, but for reasonable performance in this demo you should opt for 50,000 RUs). Finally, set the partition key to "/deviceId". This last setting ensures that all telemetry arriving from a given device always lands in the same partition. Click OK, and in a few moments your collection is ready to receive data (see Figure 8-4).

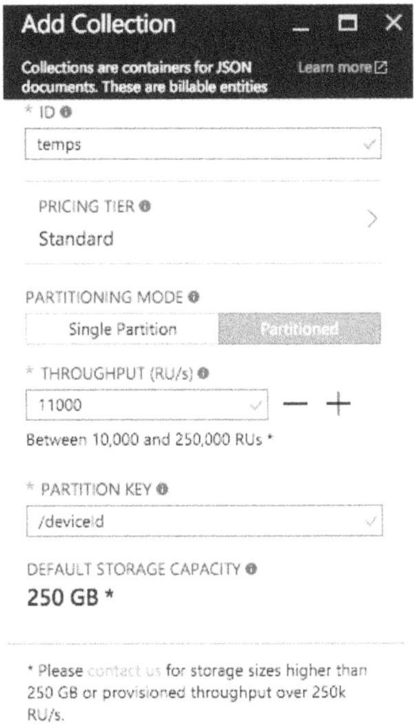

Figure 8-4. Creating a partitioned collection in the Azure Portal, and indicating the partition key.

Next, configure a Stream Analytics job to pull from your Event Hubs instance as we documented in Chapter 5. The major difference is you will want to configure your output to use your created DocumentDB collection instead of Azure Storage. You may also want to modify the query used in your Stream Analytics job, removing the where clause so that all data goes to DocumentDB (of course, you should also indicate the name of your DocumentDB sink in the query):

```
SELECT *
INTO docdb
FROM eventhub
```

Start your job and then use the Blue Yonder Airports simulator console to prime the Event Hub with some telemetry.

After a few moments, go to the Azure Portal and navigate to your DocumentDB collection. At the top of the blade, select Query Explorer. In the text area, paste the following query:

```
SELECT * FROM c
WHERE c.deviceId = "1" AND c.temp > 69.97
ORDER BY c.createDate DESC
```

Select Run Query, and you should see a listing of telemetry documents. Notice in the DocumentDB query that we include in the where clause a filter against deviceId. This enables DocumentDB to narrow the query to a single partition (because we configured the deviceId property as the partition key). If you omit a filter that includes the deviceId, the portal will throw an error indicating that cross-partition query is not supported. This is simply a restriction in how the Azure Portal's Query Explorer operates—if you use any of the SDKs or the REST API, you can enable cross-partition querying and successfully execute such a query.

Document DB in the Batch Serving Layer

While DocumentDB is scalable both in terms of compute (RUs) and storage, it does have smaller limits that make it less of a fit for the batch serving layer. While not limited in size (the 250 GB max collection size is a soft limit you can raise by contacting support), DocumentDB has limited support for batch writes, both in terms of scale (most batches are 100 records max) and in terms of swapping in the latest view to replace an older view (it has no support for this).

One consideration for either the real-time or batch serving layer is that even though DocumentDB supports querying using SQL syntax, the clients used to issue those SQL queries are not standard ODBC or JDBC clients (and in fact have a lot of DocumentDB-specific "smarts"), as DocumentDB does not offer an ODBC-compatible endpoint. This mostly means that your clients of DocumentDB are going to be custom applications where you programmatically leverage the DocumentDB client, or solutions that explicitly integrate with DocumentDB.

Another consideration is that DocumentDB does not currently provide aggregation support, so its support for analytics query workloads is fairly limited out of the box. You currently need to perform any aggregation client-side or within a stored procedure, or you can preaggregate data on write using a trigger. Take note that your aggregate calculations need to complete within the a bounded time window or they may fail.

Lumenize

You can use the DocumentDB-Lumenize library for adding support for analytic operations like group by, pivot tables, aggregation functions (sum, count, average, etc.), and precomputing OLAP style n-dimensional cubes. See the GitHub repository at *https://github.com/lmaccherone/documentdb-lumenize*.

SQL Database

Azure SQL Database is a managed, PaaS offering of the SQL Server relational database that is available only in Azure. A few years back when SQL Database launched, it had significant incompatibilities with SQL Server and lagged behind it in terms of shipping innovative features. Fast forward to today, and Azure SQL Database and SQL Server have significant feature parity and provide for a common programming surface area that lets you write the same code that will run equally well against either. More so, Microsoft has established a trend in previewing new database engine features in SQL Database first and then incorporating those into the next release of SQL Server—so you could say it is no longer just reaching parity with SQL Server, but actually introducing features in advance of SQL Server.

In the context of the serving layer, SQL Database provides support for real-time operational analytics—which is a set of features that make it particularly well suited to the write-heavy workloads combined with analytic-style queries (e.g., utilizing aggregates and group by) present in the speed serving layer.

The real-time operational analytics capability comes from the combination of memory optimized tables, columnstore indexes, and native compiled stored procedures.

Memory-optimized tables in SQL Database are created to exist in the server's active memory instead of exclusively on disk, and by operating in memory have shown to improve performance anywhere from 2x to 30x compared to the disk-based equivalent. This does not mean, however, that if the database goes down you lose your data, as memory-optimized tables have one representation in active memory and another secondary copy on disk. This duality of memory and disk is managed by SQL Database automatically and is completely hidden from your queries.

In SQL Database, memory-optimized tables are only available in the Premium tiers, and the total amount of memory available to them and their indexes is governed by the selected tier. For example, a P1 offers 1 GB of in-memory storage, whereas a P6 provides 8 GB and a P15 provides 32 GB.

So, what happens when you run out of memory? This is a condition you will have to both plan against and monitor (using the alerting features in the Azure Portal), because when you run out of memory the system will no longer allow most write operations. You will want to ensure that you are periodically cleaning up unneeded data or offloading that data to a disk-based table (e.g., by copying to a disk-based table and then deleting the copied rows from the source memory-optimized table within a transaction).

Oops, I Ran Out of Memory

If you run out of memory and try to insert a new row into a memory-optimized table, you will get the error, "Could not perform the operation because the database has reached its quota for in-memory tables." While you can still query the table, you may also find yourself blocked from cleaning up space in the table by deleting rows, because the `delete` operation itself will be prevented. It's probably unlikely you want to truncate the table and lose all of the data.

So what can you do? If you find yourself in this situation, a temporary solution is to increase the tier of your database to the next level up (e.g., go from a P2 to P4), which will increase the amount of available in-memory storage. Then delete the desired rows, and then scale back down to the original tier.

Also note that memory-optimized tables do not support partitioning, so it is truly up to your application to manage the table data and ensure it does not exhaust the available memory. For an example of the pattern to follow to offload from a memory-optimized table to a partitioned-disk-based table, see *https://msdn.micro-soft.com/en-us/library/dn133171.aspx*.

The indexing story for memory-optimized tables is extremely important to understand in order to utilize such tables effectively for your serving layer. For a memory-optimized table, its indexes are also memory optimized and exist only in active memory (the index is rebuilt when a database is brought back online). The entries in a memory-optimized index contain the memory address that directly points to the row in the table, and these indexes do not suffer from fragmentation because they do not have fixed-size pages. Memory-optimized tables support three kinds of indexes:

Nonclustered indexes

These are the familiar B-tree indexes you are likely to have used on your disk-based tables when you wanted to support both point lookups and range scans. Note that clustered indexes are not supported in memory-optimized tables because the in-memory layout of data necessarily has different requirements than when the data is stored on disk.

Hash indexes

These are available to memory-optimized tables only, and should be used when you want to perform fast point lookups and allow the fastest form of row inserts. The storage for hash indexes is preallocated when the table is created, as its size is controlled by the bucket count parameter (which explicitly defines the number of buckets the hash entries are divided into, and implicitly defines the number of hash entries that need to be searched in a given bucket). The general recommendation is to use a bucket count of 1 to 2 times the number of distinct index keys your data will have—having too few buckets means longer index lookup times, and having too many buckets means you are wasting precious memory.

Columnstore indexes

These indexes are optimized for supporting analytic style workloads because they index all columns of the table in a columnar format, which has been shown to offer gains of 10x in performance and in data compression. For memory-optimized tables, you can only create a clustered columnstore index, which is represented as a secondary copy of the data. In other words, it is not a traditional clustered index in the sense that it affects the storage layout of the memory-optimized table.

The power to support real-time operational analytics workloads surfaces when you mix the indexes, so that you have the OLTP workload using the nonclustered or hash index, while analytics run concurrently against the columnstore index. For the speed serving layer, this approach yields fast inserts, but also enables performant analytics queries against the hot data. When authoring queries, SQL Database will automatically determine the appropriate index to use for a given query so you do not have to specify, for example, to use the columnstore index when running aggregation queries.

The final piece enabling real-time operational analytics is `native compiled stored procedures`. These are stored procedures authored in the typical fashion except they indicate `NATIVE_COMPILATION` in their definition. When created in this way, the T-SQL statements that make up the procedure are compiled to machine code on first use of the procedure. The result is that subsequent invocations of the native compiled stored procedure no longer endure the slow interpretation of every instruction like their traditional counterparts. It is worth noting that a native stored procedure can only reference memory-optimized tables and cannot reference disk-based tables.

SQL Database in the Speed Serving Layer

There are a few things about memory-optimized tables that are attractive in this scenario, but the main one is the value of getting better write and analytics performance without the cost increase associated with going to a higher SQL Database tier.

Random reads benefit from the memory-optimized tables using either hash indexes or nonclustered indexes and performing analytic queries against the columnstore index. Random writes benefit from the memory-optimized storage approach, which eliminates locks and has the I/O characteristics of a memory-based access. When it comes to data expiration, SQL Database has no support out of the box, so you will need to implement the application pattern to periodically delete expired rows from the memory-optimized table.

Let's examine this flow to store the Blue Yonder Airports telemetry data from Event Hubs using an event processor host.

Memory-Optimized Tables and Stream Analytics

Using Stream Analytics to write to a memory-optimized table would seem a match made in heaven. Unfortunately, this is currently not supported. If you try it out, your Stream Analytics job will fail with the error "The table option 'tablock' is not supported with memory optimized tables." This is a known issue and Stream Analytics is expected to support memory-optimized tables in the future. In the meantime, consider using an alternate means to pump data into the memory-optimized table, such as by using an event processor host.

In the Azure Portal, you can create a new SQL Database by selecting New→Databases→SQL Database. To create a SQL Database you need to provide a name for the database, then choose a subscription and resource group. You should opt to leave the "Select source" value at "Blank database" to avoid creating a database with sample data (Figure 8-5).

Figure 8-5. Configuring the settings for a new SQL Database instance in the Azure Portal.

For the server option, choose an existing server, if you have one you prefer to use, or follow the steps to provision a new one (Figure 8-6).

Figure 8-6. Creating a new server for the SQL Database instance in the Azure Portal.

Leave the "Want to use SQL elastic pool?" option set to "Not now." Memory-optimized tables cannot be used with elastic pools. For the pricing tier, be sure to select a Premium tier (for the purposes of our sample, a P1 will suffice). You can leave the collation set at its default value and then select Create to provision your SQL Database (and related server if you chose to create one).

Firewall Rules

If you created a new server, after your SQL Database instance is ready, be sure to add the appropriate firewall rules so that the computer you are working from can access the databases it contains. This is something you can quickly configure using the Azure Portal. See the Microsoft Azure documentation (*http://bit.ly/2mtqAWu*).

With your database ready, you can proceed to the next step of creating a memory-optimized table to store the telemetry data. We recommend using SQL Server Management Studio (which is a free download) for these steps, but you can use the tools of your choice for this.

Connect to your newly created SQL Database instance and run the following script:

```
-- {"temp":65.0,"createDate":"2016-10-11T08:28:30Z","deviceId":"1"}
CREATE TABLE [RealtimeReadings] (
  -- ID should be a Primary Key, fields with a b-tree or hash index
  [id] bigint IDENTITY NOT NULL PRIMARY KEY NONCLUSTERED
          HASH WITH (BUCKET_COUNT = 30000000),
  [deviceId] int,
  [temp] decimal(8,4),
  createDate datetime,
  --  This table should have a columnar index
  INDEX Transactions_CCI CLUSTERED COLUMNSTORE
) WITH (
  --  This should be an in-memory table
  MEMORY_OPTIMIZED = ON
);
```

The aforementioned script will create the memory-optimized table. This is indicated by the WITH (MEMORY_OPTIMIZED) = ON clause. This table has also two indexes. It has a hash index on the id column that acts as the primary key for looking up specific readings, and it has a clustered columnstore index to support analytic querying against all columns. The hash index, defined with the NONCLUSTERED HASH WITH (BUCKET_COUNT = 30000000) clause, yields a hash index that, when the table is created, consumes approximately 353 megabytes' worth of memory-based storage, but it will never grow beyond that. The columnstore index is defined with the clause INDEX Transactions_CCI CLUSTERED COLUMNSTORE. Note that it does not specify any columns of the table, as the columnstore index covers all columns in a memory-optimized table.

After creating your table, you need to run the following to ensure that all memory-optimized tables auto-elevate their transaction level to snapshot automatically, which is the only level supported by memory-optimized tables:

```
--  In-memory tables should auto-elevate their transaction level
--  to Snapshot
ALTER DATABASE CURRENT SET MEMORY_OPTIMIZED_ELEVATE_TO_SNAPSHOT=ON ;
```

This makes it so you do not have to make changes to your application code that might only be written to work with disk-based tables and are likely to use transaction levels other than snapshot.

Now your table is ready for use. In the EventProcessorHostWebJob solution that accompanies this book's source code, we have provided the SqlDBEventProcessorHostWebHob project that you can run to pull telemetry out of your Event Hub and write it to your newly created, memory-optimized table. Before you run it locally or deploy it to a Web Job in Azure, be sure to update the *app.config* file with the connection string to your SQL Database, your Event Hub connection details, and your Storage account credentials. After starting up the event processor, run an instance of SimpleSensorConsole to populate telemetry in your Event Hub.

As both the event generator and event processor are running, you can perform analytic queries against the table, such as the following:

```
SELECT
  Count(*) Counted,
  DatePart(YYYY, createDate) [year],
  DatePart(MM, createDate) [month],
  DatePart(DD, createDate) [day],
  DatePart(hh, createDate) [hour]
FROM RealtimeReadings
GROUP BY
  DatePart(YYYY, createDate),
  DatePart(MM, createDate),
  DatePart(DD, createDate),
  DatePart(hh, createDate)
ORDER BY [year], [month], [day], [hour];
```

In SQL Server Management Studio, if you turn on the option to include the actual execution plan, you should see that this query correctly selects the clustered columnstore index (Figure 8-7).

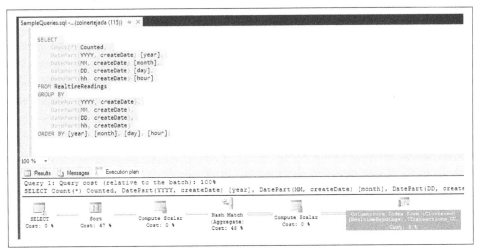

Figure 8-7. Running analytic queries against a memory-optimized table and showing how the execution plan selects to use the columnstore index.

Also in SQL Server Management Studio, you can examine your utilization of the available memory by using Object Explorer, right-clicking your database, and selecting Reports, then "Memory Usage by Memory Optimized Objects" (Figure 8-8).

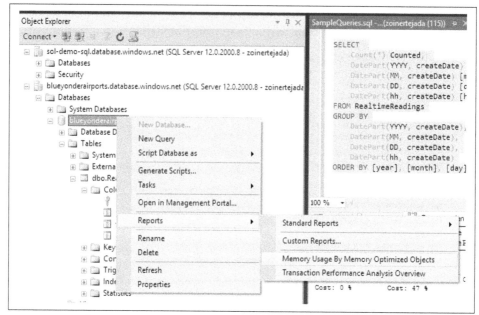

Figure 8-8. Utilizing the context menu to retrieve a memory usage report.

You will be presented with a report similar to Figure 8-9.

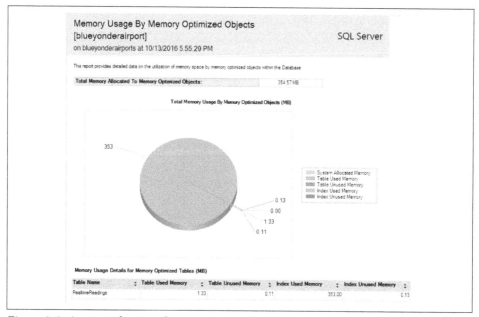

Figure 8-9. A report showing the memory used by the memory-optimized table. In this case that the data is using 1.33 MB, but the preallocated hash index is using 353 MB.

SQL Database in the Batch Serving Layer

The availability of the columnstore index for both memory-optimized tables and disk-based tables is a boon to performing analytics over large data sets. SQL Server has long had support for partitioned tables and the ability to swap in and out partitions of disk-based tables, which enables you to batch load data without having to drain and reload tables in their entirety. SQL Database also supports partitioning of tables in this way.

The application of SQL Database in the batch serving layer is a story of good up to a certain size. The largest database currently available, a P15, provides 1 TB of storage. If your storage requirements for the batch serving layer exceeds that, then you will need to use a sharding approach to divide your data among multiple SQL Database instances (each instance is a shard having the same scheme but a subset of the data), and enable T-SQL querying across the multiple shards. The good news is that SQL Database provides the Elastic Database Query feature to do just that, and it takes the now-familiar approach of using external tables to represent the table whose data spans across the shards. What's more, by using Elastic Database Query, you can still query using your favorite reporting tools as if it were a single SQL Server database.

Going Deeper on Elastic Database Query

Elastic Database Query is a robust feature, whose proper coverage is outside the scope of this book. To learn more about the feature, see the Microsoft Azure documentation (*http://bit.ly/2nK2IOA*).

The official recommendation is to use Elastic Database Query for "occasional reporting scenarios," but if your needs include heavy reporting workloads, possibly with more complex queries, then you should consider SQL Data Warehouse. This is the subject of the next section.

SQL Data Warehouse

SQL Data Warehouse is almost purpose-built to support that batch serving layer, predominantly because of the scale of the data it can serve. The maximum size of all permanent table data (i.e., excluding space used by tempdb or logs) is 240 TB once stored compressed on disk, and any given table maxes out at 60 TB of compressed disk storage. Columnstore storage, for example, provides compression of table data that yields as much as 5x compression on the raw data, so the actual uncompressed volume of data manageable by a SQL Data Warehouse database is close to 1 petabyte.

It has some limitations on random writes that are worth considering. From the data load perspective, SQL Data Warehouse is better suited for loading data in batches from files, then dealing with thousands or millions of small inserts. For example, if you try to load it with streaming data directly from your hot path, you are likely to find that it cannot keep up with that high velocity of small inserts. Moreover, the statistics that are used to optimize query execution are not automatically updated after data is inserted (in contrast to the way SQL Database and SQL Server operate). This means that your query performance is likely to suffer if significant new data is added without the statistics being manually updated.

When it comes to random reads, SQL Data Warehouse is again slightly different from its SQL Database and SQL Server brethren. It supports a maximum of 1,024 concurrently open connections, which is reasonable given a good solution design that minimizes chattiness with the database. However, only at most 32 queries can be executing concurrently. After that limit is reached, queries are queued. Queries against tables and views can queue up to 1,000 deep. This means that if you either have lots of users concurrently querying or a workload of queries that primarily take a long time to execute, then performance will not be ideal. This is where properly leveraging SQL Data Warehouse as a batch serving layer is important: you should design the tables so that all of the work needed to support good query performance occurs before you query—by way of how you load, distribute, partition, index, and create statistics for the data.

Given the aforementioned constraints, it is worth noting that SQL Data Warehouse would not make a good option for the speed serving layer.

HBase on HDInsight

Apache HBase is an open source, NoSQL database that is built on Hadoop and modeled after Google BigTable. HBase was created in 2007 at Powerset and was initially part of their contributions in Hadoop. Since then, it has become its own top-level project under the Apache Software Foundation umbrella. The goal of HBase is to provide a fault-tolerant data store hosting a few very large tables of sparse data—that is, billions or trillions of rows tall by possibly millions of columns wide—while at the same time allowing for very low latency and support for near-real-time random reads and random writes. The canonical use case for HBase was to support web search (where search engines build indexes that map terms to the web pages that contain them), but HBase has proven useful in other scenarios, including key/value storage, sensor data storage, and real-time query support, as well as situations that leverage HBase as a platform data store and layer on additional functionality (such as OpenTSDB for time series data and SQL support via Phoenix).

HBase organizes its data as rows of a table, where row data is grouped into column families and then columns. Column families represent a named grouping of logically or functionally related columns (it is desirable that they are compressed together or pinned to memory together). Thinking about it another way—within a given table, the number of column families is in the low tens at most, but the number of columns is generally unlimited. Each cell within a particular row of a column is timestamped, meaning you store a history of values for that cell sorted with the newest value coming first. Rows themselves are identified by a row key, which is represented as a byte array and must by unique within the table. Additionally, as you might expect, the row key controls the sort order of the rows. Collectively, you can think of a value as being located by this 5-tuple:

```
[TableName, RowKey, ColumnFamilyName, ColumnName, Timestamp] -> value
```

In keeping with its goal of providing low-latency random reads and writes, HBase takes a few optimizations:

- When data is updated it is first written to a commit log, called a *write-ahead log* in HBase, and then stored in the in-memory store. Only once the data in memory has exceeded a configured maximum value is the data flushed to disk and the commit logs can be discarded.

- When data is deleted, a *delete marker* (also known as a *tombstone marker*) is written to indicate the fact that the given key has been deleted. During the retrieval process, these delete markers mask out the actual values and hide them from reading clients.

- Data may be read from an in-memory cache or from the files on-disk.

The way you interact with HBase is by using the create, get, put, and scan commands. You write data to the database by using create and put, and read by using get, while you use scan to obtain data from multiple rows in a table. In other words, the mechanism is not SQL. However, by layering on Apache Phoenix to your HBase data store you get support for operational analytics that are programmed with SQL. Phoenix adds coprocessors that support running client-supplied code in the address space of the server, so it executes colocated with the data. It also adds support for secondary indexes beyond the single row key that HBase supports natively.

HBase on HDInsight provides managed HBase clusters integrated with the Azure environment. Your HBase cluster can read from and write to Azure Blob Storage and the Azure Data Lake Store. One feature worth noting is that HBase on HDInsight support private endpoints (i.e., endpoints that are not accessible via the public internet) because it can be provisioned into virtual networks.

This combination of easy querying using SQL, support for low-latency reads and writes, high scalability, and support for secondary indexes makes HBase a good candidate for both the batch serving and speed serving layers.

Let's examine this flow to store the Blue Yonder Airports telemetry data and perform an analytics query using SQL.

First, you will need to provision your HDInsight cluster. You can do this following the steps we have shown previously for provisioning any HDInsight instance. Just be sure to select HBase as the cluster type. This will include Apache Phoenix in the cluster. For our purposes here, we will use a cluster provisioned on the Linux operating system.

Once your cluster is provisioned, you will need to upload some of the flight data to query. You can use the Azure Portal to upload the provided sample file *On_Time_On_Time_Performance_2014_1_NoHeader.csv* to the container in Azure Storage that represents the root of your HDInsight cluster. We need to use a CSV file here that has no header because the import tool we will use cannot ignore the header row.

Next, look up the internal name of your Zookeeper head node in order to target the command-line tools against it. To do this, from the Azure Portal displaying your cluster's blade, select Cluster Dashboard. Log in with the admin credentials you provided during provisioning. From the Ambari home page, select HBase from the list of items on the left; then, in the Summary area, select the Active HBase Master link. On the screen that appears, the value displayed for hostname in the summary box is what you seek (Figure 8-10).

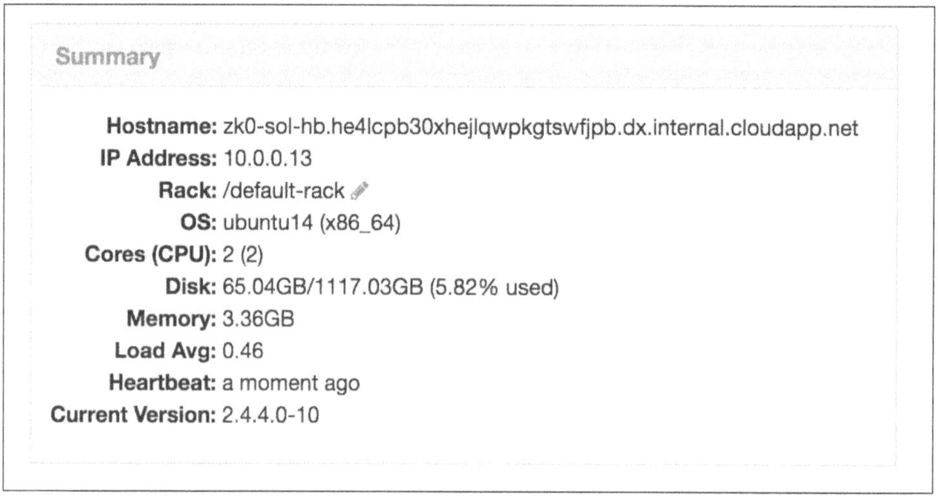

Summary

Hostname: zk0-sol-hb.he4lcpb30xhejlqwpkgtswfjpb.dx.internal.cloudapp.net
IP Address: 10.0.0.13
Rack: /default-rack ✎
OS: ubuntu14 (x86_64)
Cores (CPU): 2 (2)
Disk: 65.04GB/1117.03GB (5.82% used)
Memory: 3.36GB
Load Avg: 0.46
Heartbeat: a moment ago
Current Version: 2.4.4.0-10

Figure 8-10. The hostname value, as seen in Ambari, identifies the Zookeeper hostname needed by many HBase commands.

Next, SSH into your cluster and navigate to the Phoenix binaries by issuing the command:

```
cd /usr/hdp/current/phoenix-client/
```

From here you can run the SQLLine command-line tool to execute SQL commands against Phoenix. Run the following command, substituting in the value of your hostname:

```
./bin/sqlline.py <ZooKeeperHostname>.internal.cloudapp.net:2181:/
hbase-unsecure
```

Once within SQLLine, create the schema for the flights table by running the following:

```
CREATE TABLE FlightData
(
Year INTEGER not null,
Quarter INTEGER not null,
Month INTEGER not null,
DayofMonth INTEGER not null,
DayOfWeek VARCHAR(255),
FlightDate VARCHAR(255),
UniqueCarrier VARCHAR(255),
AirlineID VARCHAR(255),
Carrier VARCHAR(255),
TailNum VARCHAR(255),
FlightNum VARCHAR(255) not null,
OriginAirportID VARCHAR(255),
OriginAirportSeqID VARCHAR(255),
OriginCityMarketID VARCHAR(255),
Origin VARCHAR(255),
OriginCityName1 VARCHAR(255),
OriginCityName2 VARCHAR(255),
OriginState VARCHAR(255),
OriginStateFips VARCHAR(255),
OriginStateName VARCHAR(255),
OriginWac VARCHAR(255),
DestAirportID VARCHAR(255),
DestAirportSeqID VARCHAR(255),
DestCityMarketID VARCHAR(255),
Dest VARCHAR(255),
DestCityName1 VARCHAR(255),
DestCityName2 VARCHAR(255),
DestState VARCHAR(255),
DestStateFips VARCHAR(255),
DestStateName VARCHAR(255),
DestWac VARCHAR(255),
CRSDepTime INTEGER,
DepTime INTEGER,
DepDelay INTEGER,
DepDelayMinutes INTEGER,
DepDel15 BOOLEAN,
DepartureDelayGroups INTEGER,
DepTimeBlk VARCHAR(255),
TaxiOut INTEGER,
WheelsOff INTEGER,
WheelsOn INTEGER,
TaxiIn INTEGER,
CRSArrTime INTEGER,
ArrTime INTEGER,
ArrDelay INTEGER,
```

```
ArrDelayMinutes INTEGER,
ArrDel15 BOOLEAN,
ArrivalDelayGroups INTEGER,
ArrTimeBlk VARCHAR(255),
Cancelled BOOLEAN,
CancellationCode VARCHAR(255),
Diverted BOOLEAN,
CRSElapsedTime INTEGER,
ActualElapsedTime INTEGER,
AirTime INTEGER,
Flights INTEGER,
Distance INTEGER,
DistanceGroup INTEGER,
CarrierDelay INTEGER,
WeatherDelay INTEGER,
NASDelay INTEGER,
SecurityDelay INTEGER,
LateAircraftDelay INTEGER,
FirstDepTime INTEGER,
TotalAddGTime INTEGER,
LongestAddGTime INTEGER,
DivAirportLandings BOOLEAN,
DivReachedDest BOOLEAN,
DivActualElapsedTime INTEGER,
CONSTRAINT FlightData_PK PRIMARY KEY(Year, Quarter, Month, DayofMonth, FlightNum)
);
```

Now you are ready to load some data into this table.

Exit out of SQLLine by typing:

```
!quit
```

Back at the SSH command line, you will use the CsvBulkLoadTool included with Phoenix to load data into a table. Run the following command, being sure to adjust the path to your CSV file and the hostname of your Zookeeper node.

```
hadoop jar phoenix-client.jar
org.apache.phoenix.mapreduce.CsvBulkLoadTool
--table flightdata
--input /example/data/On_Time_On_Time_Performance_2014_1_NoHeader.csv
--zookeeper "<ZookeeperHostName>.cloudapp.net:/hbase-unsecure"
```

Note that in the preceding, the `--input` parameter accepts either a single CSV file or a path to a folder containing CSV files. This command will kick off a MapReduce job that, once complete, will have your data loaded into the HBase table and queryable by Phoenix.

Now you are ready to query the data. Begin by running SQLLine as shown previously.

Within SQLLine, run the following to output results in a CSV format (the default tabular format may be too wide for most displays):

```
!outputformat csv
select carrier, count(*) from flightdata group by carrier;
```

In a few moments, you should see a summary of the flight data similar to the following:

```
'CARRIER','COUNT(1)'
'AA','13299'
'AS','2977'
'B6','5377'
'DL','22919'
'EV','32323'
'F9','1362'
'FL','1449'
'HA','1610'
'MQ','20224'
'OO','30308'
'UA','9776'
'US','9330'
'VX','1272'
'WN','14773'
```

With that, you have just experienced the power of HBase, queried with the simplicity of SQL via Phoenix.

Azure Search

There is one final Azure service that pairs well with the data stores used in either the speed serving layer or the batch serving layer: Azure Search. Azure Search provides, in effect, an external index to any data. This means it can be used to provide a secondary index for data managed by data stores that do not support secondary indexes. The central object created in Azure Search is an index, and the items contained by the index are JSON documents. Index documents are loaded directly by applications on an item-by-item basis; for example, when new data is added to the source data store, the application orchestrating the input can also push the data that needs to be present in the index into Azure Search. In this case, data is inserted using either a REST API or the .NET SDK. Alternatively, data can be periodically pulled and indexed from the source using an indexer. Sources that support indexers include Azure Blob Storage, DocumentDB, SQL Database, and SQL Server in a VM. When using an indexer, you don't actually need any code—you just configure the indexer within the Azure Portal.

Loading Azure Search

For examples on how to load data into Azure Search from various sources, see the Microsoft Azure documentation (*http://bit.ly/ 2nJULcf*).

Azure Search provides for performant querying of the documents it manages. It has support for *faceted queries* (think data that has categories) and for setting up ranges/buckets and getting document counts by facets. It can provide a universal external index to all serving layer storage that provides quick, high-level summarization and navigation for a max of 2.4 TB (200 GB × 12 partitions) and 1.4 billion documents per service instance.

Querying Azure Search

For detailed examples on how to query Azure Search, see the Microsoft Azure documentation (*http://bit.ly/2n82gGI*).

In the end, you should consider Azure Search for select data sets of either serving layer to optimize the query experience of the downstream analytic clients.

Summary

In this chapter we completed our exploration of the data processing pipeline of the lambda architecture, having gotten our data to the serving layer. We looked at options for the speed serving layer (Redis, DocumentDB, SQL Database, SQL Server in VM, HBase on HDInsight) and options for the batch serving layer (SQL Data Warehouse and HBase on HDInsight).

In the next chapter, we will look at the options for adding intelligent analytics to your data pipeline, including the various mechanisms Azure offers for training and operationalizing your models, as well as the ready-made web services available from Microsoft Cognitive Services.

CHAPTER 9

Intelligence and Machine Learning

Advanced analytics pipelines often include machine learning to make predictions against data flowing through the data pipeline. Azure provides a few ways you can integrate machine learning into your data pipeline. While this chapter is not meant to provide deep coverage of machine learning in Azure, which merits a book of its own, it will provide broad coverage of the machine learning options available and the two most critical phases of most machine learning: model training and model operationalization (see Figure 9-1).

In the world of machine learning algorithms, there are two broad categories of algorithms (aka *learners*) that are defined based on the way the model is created. *Supervised* learners are like students in school—they need to be taught by example. They are shown lots of examples and the resulting outcomes, with the goal that one day (e.g., during final exams) they can be presented with new data and accurately predict the outcome (e.g., pass the test). They are called "supervised" because they need training before they can make any predictions, much like students need to be taught the subject before they hope to pass an exam on it. In machine learning, examples of scenarios that use supervised learners include:

- Examining email to classify it as spam or not spam
- Reviewing consumer profiles to predict their likelihood of default on a mortgage
- Predicting flight delays given flight and weather historical data

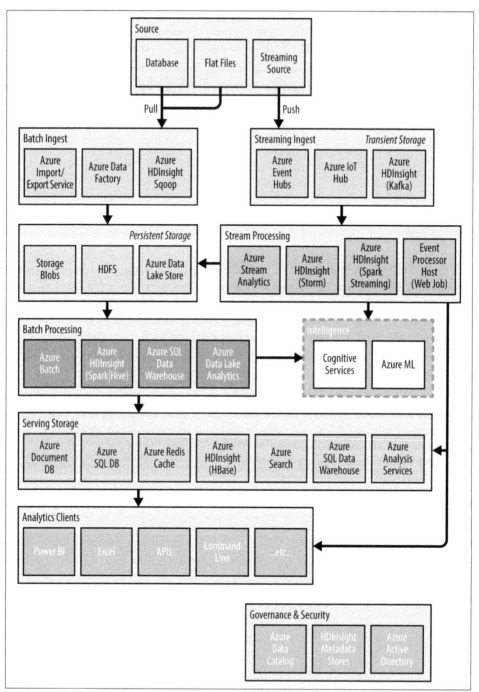

Figure 9-1. This chapter focuses on the intelligence components of the Azure analytics pipeline.

By contrast, *unsupervised* learners can make predictions the first time they see the data. They do not undergo a training phase. The most common example of this is grouping (aka *clustering*) consumers into distinct groups for marketing purposes. In this scenario, the algorithm is provided data about consumers and told to divide them into N buckets. The algorithm will do its best to create N buckets where within each bucket all consumers are very similar in some fashion, while ensuring the consumers in different buckets are sufficiently different. The outcome can be used, for example, to separate out buckets representing groups of consumers by behavior, including sale shoppers, regular customers, and patrons.

With an understanding of supervised and unsupervised learners in tow, let's define model training and model operationalization. In *model training* a supervised learner is trained, and the outcome is a model that can be used to make predictions. The integration of that model into a production analytics pipeline is called *model operationalization*. For example, the trained model might be wrapped in a web service and prediction is performed from a production application by invoking the web service. Unsupervised learners skip model training and typically go straight to operationalization.

In this chapter, we will cover machine learning with this perspective of model training and model operationalization in mind, using Figure 9-2 as a guide.

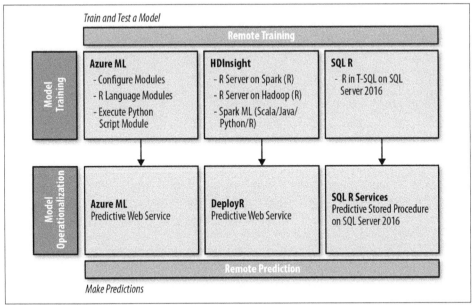

Figure 9-2. Model training and operationalization options in Azure.

Azure Machine Learning

Azure Machine Learning (Azure ML) allows you to train models using its web-based Machine Learning Studio. This interface provides a visual drag-and-drop experience that is similar to designing a flow chart, but instead of representing activities and decision points, each box is called a *module* and the flow chart itself is called a *training experiment*. Modules can retrieve data (such as from Azure Blob Storage, SQL Database, or external REST services), transform data (such as by converting data types, or addressing missing values), process data (such as by filtering or joining), train a model (using one of the 25+ built-in algorithms or pulling from the 8,000+ available in the community), and evaluate the model's performance. Training experiments can consist purely of configured modules, but also support modules allowing you to author and execute code using R or Python. When you train a model in Azure ML, the training happens in the context of a single virtual machine running on your behalf in Azure. See Figure 9-3.

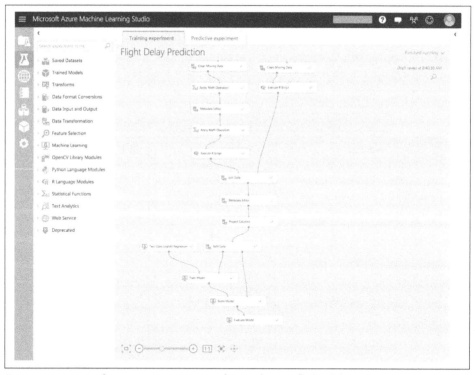

Figure 9-3. Example training experiment for predicting flight delays showing a mixture of built-in modules and modules that run R script code.

When you are ready to operationalize your training experiment, you click a button to set up the training experiment as a web service. The result is a new experiment called a *predictive experiment*, which basically wraps the call to execute the prediction against your trained model between web service input (that receives the inputs you want to predict against) and web service output (that returns the predicted results). See Figure 9-4.

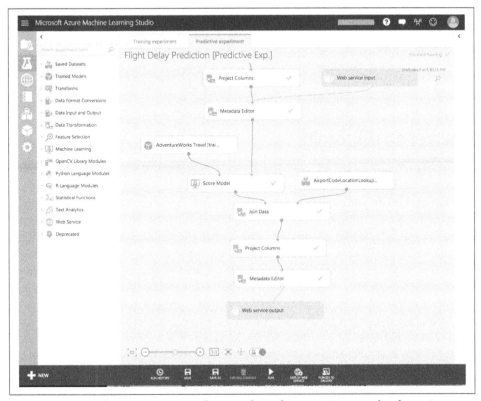

Figure 9-4. A predictive experiment showing the web service input and web service output modules that wrap the trained model.

Once you have created your predictive experiment, you publish it as a web service. At this point, your predictive web service is automatically provisioned and hosted in a scalable fashion by Azure ML. You can integrate calls to this web service into your pipeline code. It's worth noting that Azure ML can perform predictions in two ways. It can provide a prediction for a single input record (known as the *request/response API*), or you can provide it with a data source containing a batch of records to score (e.g., the path to a CSV file in Blob Storage or tables in SQL Database or Hive) and it will return a new CSV file with predictions for each row in that file (known as the *batch execution API*). Both mechanisms are available via separate web service endpoints that result when you publish your predictive experiment.

Beyond the aforementioned approaches, it is also possible to publish a web service from R Studio or a Jupyter notebook; see *http://bit.ly/2khOkuL*.

Hands-on with Azure Machine Learning

If you are interested in experimenting with Azure ML, see the tutorial in the Microsoft Azure documentation (*http://bit.ly/2nSiQu7*).

It is also worth exploring the ready-made experiments in the Cortana Intelligence Gallery (*https://gallery.cortanaintelligence.com/*), as they may provide solutions similar to your particular needs and are easily modified to suit your requirements.

R Server on HDInsight

HDInsight offers a variety of ways you can train a predictive model using the cluster of servers running in Azure. You can author R scripts that execute across the cluster to train and verify your model against data stored in Azure Blob Storage or Azure Data Lake Store by using the R Server on Spark or R Server on Hadoop cluster types of HDInsight. Deploying HDInsight with Spark enables you to author the model training using Scala, Java, Python, or R. The workflow followed here involves developing your application remotely or over SSH, and then executing your application on the cluster by using SSH. This approach enables you to train a model against data sets that are much larger than can fit in the memory of a single machine. The outcome of this training is typically a model that you serialize to disk for subsequent operationalization. Naturally, hosting your trained model as a web service within your HDInsight cluster is not cost-efficient, so the better approach is to host the model in another environment that just provides web server capabilities.

Hands-on with R Server on HDInsight

If you are interested in training a model using R Server on HDInsight, see the tutorial in the Microsoft Azure documentation (*http://bit.ly/2ndRBfd*).

When you are ready to operationalize your model, you take the serialized version of your trained model and upload it to a compatible host that can wrap prediction calls that use the model in a web service. In Azure, you deploy a virtual machine that is running Microsoft DeployR (you can find an image for this from the Azure Marketplace), which wraps a web services layer around a prediction script written in R (Figure 9-5).

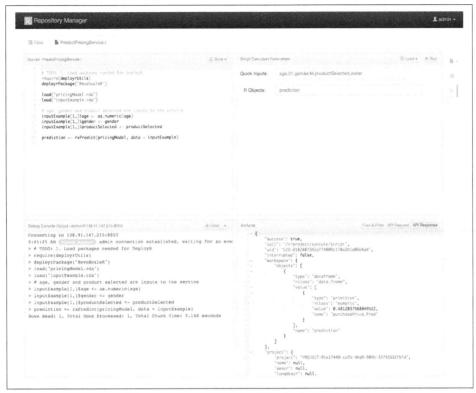

Figure 9-5. Example of the R script in Microsoft DeployR that invokes prediction against a trained model (top left), the input parameters (top right), the diagnostic output (bottom left), and the prediction results (bottom right).

SQL R Services

SQL R Services represents a new set of functionality available with SQL Server 2016 when running in an Azure virtual machine. It enables you to train and test predictive models in the context of SQL Server 2016—you literally embed your R script code within T-SQL, and SQL Server takes care of the execution. The pattern typically followed is that you package the R code that trains your model, and a call to `sp_exe` `cute_external_script` that executes the R code, in a stored procedure that saves the serialized model to a table in the database. Because the R script runs in the context of SQL Server, it has easy and ready access to data stored within the tables there.

Once you have trained your model, you operationalize it by encapsulating the R code to make predictions within another stored procedure. This stored procedure loads the serialized model from the table in which it was stored, and executes the prediction script, returning the results as tabular result sets. The net effect of this approach to operationalization is that it simplifies the integration of predictive analytics into any application that can use TDS to connect to SQL Server and invoke a stored procedure.

Hands-on with SQL R Services

Want to get your hands on SQL R Services? Get started with the great tutorial at *http://bit.ly/2ndCoLk*.

Microsoft Cognitive Services

Not all predictive analytics services in Azure require you to build your own model from scratch. Microsoft Cognitive Services provides a set of specialized web services that are already fully trained and hosted and ready for integration with your analytics pipeline or directly within your application.

Categorically, you can understand the set of services provided by Microsoft Cognitive Services by examining them in the context of these four categories:

Vision
Enables your pipeline to understand images and videos, via the Emotion API (which can detect people's emotions from a photo), Face API (which provides demographic information from a photo), and various computer vision APIs (which can analyze image content, detect celebrities, create smart thumbnails, and perform OCR).

Speech
Enables your pipeline to process spoken audio by filtering noise, identifying speakers, and understanding intent. Includes the Speaker Recognition API and the Bing Speech API (which provides various services like speech to text, intent recognition, and text to speech).

Language
Enables your pipeline to process text and understand text-based conversation. The APIs include Text Analytics (which provides sentiment analysis, key phrase extraction, topic detection, and language detection), the Web Language Model API (which provides word breaking, text conditional and join probabilities, and statement completions), and the Language Understanding Intelligent Service API (which enables you to define context models for understanding objects and actions from prose).

Recommendations
The Recommendations API enables your pipeline to apply intelligence such as frequently bought together, item-to-item recommendation, and customer-to-item recommendation.

See All the APIs

For the latest list of Cognitive Services APIs, see *https://www.micro-soft.com/cognitive-services/en-us/apis*.

Let's drill into the plethora of Cognitive Services options a little further. The current list includes a suite of 23 services, which can seem an overwhelming number of options. To help you pick the one that is right for you, here is the 30,000-foot view on each. We'll follow that with a table that will help you select which service to use based on the type of data you intend to process.

Academic Knowledge API
Supports querying of academic research papers.

Bing Autosuggest API
Provides suggestions to a partial search query based on what other Bing users have used.

Bing Image Search API
Provides a similar search capability as *bing.com/images* for submitting a query and getting back a list of relevant images from the web.

Bing News Search API
Provides a similar experience to *bing.com/news* for submitting a query and getting back a list of relevant news articles from the web.

Bing Speech API
Provides support for speech recognition and text to speech.

Bing Spell Check API
Provides inline suggestions for misspelled words.

Bing Video Search API
Provides a similar search capability to *bing.com/videos* for submitting a search query and getting back a list of relevant videos from the web.

Bing Web Search API
Provides a similar search capability to *bing.com/search* for submitting a search query and getting back a list of relevant search results from the web.

Computer Vision API
Tags/categorizes images, identifies type and quality of images, detects faces, performs OCR, identifies adult content, crops photos, and automatically generates text descriptions of photo contents.

Content Moderator

Scans text, images, and video for profanity, adult content, and personally identifiable information (PII); autocorrects text content; reviews API and web experience for human–computer content moderation workflows.

Emotion API

Detects emotions in photos or video.

Entity Linking

Detects entities in text and returns a list, along with possible Wikipedia entries.

Face API

Detects faces in photos, identifies facial attributes (pose, gender, age, facial hair, glasses), and provides face recognition capabilities (verification, find similar, face grouping, and person identification).

Knowledge Exploration Service

Builds an index from structured data, authors a grammar to interpret natural language queries, and provides interactive query formulation. Currently this is an executable that can be run locally or deployed in an Azure VM or cloud service and then exposed via a Web API interface.

Linguistic Analysis APIs

A set of APIs that provide sentence splitting and tokenization, part-of-speech tagging, and constituency (i.e., key phrase) parsing.

LUIS (Languange Understanding Intelligent Service)

Takes a sentence and interprets the intention and key entities present. Enables custom apps as well those leveraging Cortana (the personal assistant). Includes channels for news, weather, stocks, dictionary definitions, and time. Supports integration with Slack and the Microsoft Bot Framework.

QnA Maker

Enables you to quickly build an interactive bot (typically in Azure Bot Service) that can answer questions just by learning from web pages or files containing text content (`.tsv` or `.tx`, `.doc`, `.pdf`) in the typical question-and-answer format used by FAQs.

Recommendations

Enables ecommerce applications to provide recommendations such as frequently bought together, item-to-item, and customer-to-item recommendations.

Speaker Recognition API

Provides capabilities for identification and verification based on a user's speech.

Text Analytics

A set of APIs supporting sentiment analysis, key phrase extraction, topic detection, and language detection.

Translator API

Performs language translation, speech-to-speech translation, text language detection, and language translation in speech to text and text to speech. Includes an embeddable web widget for translating your own web pages in situ.

Video API

Tracks faces, detects motion, stabilizes video, and creates thumbnails.

Web Language Model API

Natural language processing operations supporting joint probability of a word sequence, conditional probability of one word given preceding words, list of completions, and word breaking of strings that are missing spaces.

One way to approach identifying which service might be helpful to your application is to take the perspective of the data used as input. In Table 9-1, the options are text (the input data is textual), speech (the input is recorded human speech), images and/or video, web search (the input is web search query), and other (those whose input is different from the aforementioned).

Table 9-1. Narrow your options based on the type of input data (first row)

Text	Speech	Images and video	Web search	Other
Text Analytics	Bing Speech API	Computer Vision API	Academic Knowledge API	Bing Spell Check API
Content Moderator	Speaker Recognition API	Content Moderator	Bing Autosuggest API	Recommendations
Entity Linking		Emotion API	Bing Image Search API	
LUIS		Face API	Bing News Search API	
QnA Maker		Video API	Bing Video Search API	
Linguistic Analysis APIs			Bing Web Search API	
Translator API	Translator API			
Knowledge Exploration Service				
Web Language Model API				

Since you will generally utilize the Cognitive Services in response to some event, like a photo being uploaded or a text chat message being input, a good way to integrate them in your application is to use the Azure Functions service. If you use the Consumption plan for hosting your Azure function, then you pay only for the time your code is running, as opposed to having a web server running 24/7 even while there is no activity. You can create these functions using either Visual Studio 2015 or directly within the Azure Portal. The latter approach can be useful during your experimentation with a given Cognitive Service on account of the minimal overhead it requires to create and deploy a function.

Visual Studio Tools for Azure Functions

If you are interested in developing your Azure functions with Visual Studio, you will need to get the latest version of the Visual Studio Tools for Azure Functions. You can read a quickstart blog> (*http://bit.ly/2nJV5Yj*) on how to install and use the tools.

To illustrate using a Cognitive Service from an Azure function, let's take a computer vision scenario where we upload a photo to Azure Blob Storage and would like to get a peek at what a Cognitive Services API would "see" in the photo. To do this we will integrate a call to the Computer Vision API. Begin by creating the Cognitive Services account (Figure 9-6):

1. In the Azure Portal (*https://portal.azure.com*), select New→Intelligence + Analytics→Cognitive Services APIs.

2. In the Create Cognitive Services Account blade, provide a unique account name.

3. Select your subscription.

4. In the "API type" drop-down, select Computer Vision API.

5. Select a location.

6. For the pricing tier, you can use any of the options.

7. Choose a resource group as desired.

8. Check the checkbox to agree to the legal terms.

9. Select Create.

In a few moments your new Cognitive Services account should be ready. When it is ready, navigate to its blade in the Azure Portal and follow these steps:

1. Select Keys from the menu bar at left.

2. Take note of the Account Name and Key 1 values for when we configure the Azure function.

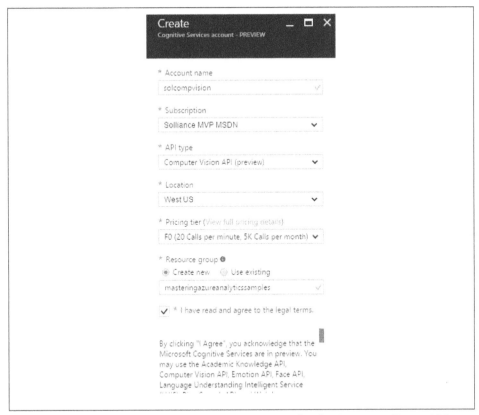

Figure 9-6. Creating a new Cognitive Services account for the Computer Vision API

Now, create a new Azure function by following these steps in the Azure Portal (Figure 9-7).

1. Select New→Compute→Function App.

2. Provide a unique name for your new function app.

3. Select your subscription and resource group.

4. For the hosting plan, select Consumption Plan.

5. Choose a location.

6. Leave Storage Account set to create a new account.

7. Select Create.

Figure 9-7. Create a new Azure function app using a Consumption Plan

Once your function app is ready, navigate to its blade in the Azure Portal and follow these steps (Figure 9-8):

1. From the menu on the left, select New Function.

2. From the "Choose a template" menu, select BlobTrigger-CSharp.

3. Provide a name for your function.

4. Under the Configure section, provide the path where you will upload images in your Azure Storage account.

5. For "Storage account connection," leave the value set to AzureWebJobsDashboard; this will enable us to reuse the Storage account created to support this function. Of course, if you want to use a different Azure Storage account, select the new link to the right of this field.

6. Select Create.

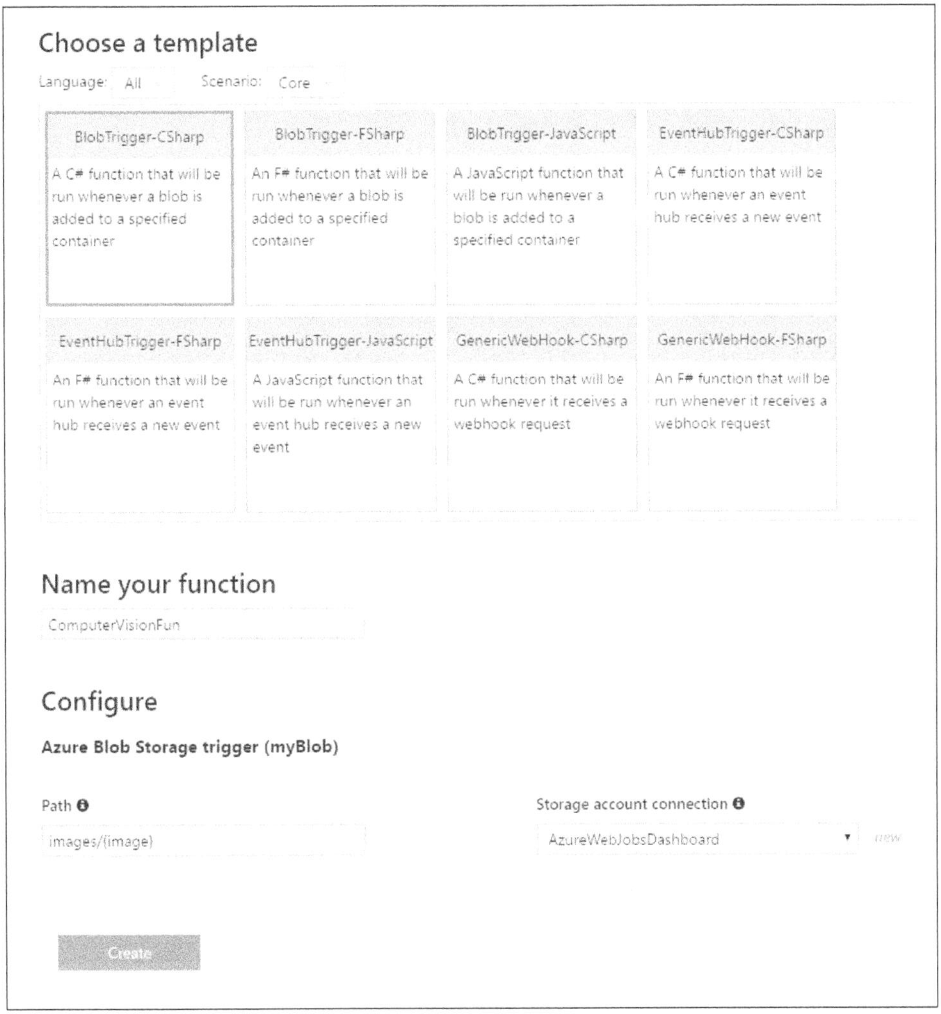

Choose a template

Language: All   Scenario: Core

BlobTrigger-CSharp	**BlobTrigger-FSharp**	**BlobTrigger-JavaScript**	**EventHubTrigger-CSharp**
A C# function that will be run whenever a blob is added to a specified container	An F# function that will be run whenever a blob is added to a specified container	A JavaScript function that will be run whenever a blob is added to a specified container	A C# function that will be run whenever an event hub receives a new event
EventHubTrigger-FSharp	**EventHubTrigger-JavaScript**	**GenericWebHook-CSharp**	**GenericWebHook-FSharp**
An F# function that will be run whenever an event hub receives a new event	A JavaScript function that will be run whenever an event hub receives a new event	A C# function that will be run whenever it receives a webhook request	An F# function that will be run whenever it receives a webhook request

Name your function

ComputerVisionFun

Configure

Azure Blob Storage trigger (myBlob)

Path ❶

images/{image}

Storage account connection ❶

AzureWebJobsDashboard   ▼   new

Create

Figure 9-8. Creating an Azure function that will trigger when a file is uploaded to Blob Storage.

In the code dialog that appears, replace the contents with the following code:

```
#r "Microsoft.WindowsAzure.Storage"
#r "Newtonsoft.Json"

using System.Net;
using System.Net.Http;
using System.Net.Http.Headers;
using Newtonsoft.Json;
using Microsoft.WindowsAzure.Storage.Table;
using System.IO;
```

```
public static async Task Run(Stream myBlob, TraceWriter log)
{
    log.Info("Before call to Vision API");
    string result = await CallVisionAPI(myBlob, log);
    log.Info("After call to Vision API");

    log.Info("Result from call to Computer Vision API: '" + result + "'");
    log.Info(result);
}

static async Task<string> CallVisionAPI(Stream image, TraceWriter log)
{
    using (var client = new HttpClient())
    {
        var content = new StreamContent(image);
        var url = "https://api.projectoxford.ai/vision/v1.0/" +
                    "analyze?visualFeatures=description";

        log.Verbose("Vision API Key: '" +
          Environment.GetEnvironmentVariable(
          "Vision_API_Subscription_Key") + "'");

        client.DefaultRequestHeaders.Add("Ocp-Apim-Subscription-Key",
          Environment.GetEnvironmentVariable("Vision_API_Subscription_Key"));
        content.Headers.ContentType =
          new MediaTypeHeaderValue("application/octet-stream");

        var httpResponse = await client.PostAsync(url, content);

        log.Verbose("Vision API Response '" + httpResponse + "'");

        if (httpResponse.StatusCode == HttpStatusCode.OK)
        {
            return await httpResponse.Content.ReadAsStringAsync();
        }
    }
    return null;
}
```

Next, you will need to provide your function the account name and key to your Cognitive Services Account that you noted earlier (Figure 9-9):

1. In your Azure Functions blade, from the menu on the left select "Function app settings."

2. Select the button labeled "Configure app settings."

3. Scroll down to "App settings" and add a new key/value entry where the key is "Vision_API_Subscription_Key" and the value is the value of Key 1 from your API.

4. Select Save to apply your new setting.

App settings

AzureWebJobsDashboard	DefaultEndpointsProtocol=...
AzureWebJobsStorage	DefaultEndpointsProtocol=...
FUNCTIONS_EXTENSION_VE...	~1
WEBSITE_CONTENTAZUREFI...	DefaultEndpointsProtocol=...
WEBSITE_CONTENTSHARE	solcomputervision
WEBSITE_NODE_DEFAULT_V...	6.5.0
Vision_API_Subscription_Key	3c0062ef12644cc99e6c4f85...
Key	Value

Figure 9-9. Adding a Cognitive Services key to an Azure function's app settings.

Now you are ready to upload a photo to try out your function.

1. Navigate back to the Code screen for your Azure function and click the Logs icon so that you can see the real-time logs emitted as your function executes. Leave this tab open as you proceed.

2. In a new browser tab, navigate to the Azure Portal and locate the resource group that contains your Azure function.

3. Select the Storage account in that resource group associated with your Azure function.

4. Select the Blobs tile.

5. On the Blob service tab, select Container and provide the name "images" for the new container that will hold your uploaded images.

6. Select Create.

7. Back on the "Blob service" blade, select your images container to view its contents.

8. From the command bar, select Upload.

9. On the "Upload blob" blade, use the folder button to launch a file picker dialog and choose an image to upload.

10. Select Upload on the "Upload blob" blade.

11. Return to the tab where your Azure function log is displayed. You should see new output similar to Figure 9-10, showing what the Computer Vision API "saw" in the photo.

Figure 9-10. Example monitoring function log output as an image is processed.

For example, in my case I uploaded the photo shown in Figure 9-11.

Figure 9-11. Sample photo submitted to the Computer Vision API

The Computer Vision API came up with the following result (formatted for readability):

```
{
  "description": {
    "tags": [
      "grass",
      "outdoor",
      "house",
      "building",
      "green",
      "yard",
      "lawn",
      "front",
      "small",
      "home",
      "field",
      "red",
      "sitting",
      "grassy",
      "white",
      "brick",
      "large",
```

```
          "old",
          "standing",
          "grazing",
          "sheep",
          "parked",
          "garden",
          "woman",
          "man",
          "hydrant",
          "sign"
      ],
      "captions": [
        {
          "text": "a large brick building with green grass in front
                  of a house",
          "confidence": 0.73412133238971
        }
      ]
  },
  "requestId": "842b2e69-2e09-441d-9c60-8a3700435c6e",
  "metadata": {
    "width": 700,
    "height": 539,
    "format": "Png"
  }
}
```

Take a look at the tags and the autogenerated caption. While it's not perfect (the API acknowledges it was only 73% confident), it's a pretty good interpretation of the photo given there were no humans involved!

Summary

In this chapter, we looked at the options for adding intelligent analytics to your data pipeline, including the various mechanisms Azure offers for training and operationalizing your models, as well as the ready-made web services available from Microsoft Cognitive Services.

In the next chapter, we will examine how you manage the metadata for your data, and keep track of your data assets.

CHAPTER 10

Managing Metadata in Azure

When you think of metadata, you probably think schema—what are the names and types of fields contained in a table, the names of tables, etc.? This is the sort of information managed by localized metadata stores, like the Hive metadata store, which manages the metadata for external tables used by both Spark and Hive on HDInsight.

However, there is a bigger-picture metadata consideration that has to do with how you manage the metadata across all of your data assets in your data lake. In this chapter we explore one approach to doing so using the Azure Data Catalog (Figure 10-1).

Managing Metadata with Azure Data Catalog

When you first start collecting your data assets, managing what data lives where is easy. You have this database for your ecommerce transactions, and that data warehouse for your analytics. Think of how you would describe that to the new person on your team. However, as your data needs evolve to encompass a data lake, you have an explosion of databases, multiple data warehouses, and hyperscale filesystems. How do you help your new hire find that transaction history log he is asking for? That is the goal of Azure Data Catalog, a fully managed cloud service that enables users to discover the data sources they need for themselves, and to be certain it is the data they are looking for, all without actually having to move the data out of the data store in which it resides.

Azure Data Catalog is intended to enable any user—from developers to data scientists —to discover, understand, and consume data, but also to empower folks in the know about a data source (such as the owners of the ecommerce database mentioned previously) to easily contribute their understanding of the data by means of authoring metadata and annotations.

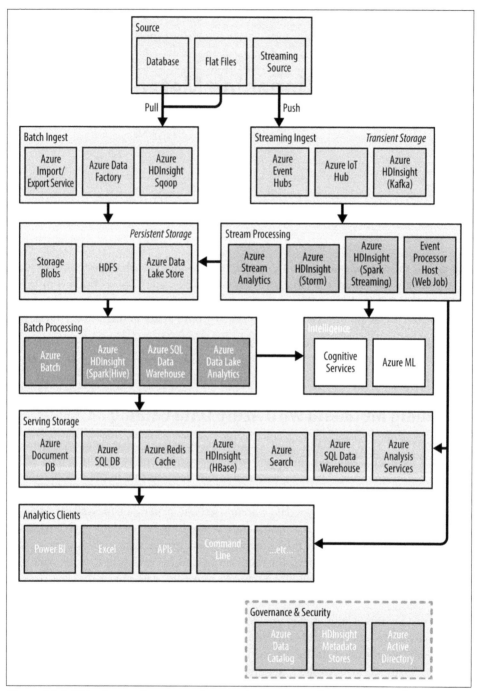

Figure 10-1. This chapter focuses on the metadata aspects of governance and security in the Azure analytics pipeline.

Users of Azure Data Catalog search for their desired data using a web portal that returns in the results descriptive metadata about the data as well as the connection information required to access the data in its native data store. For example, for SQL Database, the connection information returned includes the standard connection string format. For certain data sources, the web portal provides single-click access to open the data source using Power BI, Excel, or SQL Server Data Tools.

Search Syntax

The Azure Data Catalog supports a robust search syntax. You can search for assets whose metadata matches a term, but also specify more complex boolean expressions that match specific properties of an asset.

See *http://bit.ly/2ndOHHt* for more details on the syntax options.

Metadata publishers add metadata to the Azure Data Catalog via a public API, via an application that automates the collection of metadata, or by entering it manually in the Data Catalog web portal.

This list of supported data sources is extensive, so here is just a sampling of the supported data sources:

- Azure Data Lake Store
- Azure Blob Storage
- Azure Table Storage
- HDFS
- Hive Tables and Views
- MySQL Tables and Views
- Oracle Tables and Views
- SQL Data Warehouse Tables and Views
- SQL Server Tables and Views
- Teradata Tables and Views
- FTP files and directories
- HTTP endpoints
- OData endpoints

In addition to enabling metadata discovery and metadata publishing, Azure Data Catalog supports governance efforts by providing asset-level authorization that controls which users can view and modify any metadata asset.

Data Catalog in the Blue Yonder Airports Scenario

If you've been following along with the examples in this book, you have probably noticed Blue Yonder Airports has a lot of data stores. Let's look at the experience of using Azure Data Catalog to manage the metadata for a few of these.

You Will Need Azure Active Directory Credentials

Azure Data Catalog relies on Azure Active Directory, so you will need to try this using a work or school account. Personal accounts will not work. This restriction only applies for creating and accessing the data catalog, so if you have data stores you want to utilize that are in Azure subscriptions using personal accounts, you will be able to add metadata for those.

Begin by provisioning a new Azure Data Catalog.

1. Navigate to *https://azure.microsoft.com/en-us/services/data-catalog/*.
2. Select the Get Started button.
3. Provide a name for your data catalog, select a subscription, and choose a location (Figure 10-2).

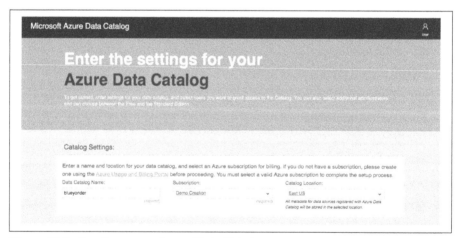

Figure 10-2. Creating a new Azure Data Catalog.

4. Select a pricing tier (you can leave it at Free Edition for the purposes of these steps).
5. Leave Security Groups, Catalog Users, Glossary Administrators, and Catalog Administrators at their defaults (Figure 10-3).

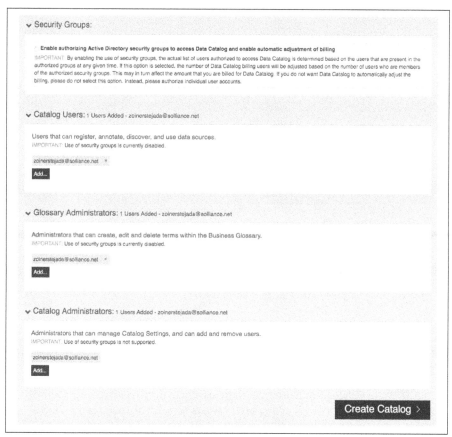

Figure 10-3. Configuring the new Azure Data Catalog.

6. Select Create Catalog. It will take a few minutes to provision.

7. When you see the home page for Azure Data Catalog, you are all ready to go (Figure 10-4).

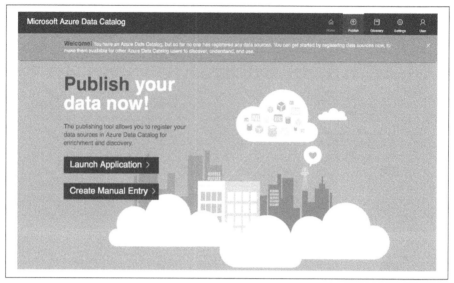

Figure 10-4. Azure Data Catalog home page

What's the Difference Between Standard and Free?

The Azure Data Catalog Free Edition includes access to all Data Catalog features except those having to do with asset-level authorization (which allows asset owners to restrict which users can discover and annotate registered data assets). The Standard Edition adds these capabilities.

Add an Azure Data Lake Store Asset

Let's add an Azure Data Lake Store to the data catalog.

1. On the Azure Data Catalog page, select Create Manual Entry.

2. Provide the Name, Friendly Name, Description, and Request Access (describing how a user should go about requesting access).

3. For the Source Type choose Azure Data Lake Store and set the Object Type to Data Lake with OAuth Authentication (Figure 10-5).

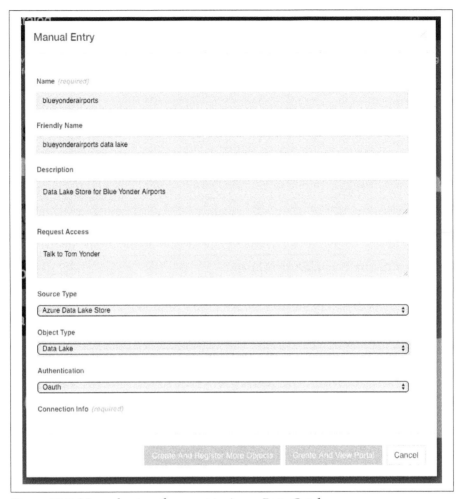

Figure 10-5. Manual entry of an asset to Azure Data Catalog.

4. For the "Connection info," provide the URL to your Azure Data Lake Store.

5. Select Create and View Portal.

6. Once the asset has been created, you will be able to see it in the catalog. Notice the search box at the top and the faceted search fields at left that you can use to find assets (Figure 10-6).

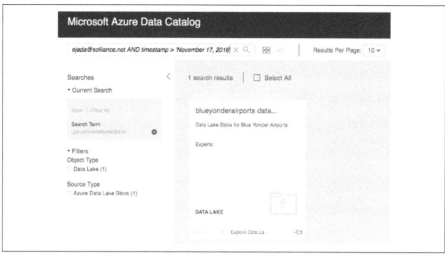

Figure 10-6. A Data Lake Store asset.

7. Click on your Data Lake Store asset to view the Properties panel with the metadata (Figure 10-7).

Figure 10-7. Properties panel for an Azure Data Lake Store asset.

8. Select the Document tab. Note that you can write more detailed descriptions about the data asset here using the rich text editor (Figure 10-8).

Figure 10-8. Documentation tab for an Azure Data Lake Store asset.

That should give you a sense of the manual approach to adding an asset, but if you are running Windows there is a ClickOnce application you can download and run that will automate the collection of the metadata. If you are running on Windows, continue with the following steps.

Add Azure Storage Blobs

Now, let's look at the similar process for adding Azure Blob Storage assets. We will add these using the Azure Data Catalog application.

1. From the menu bar at the top of the Data Catalog website, select Publish.
2. On the Publish screen, select Launch Application.
3. Download and run the app.
4. Select Install on the Application Install Security Warning.
5. The application will take a few moments to download and install.
6. Accept the license agreement.
7. On the Welcome! screen, select "Sign in." Use the credentials you used when creating the Azure Data Catalog to sign in when prompted (Figure 10-9).

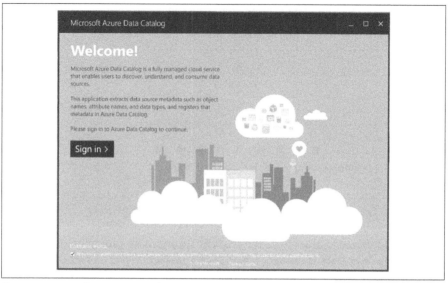

Figure 10-9. Welcome screen for the Azure Data Catalog ClickOnce application.

8. On the Select Data Source screen, select Azure Blob and then select Next (Figure 10-10).

Figure 10-10. Selecting Azure Blob to add a Blob Storage asset.

9. Provide your Storage account name and key, and select Connect (Figure 10-11).

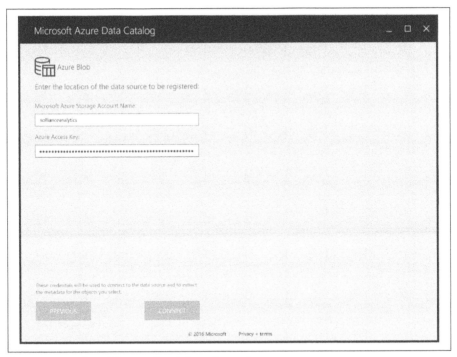

Figure 10-11. Providing credentials to Azure Storage.

10. From the list of blob containers under Server Hierarchy, select the container that has your flight delay data.

11. In the "Available objects" listing, choose the subfolder that contains your flight delay blobs.

12. To the right of the "Available objects" listing, select the right chevron to add the blob directory (Figure 10-12).

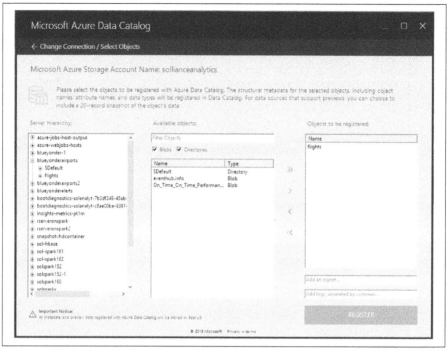

Figure 10-12. Selecting a subfolder of a container in Azure Storage to add as a directory asset.

13. Select Register. You have now registered this container.

14. To register individual blobs within it, select Register More Objects.

15. Select Azure Blob and then select Next.

16. Provide your Storage account name and key, and select Connect.

17. This time, select the *flights* subfolder underneath your container. The blobs in that folder should appear listed in the "Available objects."

18. Select the double chevron to add all of the blob files. See Figure 10-13.

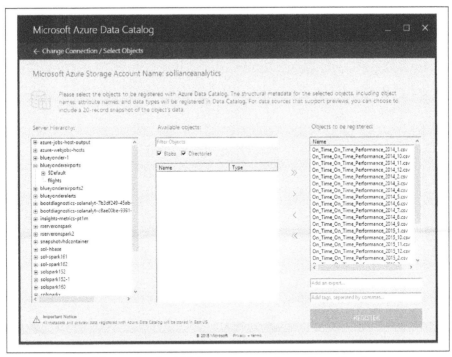

Figure 10-13. Adding individual blobs as assets to Azure Data Catalog.

19. Select Register. Wait for the registration to complete.

20. Select View Portal.

Now that you have the Blob Storage container, you can document and search for the individual Storage blobs available as assets (Figure 10-14).

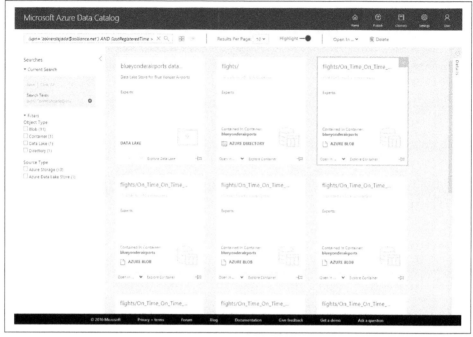

Figure 10-14. Viewing blob assets available in Azure Data Catalog.

If you select a blob, notice next to the Properties pane the Data Profile tab appears. Selecting that will show the size of the blob (Figure 10-15).

Table Profile			
Number Of Rows	Size	Last Data Update	Last Schema Update
0	207.84 MB		4/8/2016

Figure 10-15. Viewing the Data Profile for a blob asset in Azure Data Catalog.

Add a SQL Data Warehouse

Now, let's add the SQL Data Warehouse that contains the FlightDelays table.

1. Return to the Microsoft Data Catalog application and select Register More Objects.

2. This time, select SQL Data Warehouse and select Next.

3. Enter the connection details for your SQL Data Warehouse instance that has the FlightDelays table.

4. In the Server Hierarchy, select the root node.

5. In the "Available objects" listing, select your FlightDelays table and press the right chevron to add it to the "Objects to be registered" list.

6. In the "Objects to be registered" list, select the table.

7. In the "add tags" field, add the tags "historical, flight delay, DOT" to annotate this table with those tags for easier discovery later.

8. Select Register. When it is finished registering, select View Portal.

You should see two new assets, a SQL Data Warehouse and a SQL Data Warehouse table. Also, notice that your faceted search options have automatically been populated with the tags you provided (Figure 10-16).

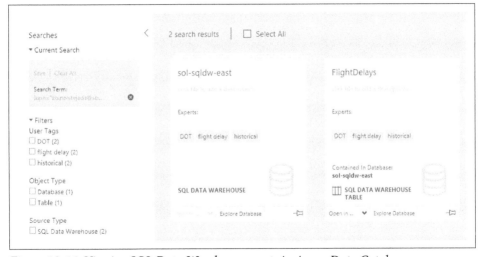

Figure 10-16. Viewing SQL Data Warehouse assets in Azure Data Catalog.

Select the FlightDelays table, and in the Properties panel select the Columns tab. Notice that the application has automatically populated the columns for you (Figure 10-17).

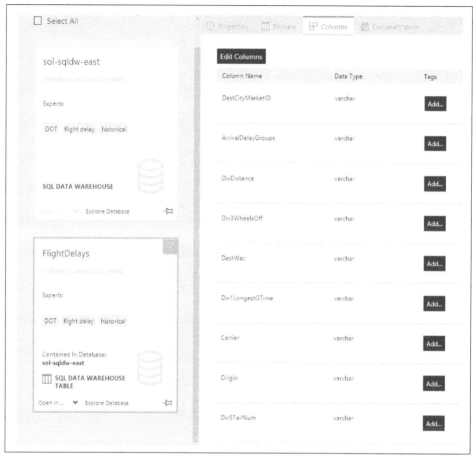

Figure 10-17. Viewing the columns of a SQL Data Warehouse table in Data Catalog.

Back on the FlightDelays table asset, select Open In and choose Excel (Top 1000). This will download an Excel file. Open the file and log in to your SQL Data Warehouse; it brings back a sample of the data (Figure 10-18).

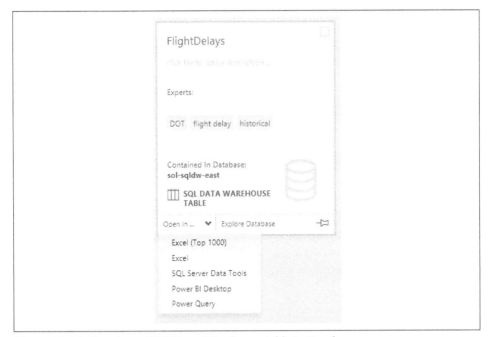

Figure 10-18. Opening a SQL Data Warehouse table in Excel.

Now that you have loaded a few different data assets in Azure SQL Data Catalog, you can see how this will help you manage the data across all of the assets Blue Yonder Airports may have in a data lake.

Summary

In this chapter we examined how to organize all of the data assets in a data lake by using the Azure Data Catalog as our metadata repository.

In the next chapter, we will look at considerations for securing the data in our data lake.

CHAPTER 11

Protecting Your Data in Azure

If you built a data pipeline following the lambda architecture guidance in this book, then odds are you view your data as a valuable asset—one that you want to protect.

In this chapter we take a high-level look at the options for protecting your data in Azure.

Identity and Access Management

Controlling who gets access to the resources in your analytics pipeline and what they can do once they have access is the goal of identity and access management. This boils down to these main concepts:

Identity
    Who are the users or groups?

Authentication
    How do you verify that a user or application is who they say they are?

Authorization
    What do you let the user or application do?

The actual mechanisms provided for defining identities, authenticating identities, and authorizing actions varies by Azure service, but can be distilled to the following, which we'll call *access management mechanisms*:

Azure Active Directory identities
    Using Azure Active Directory (AAD) to manage user identities, application identities, and group identities.

Shared keys
    Typically a username and password or a key name and secret value.

Shared access signatures

Cryptographically secured URIs that encapsulate a resource and the permissions allowed on that resource in a convenient URL format. The canonical example of this is Azure Blob Storage, which enables you to manage access to an account, container, or blob and specify what the user is allowed to do with it (read, write, delete, create, update, etc.).

Policies

Describe what actions a user is allowed to take. This could take the form of POSIX-style permissions (e.g., read, write, execute) or more service-specific permissions (e.g., IoT Hub defines manage, send, and listen).

Role-based access control

Permissions are applied to a user or application based on their membership in a role or group.

Firewall

Access is allowed based on the IP address of the client attempting to reach the service.

In this chapter, we will not go into the specifics of using each of the mechanisms (the previous chapters covered many of these by way of using the service). However, it is important to understand, for your data lake and analytics pipeline, exactly what access management surface area you need to consider when securing your solution. Table 11-1 summarizes the available mechanisms for all the services mentioned in this book.

Table 11-1. Access management mechanisms by service

Azure service	Access management mechanisms
Azure Event Hubs	Shared access policies using shared access key name and value Policy defines manage, send, and listen permissions
Azure IoT Hub	Azure role-based access control Shared access policies using shared access key name and value Policy defines registry read/write, service connect, and device connect permissions Device shared access signatures
Azure Import/Export Service	Azure Storage account key for disk preparation Personal, school, or work credentials for job creation
Azure Data Factory	Azure role-based access control
Azure HDInsight	Azure role-based access control Admin username and password SSH user and password SSH public key
Azure Stream Analytics	Azure role-based access control

Azure service	Access management mechanisms
Azure Blob Storage	Azure role-based access control Azure Storage account name and key Shared access signatures
Azure Data Lake Store	Azure role-based access control AAD native client application AAD Web Apps application with secret key AAD Web Apps application with certificate POSIX access controls on lake, folders, and files Firewall
Azure SQL Data Warehouse	SQL authentication AAD identities Firewall
Azure SQL Database	SQL authentication AAD identities Firewall
Azure Data Lake Analytics	Azure role-based access control AAD identities
Azure DocumentDB	Azure role-based access control Account endpoint and account key with read/write and read-only versions Firewall
Azure Redis Cache	Hostname and password
Azure Search	Azure role-based access control Shared keys for administration and query

Data Protection

Beyond controlling who can access your data and what they can do with it, your solution needs to consider the security of the data as it sits at rest on disk and while it is in transit between the client and the data store.

These are collectively the data protection mechanisms, and we can summarize the available options for data protection at rest as follows:

Disk encryption
　　The disk volume or virtual hard disk is encrypted.

Storage encryption
　　For file stores like Azure Blob Storage and Azure Data Lake Store, the data is encrypted prior to write and decrypted prior to read. Encryption and decryption operations are transparent to the client application.

Transparent data encryption
　　For databases like SQL Database and SQL Data Warehouse, the data is encrypted prior to write and decrypted prior to read. Encryption and decryption operations are transparent to the client application.

Similarly, the options available for data protection of the data in transit can be summarized as follows:

TLS

The connection between the client and the data store uses the industry standard Transport Layer Security, which provides secure communication across public channels like the internet.

Disk encryption

When you use the Azure Import/Export Service, your data never goes across the wire. However, the physical disk is shipped and hence the data in transit is protected by the encryption applied to the disk.

Table 11-2 sums up the available data protection mechanisms for the services covered in this book.

Table 11-2. Data protection mechanisms

Azure service	At rest	In transit
Azure Event Hubs	Not available	TLS
Azure IoT Hubs	Not available	TLS
Azure Import/Export Service	Disk encryption	Disk encryption
Azure Blob Storage	Storage encryption	TLS
Azure Data Lake Store	Storage encryption	TLS
Azure SQL Data Warehouse	Storage encryption Transparent data encryption	TLS
Azure SQL Database	Transparent data encryption	TLS
Azure HDInsight	Not available	TLS
Azure Redis Cache	Not available	TLS
Azure Search	Not available	TLS
Azure DocumentDB	Not available	TLS

For those with "Not available" in the "At rest" column, consider that you may be able to implement your own mechanism to encrypt the data before sending it to the data store and encrypt it when retrieving, such that the data store itself only manages encrypted data. Also, some of these may become available soon, as the product team has indicated support is planned, such as for HDInsight to be able to query against Azure blobs that have storage encryption enabled.

Azure Feedback

To check on the status of improvements requested, planned, in progress, or completed for any of the Azure services, see *https://feedback.azure.com*.

For example, the entry describing support for HDInsight accessing blobs using storage encryption can be found at *http://bit.ly/2n7O8Nz*.

Auditing

When it comes to keeping a watchful eye on who is doing what with your data, there are two forms of monitoring you want to perform. First, you want to monitor any operations that change or configure your Azure services. Second, you want to collect logs about who is accessing the data. Together these audit mechanisms appear under a variety of names in Azure, but can be summarized as follows:

Activity logs
> This nearly universal feature captures any changes made that affect the configuration of an Azure service. It is available through the Activity Log feature of a service in the Azure Portal.

Diagnostic logs
> Diagnostic logs capture Azure Storage account operations that interact with the data managed by the service. Typically, this includes audit logs that can indicate events such as successful and failed access by a user.

Storage analytics logging
> Azure Blob Storage provides a specialized set of audit logs that capture, for example, successful and failed requests, throttling, and authorization errors.

Auditing and threat detection
> This feature is specific to SQL Database and SQL Data Warehouse. It lets you track database events such as successful/failed logins, stored procedure executions, and SQL execution. Once auditing is enabled, the threat detection feature looks for anomalous database activities and can send you alerts about them via email.

Table 11-3 summarizes the audit mechanisms by each of the services we covered in this book.

Table 11-3. Audit mechanisms by service

Azure service	Audit mechanisms
Azure Event Hubs	Diagnostic logs
Azure IoT Hub	Activity logs Diagnostic logs
Azure Import/Export Service	Diagnostic logs
Azure Data Factory	Activity logs
Azure Blob Storage	Activity logs Storage analytics logging
Azure Data Lake Store	Activity logs Diagnostic logs
Azure SQL Data Warehouse	Activity logs Auditing and threat detection
Azure SQL Database	Activity logs Auditing and threat detection
Azure DocumentDB	Activity logs
Azure Redis Cache	Activity logs Diagnostic logs
Azure Search	Not available

Summary

In this chapter we took a high-level look at the options for protecting your data in Azure, from controlling access, to protecting the data in transit and rest, to auditing access to the data.

In the next chapter, we will examine the ultimate goal of our data pipeline—performing analytics.

CHAPTER 12

Performing Analytics

In this final chapter, we'll pull things together to see how we can perform analytics against a lambda architecture built in Azure. Throughout the course of this book, you've seen examples of the technologies that act in support of the hot path, the cold path, or both. We have also explored some of the tradeoffs you can make between low latency/low precision and high latency/high precision.

When you are performing analytics against data in a data pipeline, the tools are as varied as those we used to perform the data preparation. Examples include using Excel and packaging up access to data stores in custom apps and APIs. In this chapter, we'll take a look at using Power BI to create an analytics dashboard that reports against both hot and cold path data (see Figure 12-1).

Analytics with Power BI

Power BI provides a trio of tools for providing visualization and analytics against the data flowing through your data pipeline. There is the Power BI web application (also known as *powerbi.com*), which enables you to create and share visualizations using only a web browser. Second, the Power BI Desktop is a Windows-based, ClickOnce installed application that provides a similar user experience to the Power BI web application, but enables richer data munging and querying as well as support for an extensible library of visualizations provided by the community. Content created in the Power BI Desktop application can be published to the Power BI web application once ready. Users of the Power BI web app need to authenticate using Azure Active Directory credentials, and will need a Power BI subscription. However, if you want to share a report with the public internet consumer, you can leverage the third tool of the trio, the Power BI embedded service. This enables you to embed any report within an iframe of any web page, without requiring visitors to have a Power BI subscription.

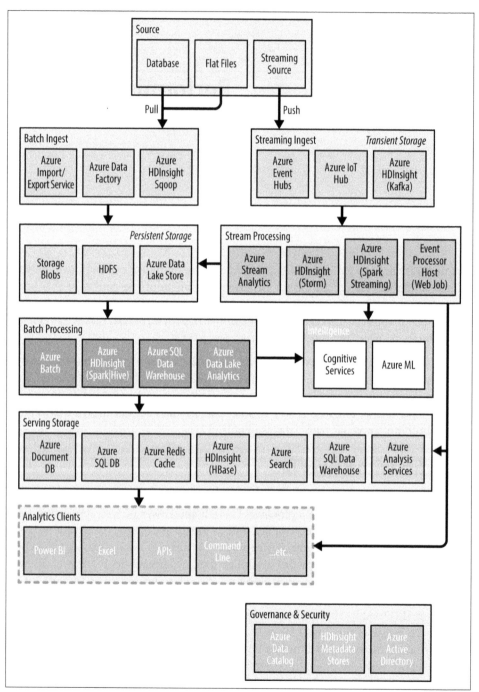

Figure 12-1. This chapter focuses on the last mile of the Azure analytics pipeline, the clients.

Power BI supports connectivity to both real-time streaming and queryable data stores.

Support for streaming data sources is only available in the Power BI web application. It provides support in two ways:

- Automatic integration as an output from Stream Analytics
- Manual integration via a REST API

More About the Real-Time Power BI REST API

The Power BI REST API enables your applications to add data to reports whose changes can be visualized in real time. To learn more about this API, see *http://bit.ly/2mtlqKa*.

The supported data stores vary between the Power BI web application and Power BI Desktop (which includes significantly more connectors), but generally both include the following:

- Azure SQL Database
- Azure SQL Data Warehouse
- SQL Analysis Services
- Spark on HDInsight

Real-Time Power BI in the Blue Yonder Scenario

Let's examine building a real-time dashboard in Power BI to visualize telemetry flowing through the data pipeline. In this scenario, we'll collect temperature events that are emitted from the device simulator and collected by an Event Hub. We'll create a Stream Analytics job that summarizes the data in one-minute windows, and then outputs the summarized result to a Power BI data set. The data produced by the Stream Analytics job consists of the window end timestamp; the device ID; the max, min, and average temperatures over the window; and the count of events collected during the window.

In order to use Power BI you will need to register at *https://app.powerbi.com* using a work or school account (personal accounts like *@outlook.com* or *@hotmail.com* will not work). Once you have signed up for Power BI, continue with the following.

Begin by creating a new Stream Analytics job (refer to Chapter 5 for a refresher on how to do this). Then add an input for the job that points to the Event Hub collecting the data produced by the SimpleSensorConsole device simulator application (Figure 12-2).

Figure 12-2. Adding the Event Hub input to a Stream Analytics job.

Next, add an output to your Stream Analytics job that points to Power BI. To accomplish this, when you add a new output, select a sink of Power BI. Click the Authorize button and log in with the same credentials you used to create your Power BI account (see Figure 12-3).

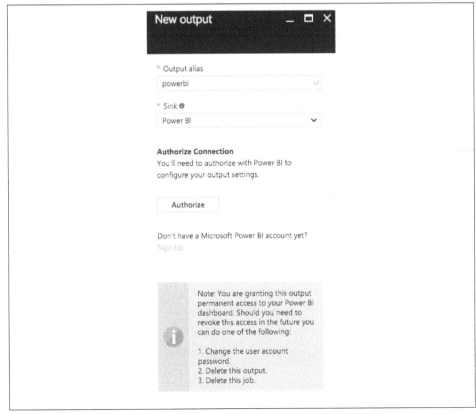

Figure 12-3. Adding the Event Hub output to a Stream Analytics job.

When the authorization succeeds, you should be back at the "New output" blade. Provide a Dataset Name and Table Name to store the hot data in Power BI. Select Create (see Figure 12-4).

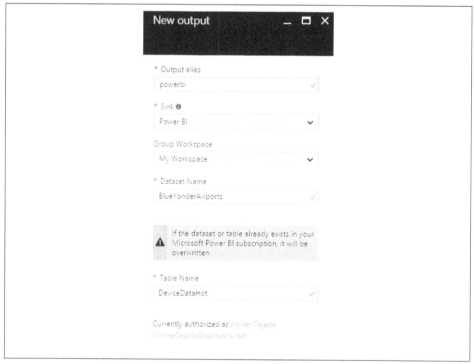

Figure 12-4. Completing the configuration of a Power BI output.

Now you are ready to define the query that will control what data flows from the hot stream of data entering the Event Hub to the data set in Power BI. For the query, use the following (be sure to adjust the input and output names as appropriate to your Stream Analytics job):

```
SELECT
    System.TimeStamp AS WindowEnd, DeviceId,
    Min(temp) AS Temp_Min, Max(temp) AS Temp_Max,
    Avg(temp) AS Temp_Avg, Count(*) AS Temp_ReportCount
INTO
    powerbi
FROM
    eventhub
GROUP BY TumblingWindow(Duration(minute, 1)), deviceId
```

Save the query and start the Stream Analytics job. While you wait for the Stream Analytics job to finish starting, open the BlueYonderAirlines solution in Visual Studio. Expand the SimpleSensorConsole in Solution Explorer and open *app.config*.

Make sure that the `SendEventAsBatch appSetting` is set to the value of `"false"`. This will ensure that data continues to stream from the simulator for at least 30 minutes (or until you close the SimpleSensorConsole). Also, ensure that `EventHubsSenderCon nectionString` is set to the correct value for your Event Hub.

Run the SimpleSensorConsole application and select option 1 to generate and send simulated telemetry to Event Hubs. Leave the console running.

Return to the Power BI web app (*https://app.powerbi.com/*). On the lefthand menu, underneath the Datasets grouping, look for "Streaming datasets" and select it.

You should see your new data set that is coming from Stream Analytics in the listing. If you do not, make sure your Stream Analytics job has started up successfully and that the SimpleSensorConsole is still sending data (see Figure 12-5).

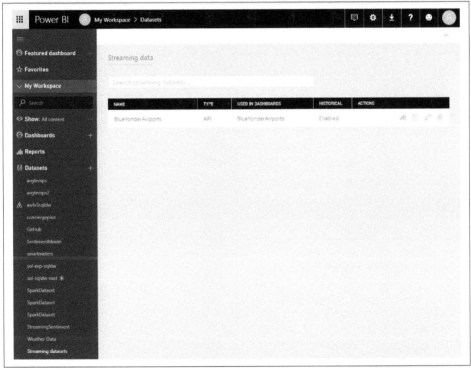

Figure 12-5. A Power BI streaming data set

Click the + next to Dashboard on the lefthand menu to create a new dashboard and then provide a name for it. In the top right of the screen, select the "Add tile" button (Figure 12-6).

Figure 12-6. The "Add tile" button used to add new streaming tiles to a Power BI dashboard.

On the "Add tile" panel, select Custom Streaming Data and select Next (Figure 12-7).

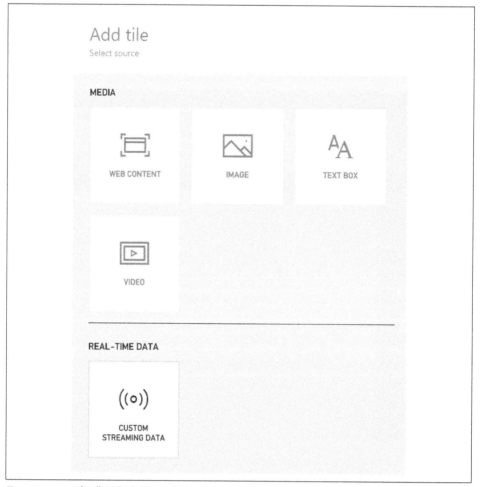

Figure 12-7. The "Add tile" panel.

On the next dialog, select your data set and select Next (Figure 12-8).

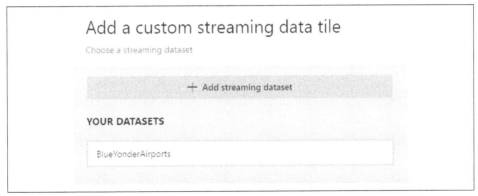

Figure 12-8. Selecting a data set for a custom streaming data tile.

On the Visualization Design, choose Card. Select "Add value" below the Fields header, select temp_reportcount, and select Next (Figure 12-9).

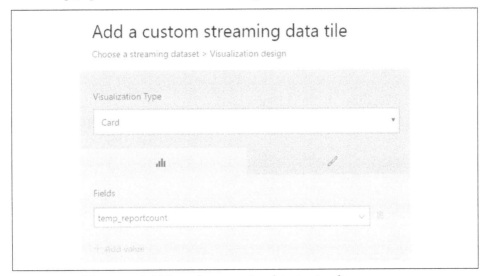

Figure 12-9. Selecting a field from the streaming data to visualize.

On the Tile Details panel, provide a title for the tile (such as "# Events in Last Window") and select Apply. What you have just created is a tile that displays the last value received for the temp_reportcount field from the input stream of data. If your pipeline is working as it should (and the simulator is still transmitting), the tile should look similar to Figure 12-10.

Figure 12-10. Example result of a tile displaying streaming data.

Now that you have one tile going, let's quickly build the remaining tiles for this dashboard.

Add another tile with a custom streaming source. This tile will report the last maximum temperature reported. Repeat the same steps as for the previous tile, except provide the following:

- Fields: temp_max
- Title: Last Temp Max Reported
- Subtitle: (Degrees F)

This tile should appear as shown in Figure 12-11.

Figure 12-11. Example result of a tile displaying the temp_max field streaming in.

Next, add another tile. This time use the following settings:

- Visualization Type: Line Chart
- Axis: windowend
- Legend: deviceid
- Values: temp_avg
- Time Window To Display: Last 10 Minutes

The result of this tile should be a line graph similar to Figure 12-12 showing the temperature reported over time for the streaming data.

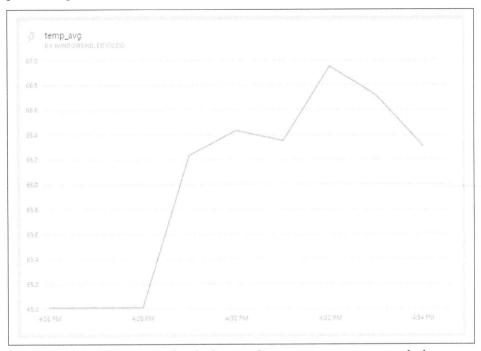

Figure 12-12. Example result of a tile showing the average temperature graphed over time.

Finally, add one more tile that shows the average temperature relative to the min and max for the window. Use the following settings:

- Visualization Type: Gauge
- Value: temp_avg
- Minimum Value: temp_min
- Maximum Value: temp_max
- Title: Last Temp Range
- Subtitle: (Degrees F)

This should result in a gauge chart similar to Figure 12-13.

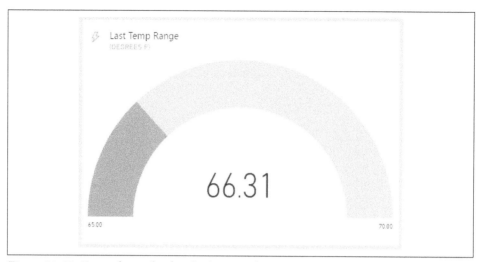

Figure 12-13. Example result of a tile showing the average temperature relative to the min and max temperature for the latest window of time.

If you arrange the tiles as desired, you should have a dashboard that looks similar to Figure 12-14 and is updating in real time!

Figure 12-14. Example completed real-time dashboard for temperature telemetry.

Batch Analytics Reporting with Power BI in the Blue Yonder Scenario

Power BI can display charts for real-time data alongside reports computed from batch-processed data. Let's look at augmenting the real-time reports with a simple Filled Map visualization showing the states with the most flight delays. In this case, we will draw the flight delay data from SQL Data Warehouse.

In the Power BI web app, from the lefthand menu near the bottom select Get Data, then underneath the Databases tile select Get.

In the list of available data sources, select Azure SQL Data Warehouse and select Connect (Figure 12-15).

Figure 12-15. Selecting an Azure SQL Data Warehouse source.

On the Connect to Azure SQL Data Warehouse screens, provide the server name, database, username, and password for your Azure SQL Data Warehouse instance that contains the FlightDelaysStaging table as created in Chapter 6.

Once the connection succeeds, select the data set on the lefthand menu named after your SQL Data Warehouse. On the Visualization panel, select "Filled map" (Figure 12-16).

Figure 12-16. Selecting the "Filled map" visualization.

In the Fields list, expand FlightDelaysStaging and drag OriginState and drop it on the Location bucket. Also, drag and drop DepDel15 from the Fields list onto the Color Saturation bucket. On the Format tab of the visualization, expand the "Data colors" ribbon. Set the diverging option to On and set your desired colors for the minimum, center, and maximum values (these will be used to color the states), as shown in Figure 12-17.

Figure 12-17. Setting the data colors for the filled map in Power BI.

Within a few moments you should be presented with a filled map that looks similar to
Figure 12-18.

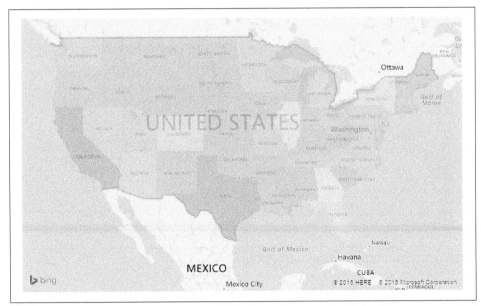

Figure 12-18. Example of the completed filled map showing the flight delays summarized by state.

Click on the Pin icon in the top-right corner of the filled map visualization (Figure 12-19).

Figure 12-19. The Pin visual button in Power BI.

In the dialog, leave Existing Dashboard selected; from the drop-down, select the dashboard you created previously with your real-time tiles, and select Pin (Figure 12-20).

Figure 12-20. The "Pin to dashboard" dialog.

From the menu on the left, select your real-time dashboard. The finished result should look similar to Figure 12-21.

Figure 12-21. An example dashboard showing visuals for both hot and cold path data.

You have just constructed a report against your lambda architecture!

A Look Ahead

The technologies available for building an analytics data pipeline continue to evolve, and new ones seem to be introduced regularly. In the last section of *Mastering Azure Analytics*, let's take a look at some of the highlights of the road ahead for building analytics pipelines in Azure.

Real Time

At the time of this writing, Apache Kafka was announced as a newly supported workload for HDInsight. This very popular open source project can be thought of as similar to the message handling capabilities provided by Event Hubs. However, given its history in the community, Apache Kafka brings with it very strong support for implementing kappa architectures where, instead of thinking of a database as your central store, you use a universal log to maintain the history of your data as it changes over time. Already many microservices and log analytics solutions rely on Kafka as the heart of their architecture, and this will certainly empower new analytics workloads on Azure.

Lower Batch Latencies

Also just announced was support for Interactive Hive—a set of features considered part of Stinger v.next in the Hortonworks distribution of Hadoop. Now, Interactive Hive is available in preview as an HDInsight workload and provides the much-anticipated Live Long and Process long-running processes, which will only serve to reduce query latency for Hive workloads, and further narrow the gap between Spark and Hive performance.

IoT

Azure IoT Hubs is introducing a Gateway SDK that, among other things, enables you to extend the reach of your data pipeline processing all the way to the edge—to where your devices live. This ability to preprocess and minimize the data flowing into the pipeline is likely to become de rigueur for any IoT-based pipeline.

Security

Recently introduced to HDInsight is Apache Ranger, which provides more fine-grained, role-based access control over Hadoop components. As HDInsight continues to evolve, we should expect tighter integration with these components and Azure Active Directory to make universally securing the data lake built in Azure a much easier proposition.

More Linux

At the time of this writing, SQL Server on Linux was just made available in public preview. It brings with it significant feature parity to SQL Server on Windows (including features like R Services, memory-optimized tables, and columnar indexes). What might make it very unique in a pipeline is the ease with which SQL Server on Linux can be deployed into Docker containers, bringing a new degree of flexibility for deploying SQL Server on a wider range of operating systems, including Linux and macOS.

The road ahead is an exciting one, with lots of new ways of mastering Azure analytics.

Index

About the Author

Zoiner Tejada has more than 17 years of experience consulting in the software industry as a software architect, CTO, and start-up CEO, with particular expertise in cloud computing, big data, analytics, and machine learning. He was among the first to receive a Microsoft Azure MVP ("Most Valuable Professional") designation and has since been awarded the MVP for five consecutive years, and now holds a dual MVP in Microsoft Azure and Microsoft Data Platform. He received his BS in computer science from Stanford University.

Zoiner is the coauthor of *Exam Ref 70-532: Programming Microsoft's Clouds* (the official exam study guide for developers seeking Azure certification), coauthor of *Developing Microsoft Azure Solutions*, and creator of the "Google Analytics Fundamentals" course on Pluralsight.com.

Colophon

The animal on the cover of *Mastering Azure Analytics* is a Philippine fairy-bluebird (*Irena cyanogastra*), a crow-sized bird found in the Philippine Islands. These animals have dark blue feathers on their back and wingtips, though the color is more vivid on males of the species. While their plumage makes them stand out in direct sunlight, they are more difficult to spot within shaded forest areas.

The fairy-bluebird lives in moist forest habitat, and eats a diet primarily made up of fruit, supplemented by insects. Figs in particular are a favorite food. Their beaks are strong and have notches to help crush fruit into smaller pieces. These birds are rarely seen alone, but forage in pairs or small groups through the forest canopy. Males court females with elaborate vocalizations, which the female responds to by building a nest. The female fairy-bluebird lays two to three eggs at a time, and both partners work together to take care of chicks.

Many of the animals on O'Reilly covers are endangered; all of them are important to the world. To learn more about how you can help, go to *animals.oreilly.com*.

The cover image is from the *Natural History of Birds*. The cover fonts are URW Typewriter and Guardian Sans. The text font is Adobe Minion Pro; the heading font is Adobe Myriad Condensed; and the code font is Dalton Maag's Ubuntu Mono.

Learn from experts.
Find the answers you need.

Sign up for a **10-day free trial** to get **unlimited access** to all of the content on Safari, including Learning Paths, interactive tutorials, and curated playlists that draw from thousands of ebooks and training videos on a wide range of topics, including data, design, DevOps, management, business—and much more.

Start your free trial at:

oreilly.com/safari

(No credit card required)

Milton Keynes UK
Ingram Content Group UK Ltd.
UKHW031840141123
432574UK00007B/222

9 781491 956656